LIVES OF THE INDIAN PRINCES

Charles Allen was born in British India in 1940, where his father served as a Political Officer on the North-East Frontier. Married with three children, he and his family have travelled widely in the country that they look upon as their second home. His previous books include *Plain Tales from the Raj*, *Tales from the Dark Continent* and *Tales from the South China Seas*.

Sharada Dwivedi is a researcher and librarian. She lives in Bombay with her husband and small daughter.

Charles Allen and Sharada Dwivedi

LIVES OF THE INDIAN PRINCES

Arrow Books Limited
62-65 Chandos Place, London WC2N 4NW

An imprint of Century Hutchinson Limited

London Melbourne Sydney Auckland
Johannesburg and agencies throughout
the world

First published in Great Britain by
Century Publishing Co. Ltd 1984
Arena edition 1986
Reprinted 1987

Photoset in Linotron Ehrhardt by
Rowland Phototypesetting Limited
Bury St Edmunds, Suffolk

Printed and bound in Great Britain by
The Guernsey Press Co. Ltd., Guernsey, Channel Islands

ISBN 0 09 946530 2

CONTENTS

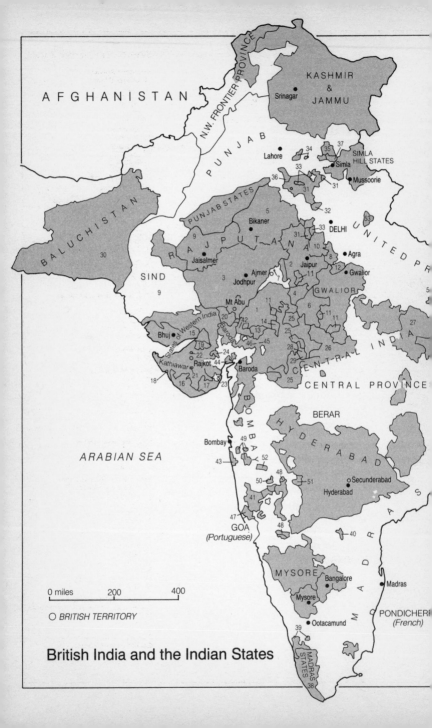

British India and the Indian States

O *BRITISH TERRITORY*

0 miles   200   400

AFGHANISTAN

N.W. FRONTIER PROVINCE

KASHMIR & JAMMU

Srinagar

PUNJAB

Lahore

SIMLA HILL STATES

Simla

Mussoorie

BALUCHISTAN

PUNJAB STATES

RAJPUTANA

Bikaner

DELHI

Jaisalmer

Agra

Jaipur

Gwalior

SIND

Ajmer

Jodhpur

GWALIOR

Mt Abu

UNITED PR

States of Western India

Baroda

CENTRAL INDIA

Bhuj

Kathiawar

Rajkot

Baroda

CENTRAL PROVINCE

ARABIAN SEA

BERAR

B O M B A Y

Bombay

HYDERABAD

Secunderabad

Hyderabad

M A D R A S

GOA
(Portuguese)

MYSORE

Bangalore

Madras

Mysore

PONDICHERR
(French)

Ootacamund

MADRAS STATES

TIBET

EPAL

BHUTAN

● Darjeeling

55

VINCES

Benares

54

PROVINCES

BIHAR

● Murshidabad

BENGAL

● Burdwan

● CALCUTTA

ASSAM

BURMA

STATES

57

ORISSA

BAY OF BENGAL

Salute States mentioned in text

Rajputana Agency
1 Udaipur (Mewar)
2 Jaipur
3 Jodhpur (Marwar)
4 Bundi
5 Bikaner
6 Kotah
7 Kishengarh
8 Bharatpur
9 Jaisalmer
10 Alwar
11 Tonk
12 Dholpur
13 Dungarpur
14 Pratapgarh

Western India States Agency
15 Kutch
16 Junagadh
17 Bhavnagar
18 Porbandar
19 Dhrangadhara
20 Palanpur
21 Gondal
22 Wankaner
23 Palitana
24 Limbdi

Central India States Agency
25 Indore
26 Bhopal
27 Rewa
28 Dewas Senior
29 Dewas Junior

Baluchistan Agency
30 Kalat

Punjab States Agency
31 Patiala
32 Jind
33 Nabha
34 Kapurthala
35 Mandi
36 Faridkot
37 Suket

Madras States Agency
38 Travancore
39 Cochin
40 Banganapalle

**States in relations with the
Government of Bombay**
41 Kolhapur
42 Idar
43 Janjira
44 Cambay
45 Baria
46 Lunawada
47 Sawantwadi
48 Sangli
49 Bhor
50 Aundh
51 Akalkot
52 Phaltan

**States in relations with the
Government of the United Provinces**
53 Rampur
54 Benares

**States in relations with the
Government of Bengal**
55 Cooch Behar

PREFACE

In this book we have attempted to show Princely India as it appeared to some of those who lived and worked within the confines of the Indian States. What we have set down is drawn entirely from the spoken recollections of eye-witnesses, including a number of ex-rulers, a larger number of *yuvarajs* or heirs-apparent brought up in the expectation of ruling in their turn, other members of erstwhile ruling families, former *Dewans* or Chief Ministers and other state servants and, at a more distant remove, such visitors from outside the states as members of the Indian Political or Civil Services. Without the wholehearted and unstinting cooperation of these witnesses and other helpers (whose names are listed on pp. 262–5) this book could not have been written. We have tried to repay their kindness by portraying Princely India not necessarily as they would wish it to be remembered, but as their own evidence suggests it was. In quoting from their recollections we have endeavoured to remain faithful to the spoken word, amending speech only in the interests of clarity and continuity. For the same reason, we have restricted names and titles to a minimum and have not always identified sources when common attitudes or experiences are quoted. We have also sought to confine ourselves to the views expressed by our witnesses, views that provide a unique insight into a way of life which was far more deeply rooted in Indian culture than has been acknowledged.

Even if such a phenomenon as Princely India cannot be wholly condoned in this democratic age, it deserves, at the very least, to be better understood. Feudal and autocratic as they were, the Indian Princes were the diamonds, emeralds, rubies and pearls that invested the imperial crowns of both the Mughals and the British with glitter and sparkle. Proud guardians of an ancient inheritance steeped in history, they gave India splendour and romance on a scale that was unrivalled in the twentieth century – and which will never recur.

Charles Allen, *London*
Sharada Dwivedi, *Bombay*

THIS MIRAGE OF THE IMAGINATION

Historic truth has, in all countries, been sacrificed to national vanity: to its gratification every obstacle is made to give way; fictions become facts, and even religious prejudices vanish in this mirage of the imagination . . .

Lt.-Col. James Tod,
Annals and Antiquities of Rajasthan, 1829

'Providence,' wrote the young Rudyard Kipling, 'created the Maharajahs to offer mankind a spectacle.' On the night of 28 December 1970, that spectacle was brought abruptly and clumsily to an end as the President of the Republic of India was roused from his bed to sign an ordinance de-recognising the Princely Order. Although they won a six-month stay of execution, this signature effectively consigned the maharajas to history, and with them the institution of Indian kingship enshrined in the word *raja*, with its original Sanscritic meaning of both 'one who rules' and 'one whose duty is to please'. As an institution it was certainly as old as the *Mahabharata* and probably as old as the early Aryans, being founded on the Hindu notion of kingship as a two-way contract between *raja* and *praja* or ruler and people. This contract traditionally required the ruler to protect his people, while they for their part were expected to reward him with obedience and a share of their cattle, gold, agricultural produce and even their women.

While successive dynasties of kings and kingdoms came and went the institution of Hindu kingship itself remained constant, providing an autocratic, paternalistic but essentially benevolent authority under which many varieties of Indian culture flourished throughout the subcontinent. It was adopted by the many waves of invaders who settled in West and Central India in the centuries between Christ and Mohammed and it survived the incursions of successive Muslim invasions from the west from the eighth century onwards. During the break-up of the Mughal Empire in India in the eighteenth century it provided a model for Muslim *nawabs*, Maratha generals and Sikh *sardars* to copy when they founded their own kingdoms.

With the arrival of the British in India this ancient concept of kingship received its first serious body-blow. British imperial rule in India, established initially by the East India Company and then in 1858 assumed by the British Crown, froze the borders of innumerable Indian kingdoms, large and small, giving their rulers a security of tenure that their predecessors had never enjoyed. The price was British paramountcy, by which the *raja* became answerable not to his *praja* but to the British *Raj* in the person of the Viceroy. In this process the Indian kings were demoted to 'Princes and Native Chiefs' and their kingdoms became Princely or Native states.

British crown rule in India lasted just under ninety years – of which the last few decades were experienced by those whose recollections fill the pages of this book. During this settled period the Viceroy exercised paramount power over two quite separate Indias. The first, comprising three-fifths of the subcontinent, was governed directly as British India. But breaking into the uniform pink on the imperial map with a confusion of yellow patches were another 600,000 square miles of what was foreign territory as far as British India was concerned. This 'Indian India' was made up of 565 Indian states enjoying direct political relations with the Government of India, who saw themselves as being 'in perpetual Alliance and Friendship' with Britain. Each had its own ruler who governed his subjects very much as he (or very rarely, she) wished but owed ultimate allegiance to the Queen- or King-Emperor through the person of the Viceroy.

The most remarkable feature of these Indian States was their diversity. At one end of the scale there were the 'Dominions of the Nizam of Hyderabad and Berar', occupying 82,700 square miles of the Deccan plateau with a population (in the mid-1930s) of 14,500,000 and an annual state revenue of 8½ crores of rupees or about £6,300,000. At the other end were minute holdings in Western India covering less than a square mile of land and yielding revenues of a few hundred rupees. Nowhere were these anomalies in size and significance more bewilderingly apparent than in the Kathiawar peninsula in Western India, where no fewer than 282 so-called Princely States jostled for attention in an area roughly the size of Ireland. The eight richest (Bhavnagar, Nawanagar, Junagadh, Morvi, Gondal, Dhrangadhara, Idar and Porbandar) together enjoyed an annual revenue that in the mid-1930s stood at approximately 5½ crores of rupees (about £4 million), whereas the remaining 274 had a total income amounting to no more than a quarter of that sum. Of these lesser statelets of Kathiawar more than half were less than ten square miles in size with annual revenues of 10,000 rupees (£750) or less. One of the smallest was Vejanoness, where a *Thakur* presided over a 22-acre estate and 200 subjects from whom he extracted an annual revenue of 450 rupees.

The British dealt with this multiplicity of states by dividing them into three main classes. At the top were the First Division States, better known as the Salute States, numbering 118 in all, their rank being measured by the firing on all formal occasions of gun salutes which descended by odd numbers from 21 down to 9 – as compared with the Viceroy's 31-gun and the King-Emperor's 101-gun salutes. In this table of salutes only five rulers (Maharaja Gaekwad of Baroda, Maharaja Scindia of Gwalior, the Nizam of Hyderabad and Berar, the Maharaja of Jammu and Kashmir, the Maharaja of Mysore) were accorded the full 21 guns, with another six (the Nawab of Bhopal, Maharaja Holkar of Indore, the Khan of Kalat, the Maharaja of Kolhapur, the Maharana of Mewar, the Maharaja of Travancore) enjoying the lesser privileges of 19-gun salutes. They were followed by thirteen 17-gun salute states, seventeen 15-gun, sixteen 13-gun, thirty-one 11-gun and thirty 9-gun salute states. Rulers with 13 guns and more to their name were generally regarded as *Maharajas* or 'great kings', the *Rajas* being confined to the ranks of the 11- and 9-gun categories. A further gradation in status came with the title of 'His Highness' which was accorded only to Salute Princes down to 11 guns, with the single exception of the Nizam of Hyderabad who was always 'His Exalted Highness'. This limitation caused so much ill-feeling among the 9-gun rulers that they too had eventually to be allowed the same honorific.

Below the Salute States there came the Second Division, made up of 117 Non-Salute States, enjoying limited jurisdiction within their boundaries and full relations with the Government of India, whose 'Chiefs' were represented either in their own right or by election in the Chamber of Princes in New Delhi which was formally opened in the spring of 1921.

Finally, at the bottom of the Princes' league there were the hereditary landowners, 327 *Talukdars*, *Thanedars*, *Thakurs* and *Jagirdars* who ruled non-jurisdictional 'Estates' rather than true states, their powers of criminal and civil jurisdiction being exercised on their behalf by Political Agents of the Government of India.

This last division completed the official table of recognised rulers, but it was far outclassed in wealth and authority by the great landowners of Bihar, Bengal and Orissa known as *zamindars*, some of whom held titles to vast areas of land for which they were required to pay annual rents to the government. Their right to govern their estates had been lost when the British overran Bengal and Upper Hindustan, but as a matter of policy many were awarded nonhereditary titles. Some, like the Maharajas of Burdwan and Darbhanga, were fabulously wealthy but, as far as the other rulers were concerned, these *zamindari* Maharajas and Rajas were not *pukka* Princes.

The British view of the Princes was neatly encapsulated by the supreme champion of paramountcy in India, Lord Curzon, when he extolled their virtues at a princely gathering in Jaipur in 1902:

> Amid the levelling tendencies of the age and the inevitable monotony of government conducted upon scientific lines, they keep alive the traditions and customs, they sustain the virility, and they save from extinction the picturesqueness of ancient and noble races. They have that indefinable quality, endearing them to the people, that arises from their being born of the soil. They provide scope for the activities of the hereditary aristocracy of the country, and employment for native intellect and ambition. Above all, I realise, more perhaps in Rajputana than anywhere else, that they constitute a school of manners, valuable to the Indian, and not less valuable to the European, showing in the person of their chiefs that illustrious lineage has not ceased to implant noble and chivalrous ideas, and maintaining those old-fashioned and punctilious standards of public spirit and private courtesy which have always been instinctive in the Indian aristocracy, and with the loss of which, if ever they be allowed to disappear, Indian society will go to pieces like a dismantled vessel in a storm.

But by 1930 such romantic notions had become largely irrelevant. The system that allowed the Princes to continue in power was 'perhaps the greatest blot on British rule in India', according to Mahatma Gandhi: 'The existence of this gigantic autocracy is the greatest disproof of British democracy and is a credit neither to the Princes nor to the unhappy people who have to live under this undiluted autocracy. It is no credit to the Princes that they allow themselves powers which no human being, conscious of his dignity, should possess. It is no credit to the people who have mutely suffered the loss of elementary human freedom.'

Undismayed by the fact that the 'unhappy people' who populated the Indian States showed not the slightest inclination to rid themselves of their rulers, the Indian nationalist leaders set about the task of demonstrating to them and to the world at large that Princely India was an anachronism that had no place in the free India of the future. In the months preceding the 1930 Round Table Conference – perhaps the most crucial period in India's freedom struggle – the All-India States Peoples' Conference produced a number of devastating reports under such titles as *The Indian Princes under British Protection* (1929) and *Indictment of Patiala* (1930) which made out the Princes to be an un-Indian excrescence on the body politic of the nation, parasitic, undemocratic and, above all, a creation of the British.

Attempts by the Princes to come to terms with this increasingly politicised India were ridiculed by writers such as Kanhayalal Gauba who in his book *HH or the Pathology of Princes* (1930) took their pretensions apart with merciless wit. The newly-opened Chamber of Princes he saw as nothing more than a 'glorified debating society', that attracted the Princes to New Delhi only because it afforded its members the opportunity to display their diamonds and ride their polo ponies:

> When the Chamber of Princes is in Session the display of royal cars which await their owners rivals that at the New York Automobile Show. All the most expensive makes are represented – Rolls-Royces, of course, Renaults, Mercedes, Fiats, Isottas. There are cars which are gold-plated and cars which are silver-plated, cars which have hoods of polished aluminium and bodies of costly woods, cars in purple, lavender, sky-blue, orange, emerald-green, vermilion, cars upholstered in satins, velvets, brocades. One has mounted on its roof a searchlight as large as those used on destroyers; another is fitted with steel shutters, presumably to save its owner from assassination; a third has on its running-board a small pipe-organ on which an attendant plays his master's favourite airs.

The Princes themselves did little to counter this highly effective propaganda. In some respects they were their own worst enemies, the names of the more self-indulgent among them constantly hitting the headlines in the period between the wars: such scandals as the blackmailing of the unfortunate 'Mr A' (whom everybody knew to be the young heir to the *gadi* of the State of Jammu and Kashmir) on his first visit to Europe; the sexual marauding of the Maharaja Bhupinder Singh of Patiala, which forced the British authorities to ban him from Simla; the shoot-out in a Bombay street over a runaway mistress which led to the abdication of the Maharaja Tukoji Rao of Indore; the bankrupting of his state by the wildly extravagant Maharaja of Bharatpur; the canine wedding fiestas of the dog-loving ruler of Junagadh; the sadistic excesses of the Anglophobe Maharaja Jay Singh of Alwar, finally deposed for what the British termed 'gross misrule'.

These and other publicised examples of princely misconduct gave credence to the necessary half-truths of political propaganda. The result is that half a century later they are now widely accepted both in India and abroad – and by default quite as much as by any deliberate political act – as the facts of history. But a way of life that directly affected the existence of a third of the Indian people prior to Independence deserves to be better remembered. Outside the states little was known about it, while to those who lived within the states it was a perfectly natural state of affairs. It is that way of life, recounted by those who experienced it directly, which forms the subject of the following chapters – together with a brief account of how it all came to an end.

I

BORN TO THE SOUND OF GUNS

Inasmuch as the prosperity of the State and the well-being of its
people are dependent on the Education and upbringing of the
Ruler, it is of extreme necessity that the child, as soon as he is
able to move about, should be kept in such a wholesome and
healthy atmosphere that he may from the very beginning tread
the proper path.

Notes on the Education and Upbringing
of the Ruler, from Maharaja Madhav Rao
Scindia of Gwalior's *General Policy*
Durbar, 1925

A male birth is always anxiously awaited in Hindu families, especially
where dynastic succession might depend on it. My own was I believe
long-awaited in the sense that His late Highness my father had
several daughters born to him but no heir. He himself had no brothers
and his father had had no brothers, so I imagine that everyone was
rather pleased at my arrival.

The birth on 3 March 1923 of a son and heir-apparent to the
princely house of Dhrangadhara in Western India was an occasion
for widespread rejoicing, as it was in every princely state when a
potential ruler was born. Provided the boy was legitimate his arrival
was publicly acknowledged on a grand scale, even though the manner
varied from place to place. Public holidays were declared, sweets
were distributed from elephants in the streets of the capital, gun
salutes were fired. In Palanpur State it was a modest 5-gun salute,
in Rampur a grandiose 101 guns, which was the equivalent of a
salute to a King-Emperor. Indeed, the King-Emperor himself was
informed, not simply as a matter of courtesy: 'You sent a telegram
to the Viceroy and to King George V or whoever it was – and if they
sent you a telegram back congratulating Your Highness on the birth
of a son that meant the son was accepted as legitimate. The British
knew that the Princes had their weaknesses, like all human beings,
so when the telegram from the Monarch or the Viceroy came to the
ruler it was a subtle way of recognising a legitimate son.'
The British Resident or Agent to the Governor-General at the

local Political Agency had also to be informed, a process that inevitably involved certain formalities. In the 21-gun state of Gwalior it was the duty of the senior-most Sardar of the state to carry the news of the arrival of a *Yuvaraj* or heir-apparent to the AGG at Indore. 'When the late Maharaja "George" Jivaji Rao Scindia was born my father went in procession riding on an elephant,' recalls the present Sardar Sitole. 'He was accompanied by liveried officers and a band all lent for the occasion by the Maharaja of Indore. He was received by the Resident in his porch, because he had what was known as "right of portico" due to his senior status. He was taken in, *thalis* of sugar and *Ittar pan* (scent, betel leaves and nuts) were formally distributed and he was again formally seen off at the porch.'

Within the state itself news of the birth was announced by proclamation and, if there was one, in the state Gazette. In the Rajput states drums were sounded. In Bikaner this took the form of beating the circular metal dishes known as thalis with rolling pins: 'In the family where the son was born they would beat a golden thali. Then people throughout the state would use whatever thalis they had and do what was called a *thali bajao*, with the idea of creating a ringing noise.' In Dhrangadhara the drumming took a more dramatic form:

> The state had two copper kettle-drums, the *Jasvant Jang Naubat* or war-drums, about five foot high, won in a skirmish from the Maharaja of Jodhpur when he was Viceroy of Gujerat in the days of the Mughals. In peacetime these are beaten on only two occasions: the enthronement of a ruler and the birth of an heir-apparent. On the *Chhathi* or sixth day ceremony of the birth they are beaten the entire day until sunset, when the membranes are pierced by a short dagger called a *katar* and silenced.

In Dhrangadhara, as in many other states, coronations and births of heirs were celebrated by the release of prisoners. 'On these two occasions all jails and lock-ups had to be emptied, then washed with milk and a black ram left tethered in them – and royally attended!', recalls the man whose birth was so eagerly awaited in 1923, the present Maharaja of Dhrangadhara, Mayurdhwaj Singhji. 'Why a ram and why black I do not know, but in our line the custom was at least as old as the accession of Amarsinhji in the early seventeenth century. When it came to my turn, a problem arose. The custom was medieval and to have released recently sentenced capital offenders would have been a travesty. However, traditionalists had also to be satisfied, so when my son was born this same ceremony was carried out in the prison in the capital and the ancestral rule duly honoured.'

When the present Maharao of Kutch was born in 1909 his grand-father, Khengarji III, attempted a similar compromise, 'but my mother, who was only fourteen or fifteen years old, heard that not all the thieves had been released so she fasted for three days until my grandfather got to know of it and had them all released'.

Other more traditional and more private ceremonies also had to be performed, among Hindus the *jitkarma* or birth ceremony at which the child was ritually cleansed before being allowed to suckle. Chichibai, an old maidservant who served five generations of the Rajput house of Pratapgarh, remembers how when the present Maharaja was born they performed the old Rajasthani custom of warding off the evil eye from the child: 'Immediately after the birth a goat kid was held over the mother and child by a Thakur (nobleman). It was rotated over their heads twenty-one times and then buried alive.' The warding-off of evil spirits also lay behind the *Pachwi puja* ceremonies that were performed – usually by the women of the household – in the Maratha states on the fifth day after the birth. '*Bhajans* (devotional songs) are sung and prayers are said and you are supposed to keep awake the whole of that night,' explains Raja Shivram Sawant Bhonsle, former ruler of the little 9-gun state of Sawantwadi, who was born in 1927 in Poona. 'The Maratha Regiment in which my father had served happened to be stationed there so people from the regiment came over to sing devotional songs all that night, while in Sawantwadi itself men from about thirty villages came to the capital with their huge war drums, which were beaten all through the night. Thus everybody was kept awake.'

The next major Hindu ceremony took place on the tenth day when the baby's mother ceased to be regarded as impure. Her rooms were washed and, in the more simple homes, the walls covered with cow-dung. This proved impractical in palaces, where other means of cleansing were employed. Padma Lokur, Princess of Bhor state, remembers how when her brother was born, 'many married women came to the palace with large vessels full of milk which was poured on the palace steps'.

On the twelfth day the infant heir-apparent – known in Hindu princely families as the Yuvaraj – had his ears pierced and was given his name. The piercing was done by a hereditary goldsmith using two pieces of gold wire, for which he was usually rewarded with a new turban, while the naming was done by an aunt on the father's side, although the actual name itself was one of four drawn up by the court astrologer. This ceremony usually began with the astrologer reading out the baby's horoscope, on which he had inscribed four

auspicious names. The father then selected one which was whispered into the child's ear by his aunt, after which she gave his cradle
a push with her hip. Here, too, evil spirits had to be deflected – and
a scapegoat found, as Leela Moolgaokar remembers from her own
childhood in Gwalior: 'A pestle used for grinding spices covered in
cloth to represent the Child Krishna was passed above and below
the cradle by the married women, saying "Govind *ghya*, Gopal *ghya*
– Lord Govind take, Lord Gopal take. Take the happiness enjoyed
when Krishna was born." Then for some reason we would all hit
the aunt in the back. After that sugar was distributed and the name
announced.' As in all such rituals and ceremonies, there were
local variations. At the infant Shivram Sawant Bhonsle's naming
ceremony it was a famous *guru* to whom his father, the ruler, was
greatly attached, who played the leading role: 'There is a thali with
rice spread on it and the father has to write the name on it using a
gold ring. But Satam Maharaj, my father's guru, not only came and
put me into the cradle, he also wrote my name in the rice himself.'
In the two neighbouring states of Travancore and Cochin at the tip
of the Indian peninsula, members of the royal house took additional
names from the stars under which they were born. 'None of us were
called by our real names,' explains Princess Rukmini Varma. 'I was
Bharini Thirunal – Bharini after the star I was born under, *nal*
meaning star and *thiru* being a title of respect used only for the royal
family.'

In Hindu princely families the continuation of the ruling dynasty
depended on there being a legitimate son to succeed his father,
which made a son 'a very precious commodity'. The only exceptions
were in the two matriarchal states of Travancore and Cochin where
succession passed through the female line, by way of the ruler's
eldest sister to her son: 'It is my grandmother Lakshmibai who is
the head of the family. Even the present Maharaja has to prostrate
himself before her. All wealth and property goes to the daughter,
so normally people want a daughter in the family, just as most people
elsewhere want a son.' Nor did the rule of primogeniture prevail in
the eighteen Muslim salute states where, in theory, the heir-
presumptive or *Walihad* was chosen by the ruler on the basis of his
personal qualities. In both Muslim and Hindu states the heir-
presumptive had to be male; although here, too, there was one
singular exception in the state of Bhopal, where a succession of three
formidable *Begums* managed to secure recognition for themselves
as rulers both from their subjects and from the British Crown
Representative in India – 'he was never referred to as the Viceroy
by us; he was the Crown Representative!'

It followed that a ruler's female offspring were generally held in much lower regard than his sons. Indeed, in the not too distant past infanticide – usually by forcing mothers to withhold milk from their female offspring – was widespread in certain parts of Rajasthan and the United Provinces. When Nandini Dev was born in the zamindari Raj of Jaunpur near Benares there was general rejoicing: 'But when it was announced that I was a girl there was great disappointment. However, I am the first female child in the family, after two hundred years, who was allowed to survive! Prior to my birth all female children were killed. When my younger sister was born, again my grandfather, the Raja, was very upset. He and my grandmother insisted that my father should marry again but he said, nothing doing.' Among the Rajput states daughters may well have been welcomed within the family but only rarely was there public rejoicing. 'Among us the birth of a daughter is not celebrated like the birth of a son,' explains Maharani Ramakumari of Wankaner, a princess from Dungarpur. 'But I, for a change, was the only daughter in a family of three sons so I was very precious to my father.' Again, it was Travancore and Cochin, where 'the gun was fired eighteen times for a girl and twenty-one for a boy', that provided the exceptions.

Direct father-to-son succession was important for all dynastic lineages and the more wives there were, the greater the chances of begetting potential heirs. Another no less compelling reason for plural marriages was the forging of political alliances. Under Islamic law, Muslims were limited to four wives, but allowed to divorce and remarry. For Hindus separation was possible, but not divorce, and there was no limit on marriages – although the due maintenance of wives and stepmothers was an inescapable obligation. But even among rulers Rama's single marriage was always cited as the ideal, as the Maharaja of Dhrangadhara explains:

The general impression needs to be corrected that Indian rulers all had several wives. For example, the late Maharajas of Kashmir, Mysore, Gwalior, Jodhpur, Nawanagar, Bhavnagar, and Porbandar – to mention a few that come to mind – had one lady apiece. But it was not at all unusual to have several wives. My father married five times. The first lady died soon after marriage. He had a daughter from the second after which she lived separately from him. Then he married my mother and later on two other ladies. So he lived with three at the same time. To us his eleven children, they were of course all mothers, commonly shared and almost undifferentiated. You might perhaps call it a small commune, except that the ladies had their own establishments and one lived in a dispersed sort of way amidst a large entourage.

By the time that the Maharaja's eldest son 'Bapa' Dhrangadhara was born, only three paternal grandmothers were still living: 'When I was old enough to take notice, my father had two mothers and one whom we only saw on ceremonial occasions and who lived apart in the *Darbargadh* (city palace). Nobody seemed bothered to tell us who was who. In every family, I suppose, everyone makes or fills a place of their own. My father's real mother was a serene, loving person, religious-minded, and fond of singing. My other grandmother didn't sing and kept everyone in their place. But she was fond of family history, told us stories and played cards with us. So they both served a wonderful purpose in our lives. We loved them all and it never occurred to me that only one was my real grandmother.'

The present Maharaja of Kapurthala, Brigadier Sukhjit Singh, remembers the same atmosphere of close communal living in the palaces of the Sikh state of Kapurthala in the Punjab, dominated in his early childhood by the personality of its ruler, his grandfather Jagatjit Singh:

> I remember very clearly four of my grandmothers living together in the same house and there was no jealousy or friction between them, despite the fact that there was a Senior Maharani who was really the person who had the pride of place. The others didn't resent it at all. I remember spending half an hour with each grandmother twice a week or whatever it was, when we used to be taken down to see them and they treated all the children just as their own children, even though some of them had their own sons. For us they were all our grandmothers and they all lived under the same roof, under the same household-comptroller who controlled the households of each one of them, though they had their separate staffs.

As well as plural marriage there was concubinage, widely accepted as a form of patronage which rulers and jagirdars of high estate bestowed on women by accepting them into their harems. Both the physically unprepossessing Seventh Nizam of Hyderabad, Osman Ali Pasha, and the magnificently robust Bhupinder Singh of Patiala maintained such harems – but were very much in a class of their own. In addition to his four legal wives the Nizam maintained forty-two other Begums in the *zanana* quarters of his King Kothi palace, as well as forty-four *khannazads* or women attendants born and brought up within the palace confines and regarded as part of the family circle. The offspring from these unofficial relationships were always well supported but never recognised as legitimate. In the Rajput states the sons were given the title of Rao Raja, a *jagir* of land and an allowance from their father but 'they could only marry at their level and not proper Rajputs', other Jagirdars' or Thakurs' children, nor eat from the same dish or drink from the same glass as the ruler's other children'. In Patiala, Bhupinder Singh's numerous natural offspring had their own palace, called Lal Bagh: 'Some were from daughters of Rajas, some from other women, and I got to know about fifty or sixty of them,' remembers Hede Dayal, who after coming to India as a refugee from Germany became a teacher to the royal children in Patiala. 'Since Bhupinder Singh cared greatly for his children he had a lot of English and Scottish nurses. He brought them all up in that style and so we hardly knew them by their Indian names because nobody could remember what they were. They were just called Dicky and Michael and so on.'

For rulers without sons of their own there was always adoption, a time-honoured custom much practised at all levels of Hindu society. There was hardly a state in India without its share of adoptions, although in every case the adopted child had to come from the same family, even if it meant going back several generations to find a suitable relation. In Northern India the ancient Vedic code of Manu was followed which stated that, 'you cannot adopt a boy whose mother you cannot marry', whereas the Maratha States followed Dravidian custom, under which it was possible to adopt a sister's or even a daughter's son. In some Rajput states potential male adoptees known as *byats* were even brought in and raised at court, just in case it might be necessary to call upon one of them to become heir-apparent: 'They were educated by the state, lived at the palace, ate with the ruler of the time, were taught how to behave and what to say and what not to say, with the idea that if the ruler did not have any sons he would adopt one of these byats.'

A classic case was Mewar, the premier Rajput state, better known today after its capital city of Udaipur, where the present Maharana, His Highness Bhagwat Singh, is himself adopted:

There was a curse on the family that no child, male or female, could be born to a ruler – and it came true. I was the eighth to have been adopted, the only criterion that I know of being simply that I was the oldest son of my father. His late Highness my adoptive father was getting old and he had an obsession that there should be no minority administration of the state. He hoped that he would live long enough for me to become a major before his death. In fact they even tampered with my age and raised it. Although when I was adopted I was hardly into my teens I was put down as seventeen-and-a-half or something like that, though the date of birth was the same. This was so that I could become a major earlier in case something happened to him.

Another royal adoptee was Setu Lakshmibai, now Senior Maharani of Travancore who, together with her cousin Parvatibai, was adopted as niece by the Maharaja of Travancore: 'The idea was that whoever between the two of us got the first child, he would be the next Maharaja.' Their adoption ceremony took place in 1900, when Lakshmibai was four and her cousin three years of age:

> The temple is in the main palace and next to it is a very large tank (temple pool) and I have vague memories of being taken there by the Senior Maharani and being made to bathe. Then we were taken into the temple where there is a huge reclining image of the family deity, Padmanabha, which is so long that there are three doors to the temple – one at the head, one at the feet and the middle one at the navel, from which there emerges a lotus. This is where the *pujas* (ritual prayers and offerings) are done. There was just a single slab of granite, very big and very famous, where all the royal children are placed when they are one year old. There both of us had to prostrate ourselves before the family deity. We thus became *dasis* (servants) of Padmanabha and every morning from then on we had to take a bath and go to the temple before we could eat. That was how the day started.

After her adoption Setu Lakshmibai and her new sister went to live with the Senior Maharani in the Sundervilas Palace – 'such a beautiful palace, full of memories, huge halls and haunting passages and corridors with beautiful parquet floors of polished rosewood. There was a very picturesque staircase going up to the women's quarters upstairs where there was a single piece of rosewood called a *tookhamanji*, like a swing with brass chains going up to the ceiling on which you could lie or sit. This was used by the Senior Maharani, who sat in it and talked to her retainers and gave her orders for the day.'

Any house in which the ruling family of a state lived was always the *Rajmahal* or palace, whether it consisted of four rooms or four hundred. It could be a medieval fort full of dark corners and narrow passages built up over many centuries, like most of the palaces of Rajputana, or an ultra-modern building designed by European architects, like the Manik Bagh palace in Indore where Richard Shivaji Rao Holkar of Indore grew up in the 1940s, which was 'extremely severe both in its exterior and interior, as was the style in Thirties Art Deco'.

Many palaces, old and new, were enormous structures, so much so that when Rajendrasinhji of Idar first came to England he was shocked to see how small was Buckingham Palace: 'I could point to ten if not twenty palaces in India, such as the palace of the Maharaja of Jodhpur or the palaces of Mysore, before which the Oueen's palace pales by comparison.' Both the palaces that Rajmata Gayatri Devi grew up in were vast buildings: her father's severely classical Renaissance-style palace in Cooch Behar – where 'you never had to get off your bicycle except when you went upstairs' – dominated by a dome said to be a copy of St Peter's in Rome, and the wildly exotic Laxmi Vilas palace in Baroda where her mother had grown up:

> The contrast was really tremendous, because whereas in Cooch Behar we used to run or bicycle all over the place, in Baroda the atmosphere was much more sedate and one felt that one had to walk slowly and running was not in order. After a few days, of course, we started running around the corridors but in the beginning one was sort of awed by the grandeur of the whole place. My grandparents were quite formal too and although our lunches used to be family lunches with my grandfather, my grandmother, my mother, my uncle, my aunt and cousins, we hardly spoke. The conversation was between my grandmother, my mother and my grandfather, more like a mono-logue than anything, and as far as the children were concerned there was complete silence. Maybe there was a little giggling and a little joke down at the end of the table but our voices were hardly ever heard.

When the present Maharaja of Baroda, Lt.-Col. Fatehsinghrao Gaekwad, first moved to Laxmi Vilas Palace with his parents from a smaller palace, he too was somewhat overawed. 'The size of the palace just hit us,' he recalls. 'It was enormous. Just within the palace itself there were over a thousand people doing various jobs and there was always a servant or two lurking behind every door. It took us children at least a year or two to find our way around and even today there are parts of the palace which I haven't been to in the last ten or fifteen years.'

Another vast structure was the Jagatjit palace at Kapurthala, modelled on the central building at Versailles and built by the Francophile Maharaja Jagatjit Singh of Kapurthala, Brigadier Sukhjit Singh's grandfather:

> The Jagatjit Palace in Kapurthala was probably the only home I know because I was brought up there from infancy and, of course, I know that palace like the back of my hand. Large as it was, it never ever gave anybody the impression of being cold or oppressive, for the simple reason that it was always bustling with activity. It was virtually the seat of governance; all the ministers had to come there and

present their papers or their problems to my grandfather who dealt with them in his office. Interviews were given, matters were decided, meetings and conferences were held in the palace and the basement was teeming with a whole spate of clerical staff, finance staff, account-ants, treasurers, people like that, who all had their respective depart-ments. I remember going in and pinching a ribbon off somebody and a rubber from somebody else or a pencil. Of course, they were terribly nice to me and spoilt me thoroughly. My sister and I would stroll down into the deeper recesses or bowels of the palace where the boiler room used to be roaring with life all the time. It was a coal-fired boiler which kept hot water running through the entire palace for twenty-four hours. Then we'd go into the stores and I remember the warmth and smell of the linen store specially, where all the linen would come in and piles from the laundry would be sorted out by suites and stocked in cupboards.

Sukhjit Singh's grandfather was probably the most widely-travelled of the Indian Princes of his time and prided himself on his good taste:

He always brought back something unique representing one facet of his travels, like the cabinet from Indonesia in the drawing room or a set of Japanese lacquer chairs or Sèvres vases. He chose very selec-tively and he tried to have each room in a certain period. For example, the drawing room was Louis Quatorze, not originals necessarily, but very beautiful copies with Flemish tapestries and things like that. Then he would have a Japanese room where all his oriental purchases would be displayed, and a Turkish smoking room which was done up in Turkish style with motifs from Morocco and Marrakesh. The main *darbar* hall was entirely Indian, with typically Indian wood carving, beautifully done. The state crest was embedded in the parquet flooring, done in different kinds of wood to give it colouring. I remember it used to be so beautifully polished that the servants used to sometimes tie their turbans off the reflection. There was a balcony running upstairs where my sister and I used to sit and peep over and observe the proceedings down below.

Sometimes at the end of a formal dinner the Maharaja and his predominantly European guests would repair to the darbar hall for a dance:

The state orchestra was under a conductor named D'Souza, a Goan. They would be in a corner in their blue and white livery and grandfather would arrive through the salon door escorting the princi-pal lady guest. He would open the Ball by dancing and then the others would follow suit, his sons and his guests and everybody, and it was a beautiful spectacle because you had this marvellous chandelier lighting up the entire ballroom with concealed lighting in the roof which resembled little stars, way up high under the central dome. My grandfather would always excuse himself at eleven o'clock but by then, of course, my sister and I would have been packed off to bed after having spent a very enjoyable evening peering through the balustrade upstairs picking out our uncles and other relations who would be on the dance floor.

During their early years of childhood both boys and girls lived in the part of the palace known as the zanana, reserved exclusively for the women of the household who lived in a state of *purdah* or seclusion. Only close male relatives and the most trusted of male servants had access and guards were always posted at the entrances. 'There were only two *huzras*, Madhav and Govind who were my father's personal servants, from whom my mother never used to keep purdah,' remembers Shashi Wallia from her childhood days in Dewas Junior. 'They were as old as my father and had been his servants from childhood and he used to say, "They are like my brothers so you can't keep purdah with them."' At Dewas Junior the zanana quarters took up two floors of one wing of the palace. On one side of an enclosed courtyard on the ground floor there was the family temple, as well as what was known as the *talghar* or cellar 'where we used to go in the summer-time and sleep in the afternoon because it used to have *khus* curtains which could be watered and kept cool.' On the first floor were the Maharani's rooms:

My mother had her own personal temple. Then there were corridors that led to her rooms, including her own personal drawing room, where she could entertain anyone who came, her sewing room, a big room where all her *saris* were kept and another room for her wardrobe, which was next to our bedrooms. She also had a little retiring room with a separate bathroom where she used to go when she had her menses. My father had rooms down below: his dressing room, bathroom and what was called his *jamdar khana* where he kept his clothes. Then we had a long hall that led into the dining room where all the pets were kept, the parrots and the mynah birds.

During the day the royal infants would probably spend their time in a separate building outside the zanana looked after by nurses, *ayahs* and attendants, seeing their parents only for a brief period in the evening, for while there was the comfort of growing up 'in a huge big family knowing you were protected', there was also the inescapable fact – of which they very quickly became aware – that they were the children of a ruler. They were growing up into a world where 'a maharaja was a maharaja even to his children' and where they themselves could never be regarded as anything but royal.

Maharani Setu Lakshmibai's grand-daughter, Rukmini Varma, remembers how as a little girl in Travancore in the 1940s she and her brothers and sisters would watch from a window as their grandmother went out into the palace courtyard below:

> We had a whole lot of *pattakars* (attendants) who wore white uniforms with silver braid on the shoulders and chest and huge flat red turbans with silver hangings like Tipu Sultan's. There were about forty or fifty just in the compound, and they would greet her by doing a *namaskar* (salutation) with folded hands starting at the tops of their heads and then bowing right down to touch the ground, with a lot of fluttering and waving of their hands in between. They had to do this seven times and it was quite an amazing sight, but they also had to do this to us when we came out into the compound and because we liked this performance we would come out and go inside and then come out again, so these poor pattakars had to keep on doing this and never stop, which was great fun for us. Then there were soldiers at the front gate who used to present arms and blow a trumpet for us, so we used to do the same thing there. I remember I once did it four times in a row and was most severely punished by being given only rice gruel for dinner, which I hate.

But as well as the privileges there were the inevitable curtailments of freedom that went with them:

> In the evenings we would be taken out for a walk at about four o'clock. There would be two pattakars in front and two at the back and two on either side so that we couldn't run off and we used to be taken like this round the compound. It was a great ceremony. The servants would also be there along with pattakars, so we were at least sixteen people going out and, of course, with all these people surrounding us we were caught if we tried to run. It was great fun trying to break away but there was this feeling of being closed in, like claustrophobia. I couldn't understand it then but I realise it now. There was no freedom. You couldn't go from one room to the next without having people following you to see what you were doing. There was not a moment to yourself.

2
INTIMATIONS OF ROYALTY

Attain good health and do not impair it.
Do not give up your religion and respect other religions.
Be neither miserly nor extravagant.
Speak out the truth and fear not.
Never tell a lie.
Always speak the truth.
Do not forget God.
Accept what is just and be always polite.
Always respect your family customs.
Be loyal to your country.
Be loyal to your Ruler.
Respect your parents and elders.
Do not easily believe everything.
Do not waste your time but use it in doing good.

Precepts for the young prince from
Notes on the Education and Upbringing of
the Ruler, from Maharaja Madhav Rao Scindia
of Gwalior's *General Policy Durbar.* 1925

It was perhaps inevitable that the young heir-apparent – the Yuvaraj or the Walihad – should be cosseted and spoiled from an early age. 'I wasn't allowed to touch the ground till I was two years old, because I was always carried around so that I didn't get hurt,' recalls Bapa Dhrangadhara. 'It was like something out of a fairy tale,' asserts Maharajkumar Rajendrasinhji of Idar:

When my daughter grows up and I tell her what it was like she's not going to believe the luxuries, the comfort and the splendour. Being the only child of the Maharaja, everywhere you went you were the centre of attraction and everyone fawned over you. You always had people hovering around you trying to see that you never hurt yourself, trying to see that you never fell sick. It was more like being wrapped up in silk rather than cotton wool. You thought the whole world was rosy; I mean you never came across anything sad or anything bad, it was that sort of life. And when we went to school and we read in the history books how the great Gautama, the Buddha, till he became a young man never saw anything sad, everybody in class used to say, 'Wow!' But I personally used to feel, 'Well, that's nothing unusual,' because till I was twelve I had never even heard of poverty and I never saw poverty. Even people who were working as menials and servants in the palaces, you never thought of them as being poor. They were all in their uniforms, and they were all spick and span.

Girls could be just as much spoiled as their brothers. 'I tell my children it was luxury such as cannot be dreamed of today,' declares Shashi Wallia, who was born and raised in the lesser of the two Central India states that went by the name of Dewas Senior and Dewas Junior. 'I always had one personal ayah (maidservant). They were changed by rote every fifteen days but then I said, "I don't want this changing. I want only one." Her name was Lachhi. She was very sweet, and she used to see to all my needs, combing my hair, seeing to my clothes. And one becomes so used to these things. Put your foot forward and your shoes were put on. Lift a finger and your hair was combed! We never raised our voices. We just had to look and by our gesture the work was done.'

Even in the 9-gun Maratha state of Sangli the first years of childhood took the form of a very pampered existence:

> The royal children had several nurses, huzras (aides) and servants and they used to behave with other common children like real maharajas. The idea was instilled in them never to do anything yourself, with your own hands, because there's always somebody around to do it for you. When anyone from the royal family called, the servants would come running and do a namaskar. Even the very aged servants had to put their head on the ground and do namaskar and they would treat even the little children with so much respect, at that young age. So the royal children realised that they were very special somebodies; that it was their birthright.

Courtiers and servants were also skilled at differentiating in their attitudes towards the various royal children: 'The Yuvaraj would always be given the most attention and the second son got less. Or if they noticed the ruler had a favourite child, then that child would get more attention and I don't think these attitudes had a beneficial effect on the little children, because they naturally grew up being jealous of each other. This estrangement really started right from childhood, which led to quarrels and strained relationships between family members in adulthood, and it certainly affected the children's minds psychologically.'

In the Muslim state of Cambay, at the head of the Gulf of Cambay in Western India, the situation was no different. 'As youngsters we were given so much attention,' remembers Princess Shahvar Sultan:

As we passed them the people, young and old, they used to *salaam* you bending down to the ground. The Cambay salaam was very peculiar. The man literally bent and touched his hand to the ground. I also remember I had this particular little servant girl that I was very fond of, and when she went away to get married, I created such a fuss; I wouldn't let her go to get married, and she even had to postpone her wedding. That's how spoilt we were really.

In Patiala, too, Hede Dayal was soon made aware that it was not their parents but the courtiers and staff around them who were spoiling the four royal children she was supposed to teach:

I remember once the three younger children came and said, 'You know what Yuvi (the Yuvaraj) did? He spat on the *Naib Saheb*.' Now the children were supposed to respect the Naib Saheb (trusted senior servant with access to the zanana). So Her Highness the Maharani said, 'Call the Naib Saheb,' and she told Yuvi, 'Now you *matha teko* him (touch his feet) and ask for his forgiveness.' But when the Naib Saheb came he was squirming and saying it was not true. He didn't want his future Maharaja to matha teko him and carry that grudge.

When the Maharaja and Maharani of Patiala left their children in their summer hill-station in the Simla hills and went off to Europe the royal children decided that they could do as they pleased:

Of course, school was out of the question. Yuvi and the others just did what they wanted. I got reports from the gamekeepers and the drivers who were all at their wits' end. The gamekeepers said, 'Memsahib, you'll have to do something. They order double-barrelled guns and they shoot wildly around. I don't know when they'll shoot somebody.' Then Yuvi was ordering the car, flying the flag and going out God knows where. The drivers said, 'They have started this terrible thing. They tie a rope to a jeep and go down over the precipice mountaineering. Then they give us a signal and we have to drive off, so that they come sailing up on the rope.' Yuvi had also heard stories of the great Bhupinder Singh, his grandfather, so they ordered food on *gadelas* (mattresses), plus drinks, plus cinema shows in the good old style. Then I said, 'Yuvi, I give you fifteen minutes and if you don't get rid of those gadelas and drinks I will inform your parents.' He was furious and wouldn't sit at the dining table but I heard his nanny, Sister Welsh, telling him in the next room, 'No, darling, we cannot throw her out. Mama and Papa have called her here and you cannot throw her out.' Then the next thing I heard was, 'I'm shooting her,' and Sister Welsh replying, 'Shooting won't do at all, darling.'

Such deference from young and old alike was not confined to the Indian States. When three-year-old Princess Gayatri Devi of Cooch

Behar – now Rajmata or Queen Mother of Jaipur – came to stay with her parents in London, she managed to escape from the house they had taken in Knightsbridge and make her way across the street into Harrods department store:

> I'd been shopping in Harrods with my mother before, and I'd heard her giving orders and I'd heard how she used to say what her account number was and I knew that the manager of Harrods was called Mr Jefferson and that he had a beard. So I asked to see Mr Jefferson, then went to the toy department and ordered a whole lot of toys. I remember there was a tub with a lot of celluloid toys floating around in it, and I said, 'I want that.' So they picked out a duck, and I said, 'No, that!' And then in the end I got impatient, stamped my foot and I said, 'No, *all* the toys, the tub, the water and all.' And at the end of my little shopping expedition I said, 'And put it down to the account of Princess Ayesha of Cooch Behar, 24 Hans Road,' as I had heard my mother saying. I had two or three little expeditions like this, until one day the governess said to my mother, 'Oh, Your Highness, you're spoiling the children.' So my mother said, 'What do you mean?' So she said, 'Well, these toys arrive every other day.' And then they found out that it was me.

Even if the indulgence that so often surrounded royal children was not always on a spectacular scale, the constant attention and respect that they were shown inevitably had an effect on impressionable young minds. 'If a young person could pass through this and not suffer from conceit it was a matter of pure luck', declares Karni Singh of Bikaner. 'Fortunately, it taught me humility – but I think that God has to help you a little bit.' In his case, as with many others, there was also a counterbalance:

> My mother always said, 'You must never let anything go to your head. Just try and be a human being.' So did my father. But then, mind you, we also had guardians who were so strict that whatever there was in the way of saluting and bands and all those things was counteracted by a Captain Whoever-he-was who would really beat us up if we were five minutes late. So on the other side there was that very, very strict discipline; stricter than an average citizen would have. We were taught to behave in public in a certain way, never to insult anybody, speak nicely to everybody and all those kinds of necessary virtues. They became part of our normal life.

The situation was the same in Gwalior, where it was instilled into all the royal children that 'no matter whether it was a poor man or a rich man, so long as he was older than you, you had to show respect. There was nobody you could call *tum* (thou). It had to be *aap* (you) all the time, even with the servants.' In Dhrangadhara, too, the young Yuvaraj had to learn that his privileged position had its disadvantages. 'The bugle would blow only for me when I came and went and the guard would turn out,' Mayurdhwaj Singhji remembers. 'But there was other special treatment in that a certain toughness was reserved for the heir-apparent who had to be more rigorously trained – and more rigorously beaten. You could not and must not be soft. So one was brought up very hard indeed and curbed on all sides.'

Playing a leading role in this character-building process were the British nannies and governesses imported especially to bring a Western influence to bear on the nurseries of the grander Indian States. Many were in the traditional mould: strict and firm with their charges, and very particular about keeping to regular schedules and administering doses of castor oil once a week.

'My nanny was from England, Mrs Dent,' recalls Karni Singh of Bikaner. 'She was an institution. She was a very kind person and she was very fond of us. If a woman is with children and stays with them for any length of time she just happens to love them. She was there from the time I was born and we loved her more than we loved our parents. In time she looked after our own children and then the grandchildren and when she got old and retired that was our saddest day. When she died we built a cenotaph for her in England.' In Rampur too, a rich Muslim state isolated in British territory in the United Provinces, the English governesses were much loved by their charges. The last Nawab's brother, Zulfiquar Ali Khan, remembers two such ladies who looked after him and his sisters: 'They were more mothers to us than our own mother. From the age of four or five I remember only sleeping near them. I still have one living with me, Mrs Simpson, who is 86. We trusted her and we had more confidence in her than in our own mother.'

Devoted to their charges as many of these nannies and governesses were, they seemed out of place beyond the confines of the nursery, 'because they didn't accommodate themselves to our culture and our understanding'. Yet their influence was undeniable, contributing to an upbringing that was a blend of East and West:

The children would get up in the morning and pay their respects to the elders with a namaskar, but at the same time wish their parents 'Good morning'. At the morning meal they would eat Indian food sitting on *chaurangs* (stools) on the floor and the other meal would be Western food sitting at table. There were two kitchens; one was the *babarchikhana* or non-vegetarian kitchen and the other was the traditional orthodox Brahmin kitchen. At the evening meal Western table manners would be taught, how to use forks and knives. This training was so you wouldn't feel awkward when the Political Agent came for dinner and when mixing with British society.

Not all the large states followed this pattern of Anglicisation. Setu Lakshmibai had a governess 'with an English complexion and strawberry blonde hair' who was an Anglo-Indian lady called Miss Watts: 'She had a very unhappy life because she elevated herself to the position of an authentic Englishwoman. She wouldn't accept any suitors from what she called the lower section, that's to say the Anglo-Indian community, and the real Englishmen considered her a Eurasian, so she remained a spinster.' But Miss Watts's influence was limited. Her charge followed all the traditional practices of Travancore, wearing 'the *mundu* which is like a sarong and with it a shawl called a *nerayuthu*, woven locally of a very fine material like chiffon with gold and black borders, which was a special combination worn by the royal family', taking her food on the ground from 'two beautiful polished plantain leaves placed one on top of the other and shaped like plates' and eating with her fingers, which were subsequently washed first in warm water, then in water mixed with herbs. As an aid to digestion she drank water in which 'cumin seed and mustard and five other ingredients' had been boiled.

Few among the lesser states ran to English or even Anglo-Indian nannies and governesses. Just south of Bombay there was the 9-gun state of Bhor, unusual among Hindu states in that its ruler came not from the warrior caste of Kshatriyas but from the Brahmin priestly caste. Here the dominant figure in the princely nursery when Princess Padma Lokur was a child was a Christian ayah: 'She was not exactly a housekeeper but she was in charge of all the other maids. They were very scared of her because she always kept popping up and scolding them. We were terrified of her but she was a very efficient woman, so we could never complain about her to my mother, who would say, "Whatever ayah says, you must do."' It was this Tamil ayah who ensured that the children kept strictly to the daily nursery routines laid down for them:

Our daily life was very interesting, but very regimented. We had to get up at 6.30 every morning and brush our teeth – that was quite a ceremony. There were no Western style bathrooms at that time, so we were made to sit on low stools called chaurangs and given black tooth-powder to brush our teeth, with a male servant standing before each one of us to pour warm water – cold water wasn't allowed. Then we would all go out riding. I was very proud of my horse which was very tall and white while my younger sister's was a little lame and very lazy. After horse-riding came the bath and then our morning meal at exactly 10.15, with very simple food after which we had to go to sleep. Every evening we had to wash our feet, recite the *Ramaraksha* (sacred texts) and recite our tables. Then there was the traditional hundred strokes to our hair with a brush or a comb which was done by ayah personally because she would see whether there were lice or scalp infections. Then before sleeping our maids Tanhu-bai and Jijabai had a regular duty which was to rub the soles of our feet with a bowl made of five metals called *kasha*. Why, I don't know, but it was supposed to have medicinal properties. This was done with pure *ghee* (clarified butter). My sister and I always tried out ways to avoid this because we never thought of it as a luxury. Then we had to have a full glass of milk with Ovaltine or if there wasn't any, with almonds.

The busiest day of the week was always Sunday, which was dreaded by all the sisters, since much of it was spent in the bathroom:

Immediately after brushing our teeth, we had to sit again on another chaurang. In fact, there were so many chaurangs in the house, there was a big room full of them. Near every chaurang there would be a *katori*, a small bowl, filled with castor oil and next to it half a lemon. Ayah would stand near us and say, 'Swallow it!', which meant that we had to immediately pick up the katori and swallow that ghastly castor oil and if we were late even by a single moment in picking up the bowl, she would shout, 'I'll bring you another katori if you don't hurry up!' So we'd swallow it fast and then suck the lemon to get rid of the awful taste. After the castor oil we were given very light food. Then at about 4 or 5 o'clock, naturally we had to go to the WC – not regular toilets but commodes. Ayah would then examine the contents and if she found anything wrong she would treat us with herbal medicines like nutmeg, aniseed or parsley seeds. If it was more serious, she would summon the palace doctor, Dr Joshi, who used to come running, poor fellow. If any of us were running a high temperature, even after we had recovered completely, our temperature would be taken by the ayah for a full month afterwards, every day in the mornings and Dr Joshi would be informed.

Poor Dr Joshi! When the states merged he came to see my mother and me and he was almost in tears. He said, 'I'm good for nothing, I don't know about the health of any other patients except your family, I don't know symptoms of any diseases except what you all got; I have spent my entire life looking into the contents of the royal thunder-boxes and I'm not fit for any other medical practice!'

Massages, baths and herbal shampoos were also part of the Sunday ritual:

> First there was an oil massage of the whole body. Each and every part was massaged by three women. One woman would hold one hand or leg, another would massage the head while a third did the back, and the massaging was very thorough: very light strokes away from the heart and pressing very hard in the other direction. Ayah would be supervising all these ladies. I still remember, we used to hate that massage so we used to try bribing the maids, but they would say, 'No way, that *Shaitan* – that she-devil is sitting outside. No, we have to massage you properly.' After the oil-massage they used to apply *utne*, which was a soft cream made out of almonds freshly ground every Sunday morning. Then came the bath, with very, very hot water. Our bathrooms were as large as bedrooms, with a big stone in the centre. We had our massage sitting on that stone and then the shampoo, using no soap only *shikakai*, a herbal shampoo. Drying the hair was also quite a procedure. We had to lie on a *charpoi* (string bed) under which they kept a coal fire with scented incense. A lot of smoke used to come out which dried our hair and left it fragrant. Perhaps these rituals were unusual by today's standards but compared to other princesses we were brought up in simple style.

Partly because of the distancing effect of being the ruling family, partly because of the close and constant proximity of nannies, governesses and servants, the natural ties between parents and children were often broken. 'We treated daddy more as a ruler than a father,' states Zulfiquar Ali Khan of Rampur. 'We always paid homage to him in the traditional way, with the *adaab* (Muslim salutation) and mummy too. We would only go and see her in the evenings, in the winter between four and six and in the summer between six and eight. They had their own way of living.' And it was very similar in the Hindu state of Dhrangadhara when Mayurdhwaj Singhji was a child:

> We had our own apartments and separate lives. We had little contact with our parents. As to being hugged, let alone kissed, it was unheard of. It would have been unmanly. Not that my sisters fared any better. We would all wait on father, after he'd had his bath and was engrossed in his newspaper. We stood in line for a while, waited for the signal, got father's nod or grunt, and were off. We had a meal together on Sundays. That's about the only contact I can remember with him, until we returned from England, when war broke out. I was sixteen then and got to know him a little bit more. But he died when I was nineteen so I never really knew him well.

The situation was not so very different in Bikaner State when the formidable Ganga Singh was the ruler. 'We used to be very frightened of him,' recalls his daughter, now Maharani of Kotah, 'but at the same time he was very affectionate and loving. As children we had fixed timings as to when to go and see my father and he always used to cuddle us and be very sweet to us. Whenever he had time he always came and saw us playing and he would always ask the nanny whether everybody was all right. He was a very busy person and was always working for the state, morning, evening and even late at night, but when my father used to come for dinner, sometimes we were allowed to sit there with him. He would have his pencils and *chit*-pads and while eating, he would write with his left hand making notes and we thought it was wonderful, sharpening his pencils and thinking that we were great office bearers.'

The larger the state, the greater the status of its ruler and the less contact he had with his children. This was certainly true of the biggest of the Indian states, Jammu and Kashmir, where the Yuvaraj, Karan Singh, was born in 1931:

> At the time when I grew up in India there was a fairly widespread custom of the princes being brought up by British guardians and that involved by definition living away from the parents, because if one lived with the parents then guardians weren't necessary. Once that decision was taken it meant that I had to move into a different house with a different establishment and that in turn meant that I couldn't see my parents very frequently. In my case, my father being particularly meticulous, he laid down exactly when and for how long I could see my parents.

This segregation from parents was, as the present Maharaja of Bikaner explains, simply taken for granted: 'The set-up was such that one wasn't able to see one's mother or father as often as one would have liked. Looking back it appears curious but the question of resentment never arose because that was the dispensation then.'

In many instances it was a grandfather who was the ruler, in which case his grandchildren were required to pay him regular but often rather formal visits. Mansur Ali Khan, better known as the cricketer 'Tiger' Pataudi, remembers visits to his grandfather, the Nawab of Bhopal, as being 'like going to see the Pope. You got dressed up in your finery, you went through corridors of servants and bodyguards and eventually the boss was sitting there with his *hooka* and you paid your respects and you sat there feeling thoroughly uncomfortable for fifteen or twenty minutes and then you left.'

Padma Lokur's relations with her grandfather, the Raja of Bhor, were almost as formal:

> If we wanted to meet him for some reason we had to send him a message through one of the *karbharis* or courtiers. Our meetings with him would last about five or six minutes and were extremely formal, but the questions he asked about our health or our education showed that he must have kept track of all our activities because he seemed to know everything about us. Since we were not allowed outside the palace grounds, we never knew how normal families behaved and I grew up with the impression that there was never a question of love in royal families. It was all duty.

It was not unusual for a ruling grandfather to take the eldest son of the heir-apparent under his wing and bring him up himself. This was what happened to the present Maharao of Kutch who, because he was the first grandson born to the ruler, was taken from his parents and brought up in the old city palace without modern baths or sanitation, 'where my grandfather lived from the time he was born to the time he passed away'.

There was a good reason for this widespread custom of the unofficial adoption of grandchildren, in that until comparatively recent times the great majority of children born to the ruling house had parents who were themselves often in their mid-teens or even younger. The mother of the present Begum of Bhopal was 'barely thirteen when she had my elder sister and was sixteen by the time she had had her three daughters. She was so young she could barely impose any sort of influence on us when we were very small, so she was more of a companion than anything else. Everything was done by my grandmother, the Begum, and my parents had very little to do with us.'

It was the same for Sukhjit Singh in Kapurthala, where almost from the moment of his birth, his grandfather made it his business to supervise the way he was brought up. Maharaja Jagatjit Singh had himself veered so far from the Sikh tradition as to shave off his beard, which had caused such offence among Sikh religious leaders that the Maharaja had taken a vow to see that if he had a grandson he would bring him up 'in the true tradition of a Sikh':

> Our nannies would take my sister and me along and he would pick us up and put us on his knee. We would have breakfast with him and then off we'd go. At night he would invariably come down to our room, sit with us for a while, taste what had come for dinner to make sure that what he'd ordered had come for us and then go away for

the evening. I still remember the entire process because just before dinner time, there would be this rustle of feet outside and the orderlies outside would open the door and say, '*Maharaj Sahib aarahe hai*', which meant that His Highness was coming. Then we would hear the patter of his Pekinese or Pomeranian preceding him and they would come straight into the room because they knew exactly where he was going. And then he would come in wearing a smoking jacket or his tuxedo or his *achkan* depending upon what function it was that night. He'd sit for a while and tell us that he was having so-and-so over to dinner, or whatever it was, and then he would kiss us both and disappear. And I still remember that marvellous whiff of his cologne which was Roger and Gallet.

Although she never enjoyed as warm a relationship with her Baroda grandparents, the great Sayaji Rao Gaekwad and his equally formidable consort, Maharani Chimnabai, Gayatri Devi learned very early on that they were a couple to be greatly respected:

My grandmother seemed to me a terrifying person. She was very strict and hardly ever laughed or joked and expected one to behave perfectly. My grandfather seemed much kinder. As I grew older I was not really so frightened of them. But I was always very impressed by my grandfather and wanted to hang on to every word he said because he always seemed so wise. I remember my grandfather playing billiards in Laxmi Vilas Palace one evening when I was told to go and say good night to him because it was bed-time. So I went along and he was just about to make a stroke. I waited for that and then I bowed and folded my hands and I said, 'Good night, *Burra Baba*', and so he said to me, 'You're going off to sleep, young lady?' So I said, 'Well, I'm not sure, I might have to think a little bit.' So he smiled and then he said, 'You don't think when you go to sleep, you go to sleep. There's plenty of time to think in the daytime.' I always remember him telling me that.

3
THE MARTIAL SONG OF THE BARD

The Rajput worships his horse, his sword and the sun, and attends more to the Martial Song of the Bard than to the Litany of the Brahmin.

Lt.-Col. James Tod,
*Annals and Antiquities of
Rajasthan*, 1829

The way I became aware of my past history was that my father put two venerable old Rajput gentlemen in my service as assistant guardians who looked after me and they were told to relate in the evenings stories about our ancestors and how we came from Chittor to Udaipur and how long we remained in Udaipur and how the quarrel and feuds between two brothers started. How the elder brother was made to leave and how he came down to the inhospitable wilds in the South and acquired a kingdom for himself. That's how I came to know about the past history of Dungarpur and of the Udaipur dynasty, the oldest dynasty in the whole of India, perhaps the oldest dynasty in the world, which came to Rajasthan and founded the State of Mewar in 800 AD.

For the young Yuvaraj of Dungarpur, growing up in Rajasthan in the early years of this century, these stories were much more than mere bedtime tales or history lessons. They enshrined examples of princely virtue and good behaviour which he and his brothers and sister were expected to follow, 'so that you didn't forget who you were, what your family tree was, that you were born in Bhagwan Ramchandra's family and that you were never to put a blot on the name and tradition of your family'. The stories also concerned Rajput chivalry, which was 'very much akin to the best traits of British chivalry: gallantry, great-heartedness, to be unassuming in victory and to show tenacity in adversity, to continue to try, try and try again to achieve your objective'. Even in a tiny Rajput state like Mansa, occupying no more than 25 square miles of fertile, flat land in Gujerat in Western India, this story-telling played a very important part in the lives of the children:

The legends and folklore of the Chavda clan, of the great founder, Vanraj Chavda, were told to us in the form of stories – stories of valour, stories of honour and honesty, stories of just how a king should behave. Certain basic qualities that we were expected to live up to were always emphasised, the very basic things of the Rajputs: generosity in victory, keeping your standard flying even in defeat, how when everything is lost the last man dies fighting, performing your religious rites which would bring happiness to the ruler as well as to his subjects. This was a very important factor in the story-telling process because there is a saying in Hindi: *Yatha Raja, tatha praja* – as the king is, so are the people. This kind of thing was told to us over and over again.

Playing a leading role in keeping alive these traditions 'which were drummed into us in childhood', were the bards who attended the court of every Rajput ruler. This ancient and much honoured institution was maintained in the Rajput states principally by two complementary castes known as Charans and Bhats, who served variously as panegyrists, genealogists, recorders and raconteurs of historic tales. They also acted as intermediaries in negotiating marriages, in guaranteeing the settlement of debts and disputes and as emissaries in times of war. Bhats would accompany travellers as guarantors against attack and robbery and Charans would act as guarantors of bonds – committing suicide and, so it was said, haunting a defaulting debtor if he failed to pay up as required. There was a well-known instance in the 1920s of a ruler in Kathiawar who defaulted on such a debt. His Charan duly committed suicide and for four years the state got no rain. His ghost was only appeased after a criminal had been executed by the ruler on the very spot where the bard had killed himself. 'We never refused a Charan,' declares Maharani Anant Kunverba, Rajmata of the coastal state of Porbandar. 'They are supposed to curse one and people are rather frightened of their curses. Even if you want to refuse or feel that they don't need any help, it's something that a Rajput never does.'

The persons of these Bhats and Charans were regarded as sacred and every Rajput would treat them with the greatest respect. Rulers would reward them with hereditary grants of land known as *jagirs*, at feasts they would be invited to eat first, and whenever they came into a ruler's presence he would rise to greet them, for 'Charans were very strong supporters of the Rajputs and the Rajputs were very strong well-wishers of this community'. Nowhere was this ancient alliance more evident than in the desert country of Bikaner, where the Charans were linked to the family deity of its Rajput rulers: 'The Charans became important to us because they were associated with the Karni Mata, a lady of Charan stock who performed miracles and was alive at the time of our ancestor Rao Bika, from whom the state took its name. Our family worshipped Karni Mata and consequently the Charans have assumed great importance in the history of Bikaner.'

The bardic roles played by the Charans and Bhats at court were shared with others who also had a part to play in preserving the past and ensuring that the present was not forgotten. In Dhrangadhara there was the *Raj-Barot*, the *Raj-Kavi* and the *Raj-Gayak*:

> The Raj-Gayak was a singer – ours was a Brahmin who was both a composer and vocalist – and the Raj-Kavi was the royal poet whose job it was to celebrate great occasions in verse. He had the right to recite and to be heard at darbars or levees – even if it made everyone squirm! He also took precedence over other Bhats and Charans who might be present, some of them better versifiers than himself. Then there was the Raj-Barot or royal herald, who was an institution in himself. He automatically held the post of *Jhala Kula Vahivanca* or genealogist of the Jhala clan. As it happened, our Barots were rare visitors since they had their lands and home in another part of India, in Malwa. The post was hereditary, so he succeeded to it by recognition not appointment. Having received the seal of recognition he would be received in private audience – because he did not recite in public, having the right to private audience of the ruler. He would sit on the floor before the gadi or throne and the vast bulk of the *Vahi* (genealogical records) would be placed before him. He would say, 'What shall I read, *Annadata* (giver of food)?' and the ruler would name some predecessor. But before looking him up he would salute the Vahi three times, touching it and then his forehead with his right hand and untie the knot of the cloth in which the Vahi was kept. For this he later received the 'untying-the-knot' fee of 1001 rupees. The first of our Barot's line, a man called Akheraj, was appointed in 1143 AD, so the size of his genealogical records, which covered the whole of the Jhala clan, can be imagined.

In his capacity as genealogist the Barot made periodic visitations upon the scattered states, estates and villages in which members of his clan had settled, noting down births, marriages, deaths and much else: 'The Vahi records wives, their fathers' and grandfathers' names, clan name and abode, sons and the provisions made for them, and major events. It also detailed the dates of recognition of the successive Raj-Barots and the gifts made to them – 15 horses, 20 camels, so many gold bangles, shawls and what-not.' Since the Barot made his rounds accompanied by a large entourage which had to be fed and entertained, his arrival in a clan village 'was feared like the coming of locusts'.

The genealogical tree was of enormous significance not only to princes but at every level of Hindu society, because 'your blood loyalties in India are colossally important'. It also reinforced the hereditary principle whereby 'a *mahant* (priest) normally takes over his father's duties, the son of a Muslim *pir* will look after the tomb that his father has looked after, the son of a *baniya* (money-lender) takes over that function. The same thing applied to the princes, because *Raja ka ladka hai* – a king's son is a king. And what does Rajput mean but "a king's son"?'

The Rajputs were the most widespread and tenacious ruling group in India. They constituted almost two-thirds of the Princes and Chiefs recognised by the British when they established their suzerainty over the subcontinent, their states being concentrated mainly in the regions of Rajputana (or Rajasthan) and Kathiawar between Delhi and the Arabian Sea, with a smaller concentration of states running in a narrow strip of land south-east from Agra to the Bay of Bengal.

To be a Rajput, to have the right to bear arms and lay claim to at least one hide of land, one had to belong to one of the thirty-six 'royal races' of the Rajputs whose pedigrees were preserved by the Barots in their charts. Each of these races or clans had its own antecedents and was divided into a number of branches. Some had withered into extinction, others had produced several ruling families, each with its own well-documented family tree reaching back into the mists of legend and antiquity. Many claimed a relationship with the sun by way of the warrior-god Rama and called themselves Suryavanshis or 'the race of the sun'; most notably, the rulers of Mewar (better known today by its lake-side capital, Udaipur) whose banner was a gold sun on a crimson field. Others, such as the ruling families of Kutch and Jaisalmer, claimed descent from the moon through the god Krishna and were known as the Chandravanshis or 'the race of the moon'.

In reality, most of the thirty-six clans were descendants of Central Asian tribes such as the Huns and Scythians who first entered India some 1500 years ago, carved out kingdoms for themselves and soon achieved respectability as members of the Hindu warrior caste of Kshatriyas. They did so in many cases with the support of local tribal people and in some areas, such as Bilkha State in Kathiawar and a number of the Eastern states in what is now Orissa, intermarried with them. Two such tribal communities in Porbandar were the Meres, warriors from Northern India, and the cattle-owning

Rabaris. Both were fiercely loyal to their rulers and won special privileges for themselves for having provided help in past crises: 'The Meres didn't touch the ruler's knee like other subjects. They put a hand on his shoulder. And when a ruler is put on the *gadi*, meaning the throne, a member of one of the Mere families cuts his finger and puts a *tikka* mark on the ruler's forehead in blood, which means "this is our loyalty to you".' The same special relationship existed in Udaipur, dating back twelve hundred years, with the descendants of the two Bhil aboriginals who helped Bappa Rawal found the state of Mewar playing leading roles in the anointing of each successive ruler. It was with these Bhil jungle-dwellers of Central India that the Rajputs established what were to become their most enduring alliances. Despite the prohibitions of caste, a Rajput would always take food and water from a Bhil's hands and would refer to him as a *bhaibund* or brother-in-arms. In all such states Bhils played leading roles as guards, keepers of state treasure and, most prominently of all, as hunters, because '*shikar* (hunting) was their domain, any beat or occasion when we went off on shikar they had to be there very happily doing the bidding of the ruler'.

The institution of monarchy in India had long predated the Rajputs. 'Our conception of kingship was quite different from European kingship,' explains Maharaja Vibhuti Narain Singh of Benares, where the *Kashiraj* or kingship of Benares was as old as Indian recorded history. 'It was more a question of family ties between a ruler and his subjects. The famous Indian poet Kalidas described kingship fifteen centuries ago as being like the sun which sucks up the water in summer from the ocean and from vegetation but in the monsoon gives back fourfold what it has sucked. That is the Indian monarch, who if he takes something gives it back fourfold to the people.' This relationship was symbolised in the way in which a ruler was addressed by his subjects – either as *Bapu* (father), *Bapuji* (honoured father), *Ma-Baap* (father and mother) or even as *Annadata* (giver of food).

Four hundred miles due east of Benares in the shadow of the Himalayas was another equally ancient kingdom, Cooch Behar, whose sovereigns claimed to have ruled the same territory since the time of the epic battle celebrated in the *Mahabharata*. When Gayatri Devi's mother was Regent in Cooch Behar in the 1920s she was always known as *Ma* and her elder brother, even as a minor, was always *Baba*: 'They called my younger brother *Chhota baba*, which means younger father and they called my elder sister either *Ma* or *Didi*, which means elder sister. I was known as *Majli Didi* or middle elder sister and my younger sister was *Chhoti Didi* – although sometimes the people also referred to us as Ma, even though we were just children.'

This ma-baap relationship with the people became central to the Rajput ideal of kingship and if there was Rajput pride – 'that used to boil our blood in childhood and gradually permeated all the cells of our bodies' – there was also the Rajput sense of inherited duty. 'Rajputs had two functions basically,' suggests Pushpendra Singh of Lunawada. 'They were a warrior race whose job was, firstly, to protect and preserve and, secondly, to rule and administer, and this is an instinct which is very, very strong in many of us. The old wives' tales always said that if you were born of a ruling family you were naturally gifted in many ways of which you were unaware and I, too, believe there is some such thing. For instance, the art of administration comes easily to me although nobody taught me this.'

Hand in hand with this Rajput ideal of leadership as an inherited right and a duty, went the understanding that a Hindu king should always be 'answerable and responsive to local sanctions'. Every Rajput ruler had, firstly, to either satisfy or contend with his landowning barons – 'king versus feudals is as chronic a theme in Indian history as king versus neighbour'. He had also to satisfy his priesthood, headed by the *Raj-Purohit* who acted as the pontiff of the state. Without this Brahmin minority the king could scarcely function, whether in a spiritual context or in administration, since it was this literate class that supplied him with ministers and a clerical establishment. Lastly, there was the power of the *mahajana*, the 'great people'. 'In our own history a *mahajana sabha* (popular assembly) and the village *panch* (council of five) are first mentioned in about 1500 AD,' states Mayurdhwaj Singhji of Dhrangadhara:

These were originally the heads of local communities although latterly it meant the mercantile urban class and, as an old Gujerati maxim has it, *darbar bap, mahajana ma* – the king is father but the mahajana is mother, meaning, you can manage without father but not without mother. The king had to heed their protest or the mahajana would 'sulk' and do what was called *risay javun*. They would close their shops and bring trade and business to a standstill. Then if this economic sanction didn't work the mahajana would declare that it wasn't worth while living in this *adharmic raj* or lawless state. They then packed their goods and chattels in carts and prepared to move out. Such a crisis was galling to a ruler; it was what we call *nak kapai gayun* or 'cutting off the nose'. He'd become an object of fun, especially among his brother rulers – and to be well thought of, and well remembered, has always been an important consideration among the Princes. Sometimes the mahajana did actually move out in long caravans and had to be summoned back when the ruler climbed down. This happened in our own state not so long ago, even after the British had taken over and all internal sanctions had been practically breached.

Another aspect of Hindu monarchy that the Rajput rulers took up was the notion of ruling as God's representative or as His *Dewan* or chief administrator. 'This is the Hindu tradition in which we submerge the individual to the Supreme Being,' explains Maharaja Vibhuti Narain Singh, who continues to this day to perform many religious functions in the Hindu holy city of Benares as Shiva's representative. 'It's not the individual who matters, so the Maharaja of Travancore, for instance, is the Dewan of Travancore as the representative of Lord Padmanabha (Vishnu). There's that famous story of how when he was called upon by Lord Mountbatten to sign the Instrument of Accession in 1947 he said, "I'm the Dewan of Travancore, not the Maharaja. How can I sign the Instrument?"' In the same way, the leaders of the Sisodia clan of Rajputs, who worshipped Lord Shiva in the shape of the stone emblem known as the *Eklingji*, referred to themselves as Dewans of Eklingji. In the Rajput state of Rewa the state deity was known as *Rajadhiraj* (king of kings) Ramchandraji. 'When a ruler is installed he does not sit on the gadi,' explains Maharani Pravinba of Rewa. 'It is the deity who sits on the throne, while the Raja takes a vow of being a servant of the deity and looking after the public. So when my husband's coronation took place, it was Ramchandraji's *murti* (image) that sat on the throne, a solid gold murti that had been in the family for generations. When there is a procession the deity leads and the Maharaja goes behind as a servant. So right from the time of his coronation my husband understood that he was merely a servant of God, serving the people as his representative.'

As Kshatriya warriors the Rajputs took their religious duties just as seriously as their temporal ones. The goddess of destruction, Mahakali, was widely adopted among them as a family deity, requiring daily prayers and sacrifices before and after every significant event. But there were many variations. In Lunawada State the family deity was the goddess Bhuvaneshwari, who was closely bound up with the founding of the state some five hundred years ago by a junior branch of the Sisodia clan: 'This was all barren jungle and when the original ruler came here it was just for shikar (hunting). The story goes that he was hunting hares on horseback when a hare stood up and faced his hound. He decided that if the hares in this area were so brave then this must be the place to build his capital.

So he entered the jungle and found a holy man on the site of the present Bhuvaneshwari temple, who blessed the ruler and made him sit before the goddess. The dog was sacrificed at the spot where now the gadi is kept when the coronation ceremony is performed.'

In Porbandar the family deity was Vindhya Vasini Devi, goddess of the Vindhya hills, while the rulers themselves claimed descent from the monkey-god Hanuman. Nor were the more powerful gods of the Hindu pantheon neglected:

> Before the time of His late Highness's great-grandfather, Rana Vikmatmatji, the ruling house worshipped Vishnu. Now every morning this Rana Vikmatmatji used to bathe, drawing 112 buckets of water himself from the well and with each bucket of water that he poured over his head he used to say one bead of the Hindu rosary. After doing his puja (worship) at home he used to get on his horse and go to a little temple of Krishna outside the palace fairly close by and, being a Rajput, he never went out without a small dagger. He was a very short little person and we still have that same stone near this temple in Porbandar with a few steps going up it, which he used to climb up and get on to his horse. Then one morning there was a new *pujari* (priest) there who said to this very autocratic ancestor of ours, 'You cannot go into the temple unless you remove that small dagger that you have in your cummerbund.' Our ancestor said, 'I have been going into this temple from the time I was a small boy. Why should I remove it?' To which the pujari replied, 'The child Krishna will get frightened.' Rana Vikmatmatji was so enraged that he said, 'If Krishna gets frightened of a little curved dagger that I have in my waist-belt, I certainly don't want to do puja to that kind of a god.' From that day the royal house of Porbandar became Shaivite and worshipped Shiva.

As the first Rajput kings began to achieve dominance in Western and Central India, so the more successful among them began to push out junior branches who carved out their own little principalities. The rulers of Idar were part of the illustrious Rathor clan which founded Marwar, better known today after its capital, Jodhpur:

> We came in about three or four centuries back from Jodhpur. At that time the house of Jodhpur was expanding in all directions, each brother or son of a ruler trying to make a stake for himself in another part of the country and it was from the ruling house of Jodhpur that we all descended. One family member went and founded the state of Bikaner, the other founded the state of Idar, other members founded the states of Kishengarh, Ratlam, Jhabua and Sailana, and so it went on. Those were very turbulent times in Indian history,

exciting times. There were no British to control and regulate and dominate. It was a free-for-all. My ancestors went south towards Gujerat and they conquered almost half of what is today known as Northern Gujerat right from the borders of Sirohi State up almost to Ahmedabad, where they established their kingdom, kept the capital at Idar and settled down. Then with the decline of the Mughal Empire the Maratha supremacy occurred. The generals of the Peshwa – the Gaekwars, the Scindias, the Holkars – these people started carving out their own kingdoms in different parts of India, and we had the Maratha invasions when we had to surrender a lot of territory to what is today the Baroda State. Then the British intervened and there was peace between Baroda and Idar and we were left with much less than what we began with.

Even more dominant as a clan were the Sisodias, divided into twenty-four branches of which the senior-most was Mewar, 'Lord of Chittor, the ornament of the thirty-six royal races'. Other branches in Rajasthan provided the rulers of Banswara, Shahpura, Pratapgarh and Dungarpur – which, according to one account, was founded in 1171 AD as the result of a misunderstanding between the Rana of Mewar and his eldest son, Samant Singh: 'At the time of marriage a coconut is always sent to the bridegroom as an auspicious symbol. It came for the prince but his father absentmindedly took the coconut without realising what it was for. The son then said, "You've taken the coconut. You must marry the girl, so I'll get out." The Rana married and got another son to whom the kingdom went – but the Dungarpur family is the senior branch.' A less romantic version of the founding of Dungarpur has the elder brother voluntarily surrendering the gadi of Mewar after his younger brother had rescued him in battle. Nevertheless, Mewar's place of honour at the head of the Rajput clans was well-deserved, for alone among the Hindu princes their rulers refused to intermarry with the Mughal Emperors of Delhi and Agra, finally emerging after eight hundred years of almost constant struggle against Muslim invaders with the same territory that their ancestors had first won for themselves a thousand years earlier. Their guiding principle throughout these centuries was 'self-reliance and independence', according to the present Maharana of Udaipur, His Highness Maharana Bhagwat Singh, the seventy-fifth in line of succession:

My ancestors believed that it was better to starve with dignity than to feed oneself like a fat dog as a slave. If we had wanted luxury we would have done what many of the other princes of India and Rajasthan did who accepted the slavery of the Delhi Sultanates of the Tughlaks and Khiljis and Mughals. There were times when almost the whole of Northern India was our kingdom and times when not even the rock or the piece of earth on which the ruler sat was his. That is why Maharana Pratap Singh is called the light and life of the Hindu community. There were times when he and his family and children ate bread made of grass. A couplet of one of the bards says that Maharana Pratap was so busy fighting for freedom that he had no time for his children. When they were starving they went to their father's famous horse, Chetak, and hugged him and cried out, 'Our father has no time for us and we are hungry. Do something to help us!' Maharana Pratap was the fifty-second ruler but fifty-one rulers before him had done the same thing.

According to the bards of Rajasthan, when news of Rana Pratap's death reached his enemy, the great Mughal Emperor Akbar – who was himself married to a Rajput princess of Amber (now Jaipur) – he 'bit his tongue, his eyes filled with tears and he gave a deep sigh for him whose horse had never any scar about it, who never turned his back on a battlefield, whose turban never went down in front of the Mughal Emperor, whose knee was never bent before him and who, while the rest of India gave in to the Mughal, never surrendered'.

But even more potent a symbol of Mewar resistance to foreign domination was the great fortress of Chittor, an extensive ruin on a mountain-top 72 miles east of Udaipur, which continues to be revered by all Rajputs for the courage of the many thousands of men and women who perished there in three most terrible massacres and mass suicides by fire; the first in 1303, the last in 1567, when Chittor fell to Akbar at the cost of 30,000 lives – 1700 of them being members of the Rana's family. 'The history of Rajasthan is something marvellous but the history of Chittor is above everything,' declares the Maharani of Wankaner, sister of the present Maharawal of Dungarpur. 'Three times in its history the women never turned their backs when they saw that their husbands were losing. Either they went into the battlefield wearing men's clothes and sacrificed themselves or they entered the pyre and threw their children on the pyre so as not to surrender to the intruders. Even girls of fifteen went out fighting or went into the fire. It is awe-inspiring to think of it. Even today when you go to Chittor you feel it. It is our holy of holies and yet in every nook and cranny in the land you'll find there were brave people who made great sacrifices.'

Among the Sisodia clan their heroic past continued to be remembered at their feasts when their gold and silver thalis were placed on platters of leaves and blades of grass put in each thali. 'This was to remind us that our fortunes can swing from high to low and not to forget the bad times,' explains Mahendra Singh, Yuvaraj of Udaipur. 'Some grass is also put under the mattress in many Rajput homes for the same reason – and a sword kept under the pillow.'

Not only in Mewar but in every Rajput ruling house there was something from the past for its bards and court poets to make much of, for the history of every Rajput clan was one extended chronicle of power struggles, invasions and counter-invasions and continual fluctuations of fortune. The Chavdas of little Mansa State looked back to a time when their ancestors had ruled the whole of Gujerat, while the stateless Raos of Patan could claim that their forebears had once ruled Delhi before the Afghans; the rulers of the Himalayan hill state of Suket could contemplate an unbroken line of succession without adoption for almost 1200 years, while the genealogical chart of the Jethwas of Porbandar showed them to be possibly the oldest ruling dynasty in existence – the last ruling Maharana Saheb, Sir Natwarsinhji Bahadur, being the 179th in succession.

The rulers of Kutch could claim that no invaders had ever successfully overrun their coastal territory, largely due to the fact that much of the 18,000 square miles of the state was made up of a desert salt-marsh known as the Rann of Kutch:

> When the rains were good we were virtually an island for about six months of the year. No one could get across except at a few known places where camels could cross. There was no direct invasion by the Mughals except once from Sind during a drought year. A very big battle was fought in which the Kutch army was annihilated but the other party was so badly mauled that they withdrew. Another invasion from Ahmedabad almost reached the capital of Bhuj but there they were defeated partly by luck and partly by nature, and they, too, thought it better to withdraw. Even in 1971, when Pakistan invaded, they thought that their battle-tanks would be able to cross the Rann but they got bogged down instead.

Two hundred miles across the desert to the north of Kutch was Jaisalmer, honoured as *Bhad Khinwad Bhati*, the 'mighty portals of the Bhati Rajputs', because 'all the raiders who came to India came from the north and Jaisalmer was the first to bear the onslaught on our fort with its ninety-nine bastions'. North again was the state of Bikaner, whose crests bore the proud motto *Jai Jungle dhar Badshah* – 'Glory to the King of the Desert' – which had been awarded to an ancestor of the present Maharaja Karni Singh by his peers at the time of the Mughal Emperor Aurangzeb:

These rulers were supposed to have gone across the Indus to Attock, where Aurangzeb intended to convert them to Islam. The idea was that all the boats were to be destroyed after they had crossed so that they would not be able to come back until they had embraced Islam. However, before they could cross, my ancestor Maharaja Karan Singh took an axe and gave a blow to the first boat, none of the others apparently having the courage to do that against the Mughal Emperor. Then of course all the boats were destroyed, so nobody went across the river and nobody embraced Islam. And as a mark of respect they built a sand throne on the side of the river and he was put on that and given the title *Jai Jungle dhar Badshah*.

South-east of Bikaner and Jaisalmer was the largest of the desert kingdoms, Marwar (later renamed Jodhpur after its new capital), whose rulers and court poets honoured the name of Durga Das Rathor, who fought his way out of Delhi and the clutches of Emperor Aurangzeb with the newly-born infant ruler of Marwar, and from the Aravalli hills of Rajasthan conducted a long guerrilla campaign against the Mughals: 'Minstrels who came begging recite this line: "*Mai ehda put jan jahda Durga Das, Bhalai Mathai rakhiyo, bina thumb akas* – Oh mother, may you have a son like Durga Das, whose spear remained upright in the limitless sky."'

Further south again was Dhrangadhara, senior house of the Jhala clan, one of whose ancestors, Ajoji, had commanded the combined forces of the Rajputs which faced the Mughal invader and first emperor, Babur, at the fateful field of Khanua in 1527. Ajoji was struck in the eye by a chance arrow, the tide of battle turned and the Mughal Empire in India began. After Ajoji, seven successive generations of his line fell in battle in the service of Mewar, so giving rise to the saying: 'What is the history of India if not the history of Rajasthan, and what is the history of Rajasthan if not the history of Mewar, and what is the history of Mewar if not the history of the Jhalas.' Among their more colourful ancestors was Raja Raysinhji, left for dead after a battle and found suffering from amnesia by some monks who took him to Delhi: 'He was a very powerfully-built man who could pick up two buckets of water in each hand and he was drawing water from a well outside Delhi when somebody noticed what a powerful man he was, so he was challenged to fight by the Emperor's men in the Red Fort. He swung with the right hand, missed and hit the wall, pushing the brick in. Then he came back with his left hand, hit his opponent's head and the entire head went into the cavity. Of course, they then discovered who this man was and he came back to Dhrangadhara.'

The annals of Rajasthan are full of accounts of military struggles, either between one state and another or against their common enemy, the Mughal invaders from the north. Dhrangadhara was no exception, each encounter with the enemy producing its own crop of heroes and horrors, as at the battle of Kuwa:

> The rule was that when the ruler was fighting a standard-bearer stood by him with a flag which was dipped only if the king fell. The flag was lowered and the eight ladies of his house thought that he had fallen. Seven of them then jumped into a well and committed *sati* by drowning but the eighth wife didn't. At the end of the day the ruler came back victorious and was horrified to find that his wives had died because of an error on the flag-bearer's part. In the ruling family's records it says that the flag-bearer had gone for a drink of water, but in the flag-bearer's record it says that he went for a pee. The ruler was particularly perturbed that his eighth wife had not committed sati on hearing of his death and so she was encouraged to jump, too. Since then we have never married anyone of her clan.

It was on this rich diet that every Rajput boy and girl, whether of royal blood or a commoner, was fed and reared: 'The importance and greatness of being a Rajput was pushed down our throats – and it went down quite happily. In the stories who were the chivalrous people? The Rajputs! Who never turned their backs in battle? The Rajputs! Other people turned round and said they'd come back to fight another day, but if our men returned from battle in cowardice the doors were slammed in their faces by their womenfolk. The great Maharana Pratap of Mewar never showed his back in the battle of Haldi Ghati and mighty Maharana Sangram lacked an arm and an eye and had eighty-four wounds on his body at the time of his death.'

But the one quality in which the Rajputs were seriously deficient was 'a sense of coming together' and a common lament among them was that their failure to unite allowed first the Mughals and then the British to conquer India. 'Whenever they have united they have been a force to reckon with,' maintains the Maharawal of Dungarpur. 'United they threw the enemy out of Rajputana within days, yet within a few months after victory they fell apart, dining and wining, with banquets and dances and merriment, embracing each other as brothers, eulogising their sacrifices and chivalry. Then gradually the intrigues started again.'

4
THE MAKING OF THE PRINCES

FIRST ARTICLE – *There shall be perpetual friendship, alliance and unity of interests between the British Government on the one hand, and the Raja of Boondee and his heirs and successors on the other.*
SECOND ARTICLE – *The British Government takes under its protection the dominions of the Raja of Boondee.*
THIRD ARTICLE – *The Raja of Boondee acknowledges the supremacy of, and will co-operate with, the British Government for ever.*

From the *Treaties between the Honourable
English East-India Company and the Maha Row
Raja Bishen Sing Buhadoor, Raja of Boondee,
concluded by Captain James Tod on the part
of the Honourable Company and by Bohora
Tolaram on the part of the Raja. Done at
Boondee, this tenth day of February AD 1818*

Although the Rajput kingdoms and principalities were to constitute the largest proportion in Indian States in British times, they were only a part of a wider panorama in which Muslim, Sikh, Jat and other non-Rajput Hindu rulers also had their place. They too had their traditions and their family sagas. Of the Muslim states the largest by far was Hyderabad and Berar, dominating the tableland of the Deccan and founded by a Mughal general appointed to be Emperor Aurangzeb's Viceroy in Southern India who, after Aurangzeb's death in 1707, set himself up as the first Nizam: 'Communications were bad in those days and rather than go back to Delhi and report to Aurangzeb's successors this gentleman stayed on with his little army, acquired the whole state for himself and failed to send any revenues back to Delhi.'

It was the slow disintegration throughout the eighteenth century of the Empire established by the Mughal Babur in North India in 1526 and reinforced by his grandson Akbar that allowed other local Viceroys and generals to follow suit. One of these new Muslim states was Bhopal, whose founder took for himself the apt Arabic motto 'Nasrum Inallahe wa Fatahoon Qarib – Give Good News, for by the

Grace of God Victory is Near'. Sited at the very heart of the subcontinent, Bhopal was to earn a unique place for itself in the history of the Indian States on account of its women rulers – as the present Begum of Bhopal explains:

> The founder of Bhopal, Dost Mohammed Khan, was with the Nizam's army that was going south to fight when he decided to break away. At the time Bhopal had a woman ruler, Kamalpati, whom he befriended and fought for before carving out a state for himself. At the time the question of who was Muslim and who was Hindu didn't arise. It was just a question of who was stronger. We had Hindu commanders and the Marathas had Muslim commanders. The tradition of the women rulers started when Kudsia Begum's father, the Nawab, laid it down as a condition of her marriage that her husband would become the ruler. He died very young leaving only a daughter, so Kudsia Begum became the Regent, ruling until her daughter came of age. Sikander Begum was a very strong person and when you look at pictures of her she looks more like a warrior than a lady ruler. She was married to one of her cousins but they couldn't get along and he also died young. She only had one daughter so she became Regent and ruler during the very troublesome times of the Mutiny and after her death in 1868 Shah Jehan Begum became the ruler. She also lost her husband early and she only had one daughter, my grandmother Nawab Sultan Jahan Begum.

The Muslim state of Janjira was an oddity, having been founded by Abyssinian pirates. By contrast, the Nawabs of Palanpur, Tonk and Rampur, as well as one or two lesser Muslim rulers, shared a common ancestry as descendants of Pathan tribesmen from Afghanistan who entered India in search of the traditional *Zan, Zar, Zamin* – women, gold and land: 'We came as plunderers,' admits Zulfiquar Ali Khan of Rampur. 'We took over the area known as Rohilkhand but during the war between the Nawabs of Rampur and Avadh (Oude) the British sided with Avadh and punished us like naughty schoolchildren by taking away ninety per cent of our territory and leaving us just Rampur to rule. That's the reason why, after losing so much territory, Nawab Yusuf Ali Khan remained neutral during the 1857 Mutiny, because he feared that what was left would also be taken from him.'

Among these Muslim states the house of Palanpur was unusual in that it was already ruling a principality named Jalor even before the Mughals came to India as a feudatory of the Muslim Sultans of Gujerat. When the armies of Akbar invaded Gujerat its ruler, Ghazni Khan II, refused to support him and eventually became his prisoner:

After a few years Ghazni Khan got his release through his mother, who was a Rajput lady and came to the court of Akbar. The Emperor took a great liking to him and gave his foster-sister in marriage to him as well as Palanpur in dowry. We have to this day a sword given by Akbar to that ruler. Unfortunately, when their son became ruler he got into bad company and drank heavily and killed his mother. The Emperor in Delhi was then Jehangir who sent for him and had him squashed under the foot of an elephant, which was one way of killing wrongdoers in those days. However, his son was allowed to rule and we continued to hold Jalor until 1704 when Aurangzeb's grandchildren were kidnapped by Durga Das Rathor, who demanded the return of Jalor to the Rajputs of Jodhpur as a ransom. So from 1704 onwards we continued to rule only from Palanpur.

Palanpur also had its bardic traditions and its court poets who recited their *rasahs* or poetical legends of princes which told with considerable artistic licence of their great deeds. One such legend concerned Palanpur's alliance with neighbouring Jodhpur and the death of their common adversary, a Maratha general:

The Rajmata of Jodhpur in those days had many camels and one went mad, killing people by trampling them with its knees. Many were killed but nobody dared complain to the Rajmata because she was a hot-tempered lady, until one day a Rajput who didn't know of this mad camel was chased by him and fell into a pit. The camel began breaking down the edge of the pit with its hooves but the Rajput saw a scorpion and, picking it up on the tip of his sword, placed it on the camel's nose. The camel was bitten and with a shriek it died. Within half an hour its meat and bones had all turned to blue ash, which was collected in jars, sealed and put in the state *toshakhana* (treasury). Palanpur was then at war with the army of the Peshwa (hereditary prime minister of the Maratha Confederacy), whose General, Pilaji Rao, was very interested in alchemy. Jodhpur joined forces with Palanpur and sent two men disguised as *sadhus* (holy men) with some poison to the camp of the Marathas. The enemy general came to hear of them and went to them because he wanted to learn how to make gold. The two sadhus said they would teach him but only in private in a closed room. In this room they lit a fire, to which they began to add the contents of the jar of poison. Then one of the sadhus went out of the room supposedly to bring back more ingredients and a little later the other left in search of him, telling the general to keep adding the contents of the jar. The sadhu closed the door behind him and within a few minutes the general was dead. Without their leader the Peshwa's army had to retire.

It was the Maratha Confederacy to the south, growing in strength and ambition as Mughal power waned, that not only put paid to

Palanpur's hopes of becoming a major power but also overran many of the kingdoms – Rajput and Muslim – that bordered the Deccan. Tough hillmen from the Western Ghats and the Deccan mountains, the Marathas were for the most part cultivators and their leaders were very different in temperament and background from the Rajputs, as the present Maharaja Scindia of Gwalior testifies: 'Unlike some of the princes who claim descent from the sun and the moon, I'm proud of the fact that we have risen from being sons of the soil, peasants really, just ordinary Maratha farmers who rose on their own sweat and blood. The original ancestor of mine was supposed to have been a village headman before he joined the services of Chhatrapati Shivaji and he rose to be a general.' Inspired and directed by the great warrior Shivaji, the Marathas united to form the first well-organised force to threaten the Mughals in two hundred years. 'It was Shivaji who put us on the map of India,' explains Sardar Sitole, whose family became the most powerful of the four Sardar families close to the rulers of Gwalior. 'Before him we were all lions in our own dens and if anybody interfered you killed him off. There was no conception of being part of a Maratha state. We were a militant race but we were not organised.' After Shivaji's death his line continued as the princely house of Satara, the other so-called Maratha states being founded either by Brahmins who had served as Shivaji's ministers, as in the case of Sangli, Aundh and Bhor, or by the Maratha generals who fought for the Brahmin Peshwas, the hereditary prime ministers of the Maratha Confederacy.

The founder of Bhor State was Shankaraji Narayan, one of Shivaji's eight ministers, who after his death and the execution of Shivaji's eldest son by Aurangzeb swore an oath of loyalty to Tarabai, the widow of Shivaji's second son. Then Shivaji's grandson, Shahu, was released from captivity in Delhi and returned to claim his Empire:

> Shankaraji Narayan was in a quandary because he had sworn an oath to Tarabai but his real loyalty lay with Shahu. So what he did was to eat a sharp-edged diamond – what we call in Marathi *hirakani* – and committed suicide at a place near Bhor called Ambevade. There we have his marble *samadhi* (cremation platform) and every year his death is remembered on a very grand scale. After his death Shahu realised that he had been very loyal and that's how Bhor State came into being, with land given by Shahu.

On the edge of the Deccan south of Bhor was Sangli, one of five small states ruled by members of the Patwardhan family, whose common ancestor had sent all his sons to serve in the Peshwa's army:

> At one time there were sixty members of the Patwardhan family in the army. They became favourites of the Peshwas, which led to a lot of jealousy. There is a story that these very people who were so jealous were invited to a feast at which they were served by many young widows of the Patwardhans. Then the guests were told that the Peshwas favoured the Patwardhan family because this was the high price they had paid to be in their service. Because of their valour they were rewarded with all the lands between Satara, Kolhapur and the Nizam's dominions.

As well as Brahmins there were also Rajputs among the Marathas, whose forebears had migrated from the north to settle in the Deccan – among them the rulers of Sawantwadi State, founded by descendants of a survivor of the first holocaust at Chittor in 1303, and the rulers of the two states of Dewas, whose ancestors also gained their land as a reward for military services to the Peshwas: 'There were three brothers, so Dhar State went to the eldest while the two younger brothers divided their portion of land between them, which came to be known as Dewas Senior and Dewas Junior.'

Though they may have lacked the antiquity of the Rajputs, the Marathas still had their own annals from the past to draw upon. One early ruler of distinction in Dewas Junior was Haibatrao Puar who, unable to stop bandit raids on his land, went in desperation to the Hill of Devi where both states shared a little temple of Kali. Here the goddess Kali appeared to him in a vision to say that she would fight on his side – but on condition that the ruler sacrificed his eldest son to her after his victory. Having duly repelled the invaders, Haibatrao Puar then had to carry out the sacrifice:

> The priest came and stood before the king with folded hands and said, 'Lord, everything is ready, but where is the sacrifice?' So the king said, 'The offering is right beside me,' and he picked up his son and swept the little crown off his head and laid him in front of the goddess. The priest was horrified and said, 'What are you doing? You are sacrificing your only son?' The king said, 'This is the goddess's wish and I have given my word,' and he lifted up his sword and cut off the head of his child, which flew from the body and lay at a distance. The priest on seeing this horrific sight fainted, but the king stood with the blade of his sword dripping with blood and cried out to the goddess in a loud voice, 'Hail Mata, I have performed what I said I would do' – and to his utter amazement, the image opened

and the goddess emerged and said, 'Well done. You are a good son, and like a true Rajput, you have kept your word. Here, I give your son back to you.' Then she picked up the head of the child and laid it against his neck and in a moment the child was up and about. From that day onwards Haibatrao came to be known as a saint and the people in the kingdom used to come to the king and ask him to lay his hands on them to heal them of various ills. Even today his *Chhatri* (cenotaph) at the place where the kings from both states are burnt, has an aura about it.

In addition to these smaller states there were the three major states founded by the ablest of the Peshwa's generals – Scindia of Gwalior, Holkar of Indore and Gaekwad of Baroda. 'All three were huzras (aides) of the Peshwa,' relates Leela Moolgaokar, recalling a story told to her as a child in Gwalior. 'When you went to see the Peshwa you left your shoes outside his office. One day Mahadji Maharaj Scindia went along but the Peshwa took a long time to see him. Waiting outside, he put his shoes on his head and went to sleep. When the Peshwa came out he saw this and was so touched that he took off the gold *toda* (anklet) from his foot and gave it to Mahadji, who put it on his head. Today you'll find the Gwalior turban worn by the Scindias and their Sardars has a little gold toda in it.'

All three of these powerful ruling families had humble origins. 'We were shepherds,' explains Richard Shivaji Rao Holkar. 'Apparently young Malhar Rao Holkar was sleeping by his flock when he was seen with a cobra reared over his head, shielding his face from the sun. Then there was a sequence of events whereby he became a military commander under the umbrella of the Peshwa.' The family name of the rulers of Baroda showed that they had a similarly lowly origin. 'Gaekwad comes from two Sanscrit words,' explains Fatehsinghrao Gaekwad, '*gae* for cow and *wad* for gate, and the story goes that my ancestor saved a herd of cows from a butcher by opening the portals of his village and allowing them to enter. The British thought this was a title and started calling my ancestors "the Gaekwars" – or even "Guickurs" – of Baroda. We were at one stage the generals of the Brahmin Peshwa at Pune – Poona, the British called it – and after we had pushed the Mughals out in 1731 our ancestors used to be sent out annually to the region known as Gujerat to collect a fourth of the revenue from the treasury at Pune. A stage came when one ancestor found the Brahmin ruler at Pune had become weak so he went to Gujerat and didn't come back.'

Once firmly established in the fertile plains of Gujerat the Gaek- wads were content to hang on to what they had won, unlike the

Holkars and Scindias who dominated and terrorised Central and Northern India for more than half a century – until finally beaten back by the sepoy armies of the British East India Company to what were to become their settled state boundaries.

It was very largely their fear of the Marathas that persuaded other Indian rulers to make alliances with this new foreign power on the subcontinent. In South India such alliances eventually left the East India Company in secure command of the Madras Presidency, well-protected from the Marathas by the extensive dominions of the Nizam of Hyderabad and Berar – always referred to thereafter as 'most faithful ally of the British' – to the north, and by the ancient Hindu kingdoms of Travancore and Cochin to the south. To the west of Madras there was the scarcely less ancient kingdom of Mysore, ruled by the Wadiyar dynasty whose founder had been a Viceroy of the once-proud Vijayanagar Empire, the bastion of the Hindus in the South, until an army of three-quarters of a million men and 2000 elephants had been scattered and destroyed at the battle of Talikot in 1562. Rescued by the British in 1799 from the usurpers Hyder Ali and his son Tipu Sultan, the Wadiyars returned to rule Mysore with model decorum. With a succession of able Dewans or Chief Ministers as powers behind the gadi, Mysore State was to become the most efficiently administered state in India, its rulers content for the most part to restrict their duties to the spectacular ceremonials and religious rituals at which Mysore excelled.

Up in Bengal the British took control by an effective mixture of bullying, bribery and military prowess which by degrees reduced such local Viceroys of the Mughals as the Nawab of Bengal and the Maharaja of Burdwan to the status of zamindars. Under Mughal rule such zamindars had exercised limited powers within their estates, but the land had always reverted to the Emperor upon their deaths – 'which led to a lot of mismanagement and horse-trading'. By the Permanent Settlement of Bengal of 1793 this system was reversed, so that a zamindar could keep his land so long as he paid his annual dues to the government on time, but lost his rights as a local ruler. Having no obligations to look after the welfare of their tenant-farmers big zamindars like Burdwan – the biggest individual taxpayer in the British Empire – Darbhangha and Dumraon became exceedingly wealthy and surrounded themselves with all the trappings of Indian royalty. Some, like the enlightened zamindars of Cossimbazar, made great efforts to provide schools, hospitals and other modern facilities for those whom they regarded as their people. Tikari Raj, near Patna, was a more typical zamindari where its

Maharajas lived well while seeing to it that their tenants were provided for:

Maharaja Gopal Narain Saran Singh's ancestors got their property with the Mughal ruler Akbar. The line of communication between Agra and Bengal went through the forests of Bihar where *dacoits* and bandits found it a very remunerative business looting all these Mughal caravans. So to prevent this the Mughal general of the time appointed probably the biggest dacoit of the area and said, 'You look after us and we'll give you this property.' So that's how the Tikaris started. They were just big zamindars and the titles of Raja and Maharaja started with the British when they helped them against other small feudal barons and landlords. They lived very much as maharajas and Maharaja Gopal Narain Saran Singh, for one, was probably better known in the European capitals than most Indian rulers. When the 1914–18 war was declared he insisted on joining up and went as a Lieutenant Despatch Rider to Field-Marshal Haig. As a present he took a loan from Darbhangha and presented the British government with a squadron of tanks. There was an incident on the Western Front when complaints were received from the Germans that some bullets were being used at a certain part of the lines in contravention of the Geneva Red Cross Convention. A senior officer went down one evening to investigate and found a lot of his staff officers gathered round the Maharaja of Tikari, who was shooting out the little steel shields that the Germans had produced with his Westley-Richards 476 high velocity double-barrelled tiger gun.

As the British advanced deeper into what became known as the 'conquered and ceded provinces of Upper Hindustan' in the latter half of the eighteenth century, they did their best to absorb local states into the Bengal Presidency. One of the few that survived much reduced in size was Benares, which was to become unique for regaining in later years part of the territories it had earlier lost to the British:

Our family never forgave Warren Hastings who said there was maladministration and took over Benares. If he had not we would have been as strong as the Nizam of Hyderabad, with territory stretching from Allahabad down to Buxar in Benares. But Warren Hastings had a quarrel with Maharaja Chait Singh and came personally to Benares to arrest him. The citizens of Benares rose in a rebellion and Warren Hastings had to make a hasty retreat. He returned with a bigger force and Chait Singh had to flee to Gwalior. So that dynasty finished and one of my ancestors who was an adopted son became the founder of the new state. He was chosen by Warren Hastings to accede to the gadi of Benares but with no powers of

jurisdiction. In addition, we lost the sovereignty not only of Benares
city but of other parts that used to fall within Benares State.

From their magnificent riverside palace of Ramnagar overlooking
the Ganges a mile upstream of the city that was no longer theirs,
the rulers of Benares fought for over a century to have their
rights restored – until eventually in 1911 the Viceroy invested the
grandfather of the present Maharaja with his original title and
accorded him all the powers and privileges of a 13-gun state.

By the opening years of the nineteenth century the advance guards
of the East India Company had begun to come up against the Rajput
states of Rajasthan and the neighbouring Jat states of Dholpur and
Bharatpur – whose rulers were among the thirty-six 'royal races'
and claimed descent from the moon, but were never accepted as
pukka Rajputs by the other clans and remained outside the pale as
far as intermarriage was concerned. Conscious that the main threat
to their existence came not from the British but from the Marathas,
the larger Rajput states began one after another to throw in their
lot with the British. Each signed treaties of 'perpetual alliance and
friendship' with the East India Company's representatives – among
them Captain James Tod, who was to become the Rajputs' greatest
admirer and champion.

In due course Gwalior and Indore also signed treaties – but as
defeated enemies. So, too, did Baroda and the larger Kathiawar
states, with Kutch falling into line in 1819, all accepting British
dominion as a *fait accompli*. In all, forty treaties which came to be
known familiarly as '*Dosti* London' or 'Friendship with London'
treaties were signed, together with a great many more *sanads* or
instruments of contract. These varied in their terms according
to the conditions under which they had been drawn up, but all
acknowledged the undisputed overlordship of the British crown as
represented by the East India Company. The last to acknowledge
British suzerainty in Central India was Bharatpur, which having
withstood one prolonged siege in 1804 fell to a second in 1825.

Finally, it was the turn of the Sikhs – the predominantly Jat people
of the Punjab who, under their one-eyed general Ranjit Singh, had
briefly regained a cohesion that the Mughals had earlier destroyed
– to become the one remaining obstacle to British control over the
entire subcontinent. Like the Rajputs, they too had a clan system
loosely based on twelve *misls*. A leader of the Phul misl founded
Patiala State, which as a result of choosing the right side in the two
Anglo-Sikh wars of the 1840s became the largest of the five principal
Sikh states to enjoy treaty rights with the British. Other family

offshoots founded the smaller states of Nabha, Jind and Faridkot. One Sikh state that fared badly in the wars was Kapurthala, founded by the dynamic *misldar* of the Ahluwalia clan, Baba Jassa Singh, who in the 1760s had won control over all the land between the Beas and Sutlej rivers – most of which was confiscated from his descendants seventy years later after the first Anglo-Sikh war of 1845:

> The only cohesive force which emerged on the scene was the Honourable East India Company. So, as a matter of political sagacity, we threw in our lot with them. At the time of the 1857 Mutiny Raja Randhir Singh himself took the field with his brother for the better part of eight months, leading the Kapurthala troops in a number of engagements and both were very highly praised in the despatches of the time to the Honourable Board of Directors.

Once the 1857 Mutiny was over the ruler of Kapurthala asked for the restoration of his land 'for services rendered'. He had before him the example of the vast territories of Kashmir to the north which only a decade earlier had fallen into the laps of the Dogra Rajput Rajas of Jammu – at the bargain price of 75 lakhs of rupees and an annual tribute of six Cashmere shawls and a dozen shawl goats – as their reward for switching sides during the hostilities of 1845. But Kapurthala was not so lucky. Instead of their former territory the rulers were offered at a nominal rent from the government large tracts in the United Provinces confiscated from the rebel landowners of Oude – not to rule, but from which to draw revenues as zamindar landlords. These zamindari lands gave Kapurthala a very handsome annual income of 24 lakhs of rupees at very little cost to the state and made its rulers far wealthier in proportion to the size of their state – 600 square miles as compared to Patiala's 6000 – than most of their fellow princes.

The Mutiny year of 1857–8 was a turning point both for the British in India and for those rulers, major and minor, who had come to terms with their new overlords. In November 1858 a Royal Proclamation was read out in Queen Victoria's name declaring an end to Company rule and the commencement of Crown rule. It also defined for the first time the new role of the Princes, who were to 'underpin and support' the British Raj: 'The British knew that they couldn't administer the whole country and they knew that the rulers were best suited to do it – provided that they could control them and satisfy them in some respects.' Because it safeguarded their authority and their future as rulers of their states Queen Victoria's Proclamation, with its solemn undertaking to 'respect the rights, dignity and honour of the Native Princes as Our own', came to be regarded as the 'Magna Carta of the Princes'.

This was the moment in their history when, in the words of one latter-day prince, 'we ceased to be kings and became princes' – and which another interprets as the start of their 'political emasculation'. By being brought under the sheltering umbrella of the Raj, 'with the British there to guarantee our boundaries, our incomes and our privileges', the Princes were given absolute security. Insurrection or opposition to the ruler became well-nigh impossible and he himself no longer required to be accountable to his people: 'Whereas the Indian Princes when they were kings were answerable and responsive to local sanctions, as they became responsible to the superior power – here always called the Paramount Power – so they paid less attention to internal sanctions.' With hindsight it was also clear that the security offered by the British umbrella was not in the best interests of those it protected, because 'giving us that sort of stability for a hundred years made us soft. We started leaning on the British, we started feeling that they were essential to our survival, whereas originally it was we who had been essential for British survival – and that mental weakness was to manifest itself in 1947 when the British left.'

The rights of the Princes that were to be so scrupulously respected related only to internal government and even here rulers were to be subject to the scrutiny and advice of the Crown Representative in the person of his Political Agents in the Foreign and Political Department – the Agents to the Governor-General stationed in their Residencies close at hand – for the British took the view that never at any time in the history of the native rulers had they been kings in the accepted sense:

> They were never at any time monarchs. What we called Indian Princes had never before the coming of the British been in the position of exercising any of the prerogatives of royalty. If there was anybody entitled to these prerogatives it was the various dynasties of emperors at Delhi and eventually, with the rise of the great Maratha Empire, the chiefs of the Maratha Confederacy, to whom they were in a state of complete subordination. At no time was the word *Badshah*, which is the Persian equivalent of king, ever applied to any of the Indian Princes as we knew them. Badshah was the prerogative of the Emperor of Delhi. Even the forebear of the Nizam of Hyder-abad who founded the dynasty was nothing more than a Viceroy or a deputy of the Emperor who was the incumbent of the throne of Delhi.

Any attempt to use such monarchical terms as 'king', 'kingdom' or 'royal', or even to refer to the gadis or cushions on which the rulers sat on formal occasions as thrones, was to be vigorously opposed over the next ninety years, as were a number of attempts by rulers to introduce 'arched crowns' as opposed to 'open crowns' on their letterheads and official state papers. A major outbreak of 'arched crowns' on princely correspondence, started by Maharaja Tukoji Rao Holkar of Indore in 1925, was deemed to be a serious infringement upon the prerogative of the King-Emperor and was rigorously stamped upon – as was an attempt by Maharaja Bhupinder Singh of Patiala in 1935 to call himself 'Royal'.

Yet while they made every effort to curtail the pretensions of the Princes in relation to the Paramount Power, the British also built them up in terms of prestige and grandeur within the states themselves. The Princes were loaded with titles, honours and gun salutes and placed in what was deemed to be an appropriate order of precedence so that 'each ruler was put in his particular orbit as a satellite'. But 'in the times of the Mughals there was no Maharaja, no Maharao in Kutch,' declares the Maharao of Kutch, former recipient of a 17-gun salute and first among the sixteen salute Princes of the Western India States Agency:

> In those days we were called Jams, like the Jam of Nawanagar who is a descendant of my ancestors. At the time of Khengarji the First who established and consolidated the state with the help of the Mughal Emperors, the Emperor said, 'You are a great Rao.' So he changed his title from Jam to Rao and this went on until the time of the British when the Rana was called Maharana, the Raja of Jodhpur was called Maharaja of Jodhpur and the Rao of Kutch was called Maharao of Kutch. It was the British way of giving a little more title to the rulers – and they liked it, because the British were very clever administrators. Gun salutes, too, were given at the time of the British. There were none at the time of the Mughals. And it became a matter of great prestige as to whether a ruler had one gun more than another. Some rulers went so far as to count the guns when they were fired, to see whether it was seventeen guns they were getting or less.

The whole question of gun salutes and who should precede whom when it came to calling on the Viceroy, or when a Prince of Wales made a royal tour, was to cause a great deal of bickering and heart-searching among the Princes. The rulers of the Kathiawar states, who fell mostly into the 11- and 9-gun category, always regarded themselves as seriously 'under-gunned' in relation to the smaller Rajput states, who came mostly into the 17- and 15-gun category – but who were themselves perpetually in dispute over who should follow the 'big three' of Udaipur, Jaipur and Jodhpur in the local order of precedence. In the 1930s an extended six-year quarrel between the rulers of Bikaner and Patiala, both outstanding and forceful personalities, over who should take precedence when they met on official occasions ended in a victory for Ganga Singh of Bikaner – and a large file of correspondence in the Political Department headed by a note that began: 'The Viceroy is getting very tired of the petty difficulties that arise over precedence.'

A further effort to draw the Princes closer into the British fold came with the introduction of coats of arms devised by an expert in British heraldry in time for the 1877 Proclamation of Queen Victoria as Empress of India, when the 102 Treaty States were provided with entirely spurious coats of arms complete with supporters of cows and elephants, scrolls often with English mottoes, and crests that had helms but no crowns.

Ultimately, it was the change of lifestyle which more than anything else 'cut the umbilical cord between us and the people' and seriously weakened the close *Raja-Praja* relationship at the heart of the ancient Hindu concept of kingship: 'In Hindu society there was always great stress laid on humility and simplicity – but that slowly changed and from the very simple way they all lived, it became very ostentatious living with one prince competing with another, which wasn't there among the old rulers.' This alteration in lifestyle varied in its timing from state to state but was nearly always characterised by the same event: 'If one were to ask when exactly this took place in a particular state I would say that the physical evidence of it is the year in which the ruler moved his residence from the centre of the city to somewhere more salubrious and more sanitary,' declares the Maharaja of Dhrangadhara. 'That's when the rulers ceased to be kings. They still had the trappings of kingship, all the ceremonies, the coronation rituals and royal anointings from ancient times, but those were shadows that remained rather than the substance of kingship. In Dhrangadhara the palace outside the city was built by my grandfather when he was a prince during his grandfather's reign, so he was residing outside the city when his grandfather died at the turn of the century, in 1900.'

A similar transformation took place in Palanpur State at about the same time, as Muzaffer Khan describes:

It must have been dramatic, that change. In Rajputana and Gujerat, all along the Western coast and in the North almost overnight there was this change, between one generation and another, from being very traditional Indians to wearing suits, playing cricket and going dancing, eating Western food and pig-sticking. In my grandfather's case it happened almost overnight when his father died and he had the opportunity to set about constructing a Western as opposed to a traditional Indian house. He started wearing Western clothes and Western cooks were called in to train up the local cooks. All these things happened in a relatively short space of time, a span of five years, in which they moved up a hundred years.

5
THE BLOOD OF GREAT MEN

Oh! the brightly shining sun of the House of Bika,
Why have you set so prematurely?

The land of Bikaner is plunged with grief,
Without you, Ganga Singhji, our noble lord of the land.

Your fame is sung far and wide,
Generous as you always were, how did you become so
*   hard-hearted*
As to leave us desolate!

On the earth there are several twinkling Kings,
But who amongst them has glorified the traditions of his
*   House*
As you did for the House of Bikaner?

On the Death of Maharaja Ganga Singh,
Ruler of Bikaner 1887–1943, by
Chander Singh, poet of Bikaner
(translated from Marwari)

'I find it quite frightening even today to think that the blood of these great men runs through my veins. It's a terrifying thing.' So says Maharaja Karni Singh of Bikaner, whose forebears drew the state of Bikaner out of the sands and arid hills of the Thar desert. Each left his mark in one way or another, but no state in India underwent such a radical transformation in its physical appearance and in the circumstances of its people as Bikaner in the years between the handing over of ruling powers to Karni Singh's grandfather, Ganga Singh, in 1898 and his death in 1943.

The fact that the rulers of the Indian States found themselves in varying degrees of subordination to the British crown did little to encourage the majority to exercise their talents. Some handed over the reins of government to a capable Dewan and turned their attentions to more frivolous pursuits; a great many more simply carried on ruling as their fathers and grandfathers had done, without much thought to the changing circumstances around them, marking time rather than making any serious effort to move with the times. But there remained a number of rulers who by dint of personality and enlightened attitudes – usually combined with the good fortune of having ascended the gadi at an early age – were able both to leave an indelible imprint on their states and to bring them out of the medieval world into the modern. Indeed, there were enough of these rulers, born at about the same time and ruling for approximately the same span of years, for this to be a remarkable phenomenon in the history of the Indian Princes. Together they dominated the princely stage from the Curzon era at the start of the twentieth century right up to the Second World War.

Inevitably, it was the rulers of large states like Baroda, Bikaner and Gwalior who captured the limelight and who today are numbered among the giants of modern Indian history. But among their contemporaries were at least a dozen quite outstanding men who, because they ruled over lesser states, are now only remembered by those who lived under their rule as children or heard about them from their parents' generation; princes of the calibre of Maharaja Bhagvatsinhji of the 11-gun state of Gondal, the only state in Western India where female education was compulsory. A highly-qualified surgeon by training, Bhagvatsinhji lived very modestly – even frugally – supported by a Maharani who was the first among the Kathiawar states to come out of purdah. To the Indian Political Officer, Conrad Corfield, he was 'so modern that it caused rather a scandal because he insisted on his daughters being educated and brought out into society'. His three sons completed their education in Scotland, like their father before them: 'One trained as a doctor, the two others as engineers and as soon as they were qualified they were placed in separate charge of the state medical services, the state roads and the state railways. They were each paid £500 a year and had to work hard under father's eagle eye.' When Bhagvatsinhji died in 1944 he left an industrially developed state that was without taxes, rates or customs levies.

Much better known both in India and abroad was Jagatjit Singh of Kapurthala, partly because his reign covered a unique span of seven decades, partly because he was an inveterate traveller, blazing trails across Europe that many of his fellow-princes were to follow – though rarely with the same degree of sophistication. Although never popular with the Political Department, as much for his dalliances with a succession of beautiful European women as for his absences from his state, Jagatjit Singh put little Kapurthala firmly on the map. Indeed, to his subjects he *was* Kapurthala.

Just as Jagatjit Singh was the maker of modern Kapurthala, so Raj Saheb Amarsinhji was the maker of Wankaner, dying in 1954 after ruling his little 9-gun state for forty-nine years. In nearby Kutch the gadi was occupied for over sixty years by the good-natured

THE BLOOD OF GREAT MEN

personality of Maharao Khengarji II, who died in 1942, and among
the Maratha states there was Sangli, where the progressive Raja
Saheb Chintamanrao Patwardhan also ruled for more than six
decades, making his state among the first in the Deccan to have
responsible government. In little Dewas Junior, Maharaja Malhar
Rao Puar died in 1934 after half a century on the throne and on
the borders of Baroda Lt.-Col. Maharaol Ranjitsinhji of Baria
presided over his 813 square miles and 150,000 subjects for forty-
four years until his death in 1952. To his grandson, the present
Maharaol, he was 'one of a group of much loved and generous
rulers who did a lot for their states' but each in a different way. For
Ranjitsinhji the main thing was accessibility and justice:

> He used to have a system whereby he camped in different parts of
> the state, a week in each place annually. He literally camped under
> canvas and anybody who had any complaints would come and see
> him. These were very elaborate camps because the officers and the
> Prime Minister and everybody was there, so there was a huge area
> which was a permanent campsite where a tent city used to spring up
> every year. There would be sections where the Maharaja with his
> family would be living and where the staff and the officers would be
> living and then in the middle somewhere there would be a court
> where people could gather and talk and where these big *shamianas*
> (open-sided tents) used to be put up. I remember people coming in
> hundreds every day with their problems. There were no petitions
> written down, they would be called in turn and then they would
> explain verbally their problem. It would be sieved through the officers
> to see whether it was something to do with revenue or something to
> do with social life. Then he would sit and hear them all. In many
> cases he would give decisions immediately on the spot. Sometimes
> it would take a little longer because they would have to check up the
> records, although they used to travel with all the records for that
> area.

As well as the week-long camps the Maharaol also liked to make
daily excursions in his car:

> He had a very good system of roads in the state, and he used to go
> on different routes and drive nearly 200 miles every day like a clock,
> 100 in the morning and 100 in the evening. People knew the routes
> on which he would be going on certain days and he was always so
> precise with his timings that people would almost set their watch by
> his visits and people would be standing on the roadside at different
> places, waiting for him. He never drove in a sedan car. All his life,
> right till the last day he was always in an open tourer – and it didn't

matter whether it was raining, still he wouldn't put the hood up. Even in the rains he would wear his solar hat and put on a mackintosh and let the rain fall on him. A very funny thing that I remember was that in those days he had cars with footboards and these men used to talk to him and if he found that they were taking a little too long and he might get late to the next point, these four or five people would get onto the footboard and the car would drive on and they would stand and talk to him as the car drove along. So his mass contact was absolutely phenomenal and people got very cheap and quick justice.

The outstanding characteristic of rulers like the Maharaol of Baria was their self-confidence: 'In spite of the educational handicaps that they may have suffered from they had tremendous confidence in themselves, and while they were willing to recognise British sovereignty over the subcontinent they were nobody's puppets. They went directly to the heart of the matter and they were so confident of success that somehow success came to them.'

No one displayed this self-confidence to greater effect than the gallant, bow-legged swashbuckler Sir Pratap Singh of Jodhpur, the great-grandfather of the present Maharaja of Idar, who personified in his life and character the traditional virtues of the Rajputs but nevertheless managed to bridge the gap between the old ways and the new. Born the third son of the ruler of Jodhpur in 1845 he showed absolute fearlessness as a child to the point of foolhardiness, going after leopards with swords and wrestling wild boars to the ground. When he grew up he took charge of the Sardar Rissala, the regiment of lancers that Jodhpur, along with a number of other leading states, provided to the Government of India from time to time as imperial service troops. At the age of seventy he even accompanied his troops into the trenches of France and later to Palestine: 'Basically, he was a soldier – and a prince only incidentally. He had certain values in life that he stuck to and when the Jodhpur Lancers fighting at the siege of Haifa fell back he gave a very simple order to his troops: "You can go forward and be killed by the enemy's bullets or you can fall back and be executed by me." That's how the Jodhpur Lancers took Haifa.'

A quarter century earlier Sir Pratap – whom the British knew as 'Sir Pertab' – had used the same directness when he first came to London to attend Queen Victoria's Golden Jubilee at the formal invitation of the Queen-Empress: 'Most of the rulers in those days used to stay at the Savoy,' explains Rajendra Sinhji of Idar. 'Or in Claridges or one of the great hotels of London, but my great-great-grandfather when he arrived in England said he would stay at Buckingham Palace. Somebody politely told him that Her Majesty had not invited him to stay in Buckingham Palace, to which he replied, "Supposing I were to invite Her Majesty to Jodhpur, would I expect her to stay in somebody else's house or hotel? So, obviously, Her Majesty will not expect me to stay in somebody else's house or hotel." Upon which he forthwith entered Buckingham Palace.'

As a child Iris Portal used to see Sir Pratap whenever he came to stay with her uncle, Sir James Dunlop Smith, ex-Indian Political Officer and former Viceroy's Private Secretary, in London during the First World War: 'He was always accompanied by his two sons and my Aunt Minnie used to say to us before they came, "Please observe their manners, they are never allowed to speak in front of their father, and if he were to order them to do anything – even to go to their death – they would unhesitatingly do so." So we goggled at these two silent young men and I said to my elder brother, "If we took them aside and told them that their father wanted them to jump out of the second-floor window, do you think they would do it?"' But Sir Pratap was also a figure of great romance as well as authority:

> There are many wonderful stories about Sir Pertab, his courage, his chivalry, his courtesy – but my uncle told Sir Henry Newbolt this story which Sir Henry turned into a poem: 'A young Englishman came to stay with Sir Pertab in Jodhpur. They went out shooting and pig-sticking together and there he died of some sudden fever and a terrible problem arose. There were not enough Englishmen in the place to carry his body out to burial – there were three but a fourth was needed – and Sir Pertab said, "I will be the fourth bearer of my friend's corpse." The Englishmen said, "You will lose caste if you touch his body," but Sir Pertab refused to pay any attention. Next morning the Brahmin priests were on his doorstep and said to him, "You will have to do very severe purification." Sir Pertab told them to go away and never speak of it again, because there is a caste that is higher than any other caste and that is the caste of the warrior.

Sir Pratap Singh's gallantry and old-world charm won him many admirers in Britain, including the Royal Family, but he never ceased to speak frankly when the situation demanded it – as on the occasion in 1921 when the Prince of Wales came to Jodhpur and was taken pig-sticking, a dangerous sport at which Sir Pratap excelled. When the future Edward VII made a blunder that left him exposed, the seventy-seven-year-old Rajput pulled him up and admonished him with the words: 'I know you are the Prince of Wales and you know that you are the Prince of Wales – but the pig doesn't know that you are the Prince of Wales.'

Sir Pratap was unusual among the Princes in that he was honoured as a head of state and yet was only very briefly a ruler. The Rathors of Jodhpur were closely related to the rulers of Idar and when the gadi at Idar became vacant without any direct heir to take over Sir Pratap Singh was one of several claimants: 'While the other claimants were fighting it out and trying to make good their claims in India with the Viceroy, my great-great-grandfather went over his head and appealed straight away to the Queen. He sent her a cable saying simply, "Idar is mine" – and somehow it worked, because we got it.' Nine years later the Maharaja abdicated to take over as Regent in Jodhpur: 'Our motto in Idar had been the same as that of Jodhpur – "Victorious in battle are the Rathors". Sir Pratap Singh introduced another motto which was "A hundred good deeds cannot weigh equal to loyalty", and it was out of his sense of loyalty towards his family and the people of Jodhpur that he abdicated the throne of Idar and went back as Regent when his nephew was a young boy. He needn't have. He could have stayed on in Idar and enjoyed life but when duty called him he went back to Jodhpur.'

A contemporary of Sir Pratap Singh who was as much concerned with Rajput honour – although displaying this in a very different way – was the ruler of Udaipur, Maharana Fateh Singh of Mewar. Born in 1853, he succeeded to the gadi in 1885 and was to rule for forty-five years. As Sir Pratap was the personification of the Rajput warrior, so Fateh Singh was the essence of Rajput kingship, a worthy occupant of the premier gadi in the land: 'The old man knew his power, he knew his position not only as the ruler of Udaipur but as the head of the Rajputs and virtually as the head of the Hindus. He could not accept his position as head of the Indian fighting class and yet subservient to a foreign power, so at every opportunity he went against the British.' He died when the present Maharana was still a small child – too young to remember anything other than the fact that his grandfather liked to cuddle him and that he inspired 'a certain amount of awe and reverence' in those around him. But Maharana Bhagwat Singhji did hear stories of Fateh Singh from his father:

> He fought battles which under the circumstances were as great as any fought by his ancestors. In 1903, when the Curzon Durbar was held in Delhi, Maharana Fateh Singh was totally torn in his loyalties. He was very friendly and respectful yet his own pride would not let him go to Delhi as a vassal – just as no ruling Maharana had gone to Delhi at the time of the Mughals. I believe he went as far as the station and then returned under some pretext. The British respected

his sentiments and when the next Durbar took place in 1911 they offered him a chair alongside King George V and Queen Mary – but even that he declined, and in the museum that we have set up there's that chair made for Maharana Fateh Singh to sit in at the Durbar, which he never occupied.

Maharana Fateh Singh also had a low opinion of the honours and dignities handed out by the British, for which so many Princes vied. During the First World War he was one of the few rulers who failed wholeheartedly to support the British war effort:

> He refused point-blank. He said, 'When there is a fight in India, Europeans don't come here to die, so why should we send our Indians to die when Europeans fight?' But at the end of the war the British sent him the highest decoration for war services and when they brought this GCIE in a velvet case he looked at it and said to his interpreter, 'It is the sort of thing that *pattawalas* (attendants) in offices wear. Put it on the horse. It looks better on a horse than a king.' The interpreter on his own told the British officials that this was not an auspicious day, so His Highness would put it on some other time. Later when somebody asked him why he had got such a high honour for doing nothing, he said, 'Because I rendered the British the highest service. While the British were away fighting the war in Europe I didn't take over in Delhi. Isn't that a big enough service?'

As a ruler Fateh Singh was a traditionalist who made decisions in what he believed were the best interests of his subjects. When the British recommended a scheme to install a modern water system in Udaipur City he made enquiries and found that the scheme would put a large number of water-carriers out of work, so its implementation was deferred until such time as the water-carriers had been found alternative employment. Nor was Fateh Singh entirely free of old superstitions. A story was told by the administrator Sir Edward Wakefield to his nephew, John Wakefield, of the time when as a settlement officer working in the state of Udaipur just after the turn of the century he was summoned by the Maharana and told to fetch the British Residency Surgeon from Ajmer because his only son and heir was stricken with appendicitis:

> So a fleet of the fastest racing camels were arranged and they galloped and rode all night and brought the Residency Surgeon from Ajmer to Udaipur, where he operated in the hall with the eyes of all the womenfolk looking down from above. He was so anxious and nervous at having to do this operation on the only male descendant of the

house of Udaipur, that whilst he was operating he kept whistling a tune which was 'Mary had a little lamb'. After the operation was over, my uncle was sent for again by Fateh Singhji who said, 'Could you please ask the Residency Surgeon to come over again, I must see him.' So they brought him in and he had to whistle the whole tune over again, and it was recorded onto one of those cylindrical discs that go round and round, wrapped in velvet and kept as part of the treasure of Udaipur as some magic incantation that had saved the son's life.

Fateh Singh did not make life easy for the British Political Agents who served as Residents in Udaipur and several attempts were made to have him deposed. To one Resident who asked for a map of the state he presented a fried *papadum*, explaining that its wrinkles were as accurate a description of his country as anything else. Perhaps the only Englishman who came close to the Maharana was an outstanding Political Officer named George Ogilvie, whose daughter came out to stay with her parents in Udaipur just after the First World War. 'The Maharana was a wonderful old man with a long white beard and an extraordinarily benign personality that put one totally at one's ease,' remembers Vere Birdwood. 'He was very proud, of course, and regarded himself as the Pope of the Hindus and he was always surrounded by numerous courtiers dressed in full Rajput kit with long white pleated skirts worn over jodhpur breeches. Whenever a member of his staff addressed him his mouth was always covered so that his breath would not be breathed by the Maharana. We didn't cover our mouths but we did show him great deference because he was the essence of dignity.'

As a young man the present Maharawal of Dungarpur often had dealings with George Ogilvie and they once talked at length about Ogilvie's relationship with the Maharana:

He could be a very difficult person to deal with over ceremonial, but when Sir George Ogilvie had to deal with the Maharana he would say to the Residency *Vakil*, 'May I go and see the Maharana all by myself in an informal manner? I am like his son, I want to discuss things completely informally.' Sir George used to talk Hindi very well and when he used to go to the Maharana he found him like any other human being. 'What is it you want?' he would ask and Sir George Ogilvie would fold his hands and say, 'How would it be, Your Highness – *Agar hum aisa Kare toh aap kya sochte hai Maharanasaheb? Aap ko pasand ayega?*' Meaning that if he did a particular thing would the Maharana like it? The answer would promptly be, '*Jo marzi*, do as you wish.' When Lord Irwin was the Viceroy George Ogilvie went to meet the Maharana informally and told him that the Viceroy's daughter was coming to Udaipur. 'She is like your daughter, how should we entertain her?' The Maharana said, 'Do exactly as you like.' So Ogilvie said, 'Would Your Highness come to the banquet?' He said, 'Do exactly as you like.' So Ogilvie turned round and said, 'You should do in this respect exactly as *you* like' – and the old man turned up! This seventy-six-year-old Rajput gentleman took this nineteen-year-old girl's arm and walked right up to the dining table, moved her chair and said, 'Please be seated.' And then he said, 'I hope you will have a pleasant evening. May I now take leave of you because I don't dine in the Western style.' And then he left.

Sir George Ogilvie also told me that Maharana Fateh Singh was the only ruler in India that he knew of who had no such thing as a private life for forty years! When I said, 'It is impossible,' he said, 'Listen. That man slept with four of his Sardars surrounding his bed, and another two Sardars who kept awake by rotation every two hours. The only time he had his private life was when he retired to the bathroom for ablutions.' On his birthday Ogilvie used to go and dine with him. The Maharana and the Maharani sat and dined in very dim candle-light and there were a hundred maidservants standing all round saying, 'May the Maharana and the Maharani live for ever. God bless them.' Every morning he used to get up at five o'clock and say prayers for a full hour and every morning there were at least fifty people who came and saluted him. He had lunch at twelve o'clock, with at least one hundred men, and before he started his lunch two hundred poor people including children and widows were fed. 'I did not look upon him as a man,' Ogilvie told me. 'I thought he was a demi-god.'

In their different ways Pratap Singh and Fateh Singh represented the best of the old school of rulers who really had no place in twentieth-century India. Even as the new century dawned, a new kind of ruler was beginning to emerge on the princely scene. The two great pace-setters were both rulers of large states and it was no coincidence that both were Marathas, less overburdened by the autocratic traditions of the Rajputs and more receptive to new ideas. One was to rule for sixty-four, the other for thirty-nine years.

The first was Sayajirao III of Baroda, born in 1863 and the great-grandfather of the present Maharaja of Baroda. At the age of thirteen he was taken from his father's village farm – where reputedly he used to herd the cows – and placed on the gadi of the second richest state in India:

The dowager Maharani was given the right to adopt and about fifty or sixty boys were produced from the closest branches of the family first, until in desperation they found three brothers in a remote village about 350 miles from Baroda. These three boys were brought before the dowager mother, and the story goes that she saw them separately and asked each the same question, why he thought he had been brought to Baroda? The oldest replied that he'd been brought to be shown Baroda, the youngest said he didn't know why and the middle one promptly replied, 'I've come here to rule.' And that was great-grandfather.

Under the remorseless care of his adoptive mother, Sayajirao was moulded into the epitome of an enlightened and Westernised ruler:

The training of Sayajirao was the most important part of his making. For five years an English tutor, Mr Elliott, and the Dewan, Sir P. Madhavrao, trained him so that he got all that an ideal prince should get. He absorbed everything. There was a book published by the *Khangi* or Private Department of the State called *Rajaputras Upadesh* (Advice to a Young Prince) and Sayajirao to the end of his days followed the advice given in that book. For instance, when proposals came before the Maharaja advice was given to him. In the book it says, 'Ask your private secretary to explain, remain absolutely calm without showing your preferences, then ask him his opinion, discuss with him why he has this opinion, but never let him know what you have in your mind.' Sayajirao discussed, took opinions. He never said, 'What a fool you are. How can you give such an opinion?' He would say, 'Oh, is that your opinion? I'll think about it, I'll keep in mind what you have said.'

But concentrated learning alone could not explain how it was that Sayajirao became the great social reformer of Baroda. His intelligence and his voracious appetite for Western literature and new ideas played a part, but there was more to it than that. 'The reason I have arrived at is very simple,' states Fatehsinghrao Gaek-wad. 'In his childhood in this little village he must have seen poverty and the maltreatment of the lower classes by the upper-class Hindus. That was why, long before Gandhi, he was one of the first to bring in reforms for the Untouchables, as they were known then. But when he tried to force these reforms through he discovered that there was resentment which led to rebellion. He found that if he wanted to bring about social reform he had to put this across to his people first – and education was the only way.'

As a first step – and for the first time in India – Sayajirao made primary education not only free but compulsory throughout the state. At high schools and colleges fees were nominal and supported by generous grants and scholarships which came directly from the Maharaja's private purse. 'Practically half the people of Baroda were getting free education,' claims Dr N. G. Kalelkar, who as a student in the 1930s went to Paris on a scholarship awarded by the ruler. 'Before anybody else did it, Sayajirao said that Untouchables must be admitted and taught in the same schools as other students. But he was not a hasty man. When there was opposition he would talk to people and consult them and proceed very cautiously. And having made his people literate he knew they must have books, so he started the village library movement.'

One other outstanding gift that Sayajirao possessed was good judgment. Both physically – being short and inclined to plumpness – and in his manner of speaking, which was jerky and rapid, he lacked authority. However, 'he was that rare type of leader who understands his limitations but has the foresight to pick people who are not only highly intelligent but the right men for the job.' Provided with able Dewans and administrators Baroda developed within the space of half a century 'from a village society into a modern state', one that was regarded by many as being in advance of anything that British India could boast of.

In his personal life Sayajirao was moderate and regular in his habits, as Nirmala Raje, one of his many grand-daughters, remembers. 'My grandfather was very particular about time, one minute late here or there and he didn't like it. When he went to the office people would say, *"Maharaja saheb office la chalale ahet-daha wajle astil* – the Maharaja is going to the office so it must be ten o'clock."' One of his problems in later years was that he found it increasingly difficult to keep himself busy. 'There was hardly anything left for him to do, so he started thinking about things like window-dressing for the shops or growing soya beans.' With less need to be present in the state Sayajirao took to spending much of the year abroad, which led to what Nirmala Raje regards as unjustified criticism. In 1938 she accompanied her grandfather on a holiday to Europe:

I remember one day in London he said, 'Now, girls, let's go and see a drama', so we went to see a play called *Banana Ridge*. But about ten minutes after it had started my grandfather turned to the ADC who was sitting behind him and said, 'What happened about that order I sent to Baroda?' The ADC knew we were not supposed to talk so he just said he didn't know. About ten minutes later my grandfather remembered something else and said, 'No reply has come. How is that?' Then people started saying, 'Shhsh! Shhsh!' and my grandfather asked my grandmother why all these people were making such a noise. She said, *'Maharaj, apan bolayche nahi ithea* – we are not supposed to talk here.' So he kept very quiet for half an hour and then said, 'Now, girls, you had better stay and see the drama but I have important things to do' – and he got up and left.

Baroda also led the way in the emancipation of women and here Sayajirao was admirably matched by his second wife, Maharani Chimnabai, the daughter of a Sardar from Dewas: 'My grandmother was a very proud woman, I wouldn't say beautiful but very handsome and dignified and she stood no nonsense. She didn't come from a very enlightened or cultured family and what education she had she got mostly in Baroda from my grandfather.' But this lack of education did not prevent the Maharani from playing a leading role in the breaking down of the barriers of purdah and in writing a powerful polemic on the role of women in Indian society. She was also reputedly the best woman shot in India and made more of the luxuries that were available than did her more puritanical husband, whose abstemious drinking habits had once upset a Viceroy when he had drunk the health of the King-Emperor in water! Gayatri Devi of Jaipur remembers how her grandmother used to love to gamble: 'I'll never forget when we were staying at the Dorchester how she'd be standing in the drawing room after dinner longing for my grandfather to go to bed. He always took his time because he knew that the minute he was gone she would be out and off to Crockfords or one of the other gambling clubs.' One of her other hobbies was the collecting of pearls, for which she had an obsession that ended in disaster. Like all the other ruling families during the Viceroyalty of Lord Willingdon she learned to dread the depredations of Lady Willingdon who had 'a very nice way' of extracting gifts from her hosts:

If there was something she particularly admired, she would say, 'Oh, Your Highness, how lovely this is,' and of course, whoever it was would immediately have to take it off and say, 'Your Excellency, with my compliments.' So Chimnabai was in a panic when she heard that Lady Willingdon was coming to Baroda and what she did was to keep a few pearl necklaces and the rest she put in a velvet-lined box which she buried in the palace gardens. Now when Lady Willingdon's visit was over Chimnabai kept putting off taking out the box, with the result that about three months elapsed and the rains had come. When eventually the velvet-box was unearthed, it was water-logged and the pearls had disintegrated and rotted away!

Born a decade later than Sayajirao but also ascending to the gadi in childhood, Maharaja Madhav Rao Scindia of Gwalior was an altogether more ebullient and lively character. 'He was always my ideal,' declares the present Maharaja of Gwalior:

My grandfather was a down-to-earth, practical type of man, full of common sense, and he had a very democratic relationship with the people of Gwalior. He mixed continually with the public and, unlike some rulers, he only twice went abroad in his life. For six months of the year he used to be under canvas or in small inspection bungalows, where the poorest of the poor could approach him. Now, even if you can't alleviate the sufferings of the poor, if you've offered them your shoulder to cry on and listened to them, they're terribly grateful – and that was why he was so very popular.

It was at one of these inspection bungalows that Madhavrao Scindia, accompanied by only two aides, once held a peace conference with a band of armed *dacoits* or brigands: 'There was no police guard and no army protection and they say that over three hundred dacoits assembled at the Karera *dak* bungalow, all armed to the teeth. He told them that dacoity in the state must stop and made them select a committee to sit in judgment over all the crimes that they had done. They accepted that and so the committee decided that this man should be given ten lashes of the whip and let go and that man sent to the Central Jail to be tried.'

Madhav Rao's improvements to his state were essentially practical. He did a great deal to encourage the development of modern industry and improve farming methods, while at the same time introducing democratic government to Gwalior to a degree that was virtually unheard of elsewhere in India: directly elected municipal councils in 1903, the *panchayat* or five-man council system of local government in 1907 and, in due course, an Upper House of Representatives that was nominated and a Lower House that was partly elected and partly nominated. He also had his privy purse fixed in the annual state budget and made sure that he stayed within it: 'Once the money was given to the ruler every item of expenditure was very closely monitored. At one time the accountant discovered a discrepancy in the household accounts affecting his mother, the Rajmata, to whom he was devoted. Even so, my grandfather passed an order in the file imposing a token fine of one rupee on the person in charge of household accounts – whereupon all hell broke loose and my great-grandmother refused to see him for a fortnight.'

Outside office hours, Madhav Rao's two greatest pleasures in life were organising tiger shoots – which he virtually developed into an exact science, killing eight hundred himself and providing another six hundred for his guests – and playing practical jokes on friends and visitors. He was known to have dressed as an engine-driver and taken over the cab of his own state locomotive to convey important guests from Gwalior City to his summer capital of Shivpuri, driving the engine at great speed and shouting to his alarmed guests, 'Never fear! Scindia is driving!' He also enjoyed playing at Harun-Al-Rashid and going into the city dressed as a *tonga*-driver complete with horse and cab – 'to hear what the people were saying about the administration and his officers'. It was said that on one occasion this prank misfired and he found himself refused admission into his own residence – the imposing Jai Vilas palace with its enormous Darbar Hall and dining room complete with miniature silver train for circulating port, cigars and sweets.

This good humour withstood the severest tests as on the occasion, remembered by Conrad Corfield, when he was thrown out of a carriage by an Englishman:

> He was returning from Bombay to Baroda dressed only in a shirt and coat like the poorest Indian traveller when his compartment was invaded by a truculent young British subaltern who had not yet learned his manners and who insisted that this Indian leave the compartment. At the next stop, where the train halted to allow passengers to have a meal in the restaurant, the subaltern was surprised to be met by a magnificently uniformed retainer who bowed deeply and informed him that His Highness the Maharaja Madhavrao Scindia of Gwalior would be deeply honoured if the Sahib would deign to dine with him. He was ushered into the Maharaja's presence and recognised the Indian he had turned out of his compartment.

Politically, Madhav Rao Scindia was more open in his support for the British than Sayajirao of Baroda, who was always more conscious of the changing political circumstances outside his state. The Gwalior tiger shoots, organised with meticulous precision so that the largest tigers always seemed to put in an appearance opposite the right shooting butt at the right time, ensured that Madhav Rao dealt direct with Viceroys rather than their Agents. The continuing support of the British Royal Family was also ensured when Madhav Rao asked George V and Queen Mary to be godparents to his two children, whom he named George Jivajirao and Mary Kamlaraje, and reinforced a decade later when the young Prince of Wales on his royal tour of India was given a welcome in Gwalior more lavishly magnificent than that laid on by any other prince.

Before coming to Gwalior the Prince of Wales had stayed for three days in the neighbouring state of Bhopal as the guest of the only woman ruler in Asia, whose public appearance – always totally concealed under a veil known as a *burqa* worn over a pale blue robe – was very much at odds with her record as a progressive ruler of a

Muslim state. This record was all the more remarkable in that Nawab Sultan Jahan Begum had come to the throne of Bhopal at the age of forty-three and belonged more to the older generation of Sir Pratap and Maharana Fateh Singh than to the new generation of progressives. Despite being extremely orthodox, she laid great stress on women's education and 'uplift' in the state, as the present Begum of Bhopal testifies:

> People talk about liberation but we had had it for generations and because the women ruled the men were more domesticated than the women. We had ladies' schools and clubs but all in purdah, because my grandmother was in strict purdah until she abdicated in favour of my father in 1925. Then she gave it up so that my mother and all of us could also give it up without people talking about it. Yet even while she was in purdah she gave us the widest freedom to shoot, ride, play hockey and football and all sorts of rough games.

Despite keeping in purdah whenever she was in the company of men, this in no way prevented the Begum from carrying out her duties as a ruler: 'She used to hold her office, or *kutcheri* as we used to call it in those days, every day from morning to lunchtime. When her ministers came to see her she used to be sitting behind a purdah screen listening to them, giving orders and instructions. Every year in summer just after the harvesting she would go out on a tour of the countryside, when we used to camp in tents for a couple of months, and every evening she used to sit and chat with the village folk and listen to their grievances, but always wearing a burqa when with men.'

In the Bhopal tradition, Sultan Jahan Begum was a very strong-willed ruler whose authority was absolute within the state and within the family:

> Whereas my great-great-grandmother used to live in luxury, I think my grandmother reacted against it and so we lived very austerely, with very simple food and very simple clothes, mostly cotton rather than silk and no fussing around. My father lived with her. He had married my mother when she was very young. She belonged to the Afghan royal family and my grandmother brought her over when she was about five so that she could be brought up in the tradition of the family. All our education was done under her guidance and she was very strict. She used to beat us up and we were terrified of her – but then everybody was terrified of her!

If Sultan Jahan Bagum overawed her subjects in Bhopal, so did the moustachioed figure of Ganga Singh in Bikaner – while at the same time inspiring a devotion close on idolatry. Born in 1880, the Maharaja of Bikaner was one of a very select group of rulers of prominent states all born within a few years of each other: the ill-starred rulers Jay Singh of Alwar and Tukoji Rao Holkar of Indore, born in 1882 and 1890 respectively; the miserly Osman Ali Pasha of Hyderabad, born in 1886; both the concupiscent Bhupinder Singh of Patiala and the saintly Sir Udai Bhan Singh of Dholpur in 1893. All were highly intelligent and commanding personalities in their own right, but none could match Ganga Singh of Bikaner.

'What a towering man!' remarks M. M. Sapat, who came from Jaisalmer in 1924 to work in the Bikaner Secretariat. 'If you were to see him in just a vest and pyjamas among thousands of people you'd say, "Yes, there's a personality." What a man he was – with a voice like a tiger's.' But it was not character alone that distinguished him. 'My grandfather was the patriarch,' declares the present Maharaja of Bikaner. 'The people treated him like a father figure and it's never difficult to talk to a father figure. Consequently he treated them like children. He always said to them, "I see no difference between my son and my grandchildren and you. You are all my children and your welfare is my first responsibility." He believed that, because he was a proud Rajput and the Rajput tradition means to protect. He could be a tyrant if he wanted to but at that time it was the only way to get work done. Anybody who stood in the way of progress he had to sweep to the side.'

M. M. Sapat remembers Ganga Singh as a hard task-master:

He made us work like slaves when he wanted work done on time. I used to come home sometimes at four in the morning and leave again at nine and not see my children for over a fortnight. Nor did he like to be contradicted, as happened with me once when I was Finance Secretary. He got very angry, but afterwards, although he would never say that I was right, he spoke to me quietly and said, 'Look, I'm not a lion. I won't eat you up. You are like children and unless I go after you you won't understand.' Then he asked me to come to dinner that night, which was a great honour, and he also raised my position. So that was the kind of man he was. You could throw all your heart behind a man who appreciated you like that.

Progress for Ganga Singh meant transforming Bikaner from a desert state into the granary of Rajasthan, a challenge that he first faced as a youngster in 1898:

We had this terrible famine called the *Chapna Kaal* when my grandfather as a youth of eighteen went on camel-back from village to village and saw how hundreds were dying because of the famine. He came to the conclusion that the only answer to this was canals – and railways so that you could bring food in quickly. So when he got his powers the first things he worked on were the canal and the railway. Bikaner had no riparian rights but because he had that magnetism and personality he was able to influence the King and the Viceroy to gain access to the river Sutlej. That's how the Ganga Canal, which irrigated a thousand square miles, came about.

The Ganga Canal system was finally opened in 1927. 'The whole of that part of the country turned green,' remembers M. M. Sapat. 'As far as the eye could see there were green fields where the desert had been. And what a matter of pride it was, not only for him, but for all of us who went there and saw it.' In later years Sapat was one of a privileged circle of courtiers who attended the Maharaja's morning toilette:

In summer he would wear a *banyan* (vest) and a pyjama, but in winter he used to dress himself well. Before going for his bath, the ADC in charge of his wardrobe would come, and there would be a lot of bearers standing behind him who would take in hangers with about fifty or sixty waistcoats and suits. H. H. used to be sitting on his chair saying in Hindi, 'I don't want to wear grey today, not the blue either.' He would select one jacket by just touching it and then the bearer would brush and iron that particular suit. Then a tray would come with detachable collars, and if by any chance the ADC gave the wrong tray after H. H. had selected the suit – 'What an oaf,' he would say. 'Don't you know anything about wearing clothes?' Then he would select a shirt and then the tie-rack would come, hundreds of ties, and he would select one, and a matching handkerchief and the socks. Then would come the velvet tray of cuff-links and buttons, and he would choose. Then he would go for his bath – and when the door opened again, what a fragrance! Every day for at least ten minutes he would set his moustaches with very fine netting with elastic that went behind the ears and pressed down the moustache. We used to sit and watch him dress and while he dressed he would dictate to the stenographer. After he had put on his clothes he would go to the room where the shoes were all in a row, and there was a long pointer like you have in school, he would just touch one of the shoes with it, and that pair would be polished and brushed. Then in the lobby, there was his collection of walking-sticks, and he would pick out one. Then a tray containing cigarette cases, one of which he would select. So he was very particular. He did not like his officers to look shabby, so we always had to dress well, shave cleanly, otherwise we wouldn't dare go before him. And he was very insistent that we always took notebooks with us and a pencil. 'Don't trust your brain, write it down,' he would say.

Ganga Singh's interests were wide-ranging and extended far beyond the confines of his state. But the greening of the desert remained his most cherished dream and long before the Ganga system was operating he was already deeply involved in planning and raising funds for a second system: 'Right up to the end he was obsessed with the idea of getting water in the desert and in 1943 when he was dying of cancer in Bombay, I remember that he came briefly out of his coma and said, "Get me the Bhakra Dam file." That was his last wish and he died the same day.'

Maharaja Karni Singh was nineteen when his grandfather died, old enough 'to understand and feel the impact of this traumatic event. You see, Maharaja Ganga Singh signified Bikaner. He was synonymous with the state and we couldn't quite imagine how anybody as powerful, so strong as he could actually die.'

6

THE ENLIGHTENMENT OF PRINCES

The guardians should always take care to set his manners right and teach him appropriate manner of speech. When he is more than seven years of age, he should be set to his regular studies.

Notes on the Education and
Upbringing of the Ruler, from
Maharaja Madhav Rao Scindia of
Gwalior's *General Policy Durbar*, 1925

The formal education of the children of ruling families usually followed English upper-class convention and began at the age of seven or eight, but their earlier years were not wasted in idle play: 'A regular programme was drawn up every day and we had to go according to that, with our playing periods and our sleeping periods and our tutoring periods.' For those of the Islamic faith, the first stage in this process began with the Bismillah ceremony at the age of four-and-a-half when all Muslim boys and girls were initiated into their religion and first began to study the Koran. In Cambay the Bismillah ceremony was performed in style. 'We were dressed up to ridiculous lengths,' recalls Princess Shahvar Sultan. 'The boys in their tight *achkhans* (buttoned tunics) and we girls in brocade *salwar-kameez* (pantaloons and blouse). Sequins were pasted onto our foreheads and garlands of flowers were tied round our heads – and you can imagine what that was like for a child of four. Then we were taken in procession in a carriage with camels and a lot of music from the house known as the Palace, which was where my father had started living, to the *Durbargarh*, the old palace where all his ancestors had lived and where all the ceremonies took place.'

It was at one such Bismillah ceremony in Palanpur that Muzaffer Khan, son of the present Nawab, received his name: 'The Bismillah ceremony involved the reading of the first *sura* or chapter from the Koran. My father with the *Pir* (holy man) and the *Mullah* (priest) had selected half a dozen names from the Koran and these slips of paper with the names on were handed to my grandfather, who chose the name Muzaffer. Before then I had been known simply as *Baba*.' The education Muzaffer Khan received during the next three years followed a pattern that was well-established in those Muslim-ruled states like Palanpur which had a predominantly Hindu population:

> My education was mainly in the hands of four people. There was an Irish lady who taught me English, a master who taught me almost every other subject, the Mullah who taught me the Koran and the Hindu *Kaviraj* or court poet. So by the time I was six or seven the English side, the Islamic side and the Hindu side were all taken care of. As well as teaching the Koran the Mullah also taught Urdu, Hindi and Arabic and in the process would tell us tales that were part of Islamic lore – stories about the founding figures of Islam and of the Muslim emperors of India. Most of them had a moral, with the helping of the poor as the central theme. The state Kaviraj was a jagirdar who had his own property six or seven miles from Palanpur city but he lived in the palace day and night. His father had also been with my father. He was very articulate with a great sense of humour and the *Mahabharat* was his favourite subject. He frequently quoted from it and knew entire passages off by heart. He also tended to moralise more than anyone else and speak about the kind of justice that he equated with the 'Great Truth' period of history – the *Satya Yuga* (truth epoch) and *Ramrajya* (period of ideal kingship) as opposed to the *Kali Yuga* (dark epoch). I'd have him for an hour during the day and again between dinner and going to bed – for story time, as it were.

A contemporary of Muzaffer Khan was Ambika Pratapsinh, the present Maharawat of Pratapgarh, who spent much of his first seven years of childhood in the Hindu state of Dhrangadhara where 'there was nothing that wasn't taught us. Our routine started at six o'clock and followed a very strict schedule. We had physical training and played football, cricket and hockey mainly in the morning. Then we had our studies which on the language side meant Hindi, Gujerati, English and Sanscrit taught by specialist tutors. Then in the evening we had to play games again, including archery and shooting.' Just as important was learning about the complexities of court etiquette – 'how to behave, how to talk, how to write letters, to say thank-you, how never to be late, how to meet distinguished guests' – as well as the intricacies of official ceremonial where 'everything was rehearsed and timed to a fraction of a second; how long it would take you to walk up to your father for the presentation of the *nazar* (homage), how long to walk backwards to your seat holding your sword without tripping and falling.' When the actual ceremonials took place there was sweet revenge for those who felt that their tutors and guardians had been pushing them too hard, for then the tables were reversed, their tormentors having to offer respects to their charges. 'We got a helluva kick out of it!' admits the Nawab of Rampur.

Mayurdhwaj Singhji of Dhrangadhara had two English tutors: 'The first was Mr Mayne, a mild man, but the next one, Mr Mayer – an MCC player, hence his choice – was very hard, or perhaps harsh is the right word. I don't think he ever forgave us for being princes. He once asked me out of the blue, what I would do when I had a lot of money, buy cars or dig wells? "Dig wells", I said – and got full marks. He actually put us through the hoops. We had to be up and ready by 6.30 for riding one day and drill the next. Lessons until tea-time, then cricket or other field sports.' Great emphasis was placed on cricket:

> The ground was always full of school-children from the city, with boys at nets and practice games. I remember one practice game when I went in to bat. There was one young fellow, a Dewan Sahib's fourth son, who used to send cannon-balls down the pitch. When they came, I sort of stepped back and my English tutor said, 'Did I see you step back? Don't do it again.' But I stepped back again. 'Are you a Rajput?', he said to me, which was quite galling because all the other boys would understand. He said, 'Don't step back again,' and I did. So he took my bat and said, 'Stand over there,' and he started hitting cricket balls at me, saying, 'Why are you afraid? The ball is not going to hit you that hard!'

In Dhrangadhara the young princes and princesses had their own Palace School: 'There was myself, my brother and four sisters, my cousin the late ruler of Jhalawar and a couple of his lads, the minor ruler of Wadhwan and his brother, and a few others. There were all sorts of teachers, including carpenters because my father wanted us to know everything: being boy scouts, ploughing with bullocks and tinkering with the internal combustion engine, of which he was inordinately fond.'

Princesses, both Hindu and Muslim, received an early education that was often on a par with that given their brothers. Growing up in the comparatively orthodox Muslim state of Bhopal, the present Begum was put through an organised schedule of learning devised by her formidable grandmother which in addition to languages included cookery, music and arts and crafts such as needlework, silver-work and leather-work; also religious instruction provided by her grandmother, the Begum herself.

The restrictions of zanana life did not greatly affect these younger girls. 'Until the age of eight or nine I was treated more like a prince,' remembers Shashi Wallia of Dewas. 'Of course, the timings and discipline were all there because from the beginning we had tutors and governesses, but I had the run of the palace. My father taught us to fly kites as well as archery and how to wield a sword and to fence.' In Jodhpur, too, the young princess Rajendra Kumari had free rein: 'My father was very broad-minded and encouraged me in everything: riding, tennis, pig-sticking, shooting. Whatever it was, he did it with me and corrected my faults and if he didn't object, who else would dare? My mother used to tell me, "You never listen to me and if you don't listen to me now, how are you going to be obedient to your mother-in-law? *Aur mera naak katwaige* – I'd get my nose cut off!" Then I used to go to my father and say, "Father dear, mother is getting out of control," and he'd say, "*Achha* (all right), I'll see to it."'

When the present Maharani Rama Kumari of Wankaner was growing up with her brothers in Dungarpur the chief influence was her mother, the Regent of the state:

My mother was a great believer in Saraswati, the goddess of wisdom and learning. My father died when we were quite young and she was very particular and very strict about our education. I had two or three governesses. Miss Atkinson was there in my father's time when we were tiny kids and we simply loathed her because she was terribly strict, but she didn't stay for long. Then we had a Scottish lady, followed by Miss Cohen who was Jewish, a wonderful lady who stayed right up to the time I was married. Don't for a moment think that we led an idle life, by no means. The hours were fixed; two hours for Sanskrit, two for Hindi and two for English. I was made to write essays, I was made to write all the Sanskrit poetry and sometimes I used to be so overworked that I used to cry as a small girl – but my mother saw to it that I did whatever the teacher or the *pandit* gave me to do. She made me write the whole Ramayana and Bhagvad Gita which I think was a great blessing, and she and my tutor told me that anything that you recite in the mornings for three days, you will know by heart and today the verses that I memorised in childhood I still remember!

In Kutch, too, Princess Pravinba had to follow a strict regime imposed by her English governesses which included practical cookery: 'Every week we girls had to go to the kitchen to cook and the dishes we prepared were brought to the table and then passed or not passed. But at the same time we were taught to ride, swim, shoot and other sports along with our studies.' All these activities took place within the confines of the palace walls:

We were not allowed even to walk about the gardens without our 'guardian angels', as we called them, following us. One day I decided that I would somehow get out. The palace gates were well-guarded by *chowkidars* (watchmen) and guards and I don't quite remember exactly how I got out but I went into this huge garden and I roamed all over there for nearly two or three hours. In the meantime, everybody knew that I was missing in the palace and servants and guards had been sent all over; even mounted police were looking for me. Then I went to my servant girl's house and she was astonished to see me. When I told her to come with me she was terrified but I forced her to come, so both of us went hand in hand shivering to the palace. Of course, I was punished and told never to do such a thing again. The elders explained to me that 'you come from a very high family, you may come to some harm,' but I could never understand. There were these lovely gardens which I could see from my window, but why couldn't I roam around freely in them?

In the hot weather months before the summer monsoon, Princess Pravinba and the other royal children were taken to the hill-station of Mahabaleshwar, but here too their freedom was restricted: 'Our English governess used to fix our programmes – picnics and outings and everything that children liked – but it wasn't my choice and I resented it.' In Travancore, Setu Lakshmibai also grew up surrounded by prohibitions: 'Outside companions were strictly forbidden because it was a time of great intrigues and conspiracies and they feared the influence of other factions. But I had my brothers and sisters, so it was not a barren or lonely childhood.'

Despite all the restrictions, there was usually the compensation of growing up in 'a huge family knowing that you were protected' that made childhood for most royal offspring a happy experience – even if 'at the time it seemed tyrannical having strict governesses and guardians and tutors all breathing down your neck'. This was particularly true in those larger states like Gwalior, Patiala and Baroda where there were enough royal children and associated nobility for the main palaces to have their own kindergartens and infant schools attached. In Baroda six miles of walls surrounded the old Moti Bagh Palace, 'so there was ample scope for doing a lot of mischief, eating tamarinds and *bors* and running about the lawns and gardens with huge *bakul* trees. In the same compound was Princes' School, where we went for our education up to the primary stage – and where grandfather himself had been educated.'

Greater freedom prevailed in the far wilder country of Cooch Behar, where Gayatri Devi and her brothers and sisters had their early education: 'There were these wonderful grounds all round where we used to ride, as well as a tennis court and a Canadian squash court. There were lakes in which one could fish or swim and because the palace grounds were surrounded by jungles, there was much wildlife and a lot of shooting. So we really grew up in the open.'

Not only in Cooch Behar but in almost every state, great emphasis was placed on learning to ride. 'Our basic education started with horse-riding,' explains Shivram Sawant Bhonsle of Sawantwadi. 'In fact, we were put on horse-back before we even started walking. We had what were called ring saddles and we were just dumped on a horse and made to ride. Every morning was a riding day and it was compulsory, except on Sundays.' It was the same for the little Yuvaraj of Gwalior. 'I was loaded like a sack of potatoes onto a Shetland pony,' remembers the present Madhavrao Scindia. 'Once when I was six the horse took off with me on it and I started weeping. My father was so furious that he didn't speak to me for a week.' Nor were the girls spared. Leela Moolgaokar remembers being put on a horse without a saddle at the age of four: 'We were told by our riding teacher, Sayyad, that if we stuck on to the horse we'd be riders and if we fell down there was a bowl of iodine and cotton wool waiting for us, and so we stuck on and eventually when we got saddles we felt as if we were sitting on an easy chair and we didn't get scared of the horses at all.'

Ambika Pratapsinh of Pratapgarh learned to ride by means of a slightly less dramatic method: 'The main thing about riding is holding on to the horse with your knees, so a rupee coin was put on the insides of each of our knees. A lancer always rode along with us holding a lead rein in his hand and this is how we were taught to ride. If the rupee fell he would give us a little tap to show that this shouldn't have happened – and this was all before the age of six.'

Once the skills of riding had been mastered it became possible to go out riding in the early morning into the surrounding countryside and through nearby villages, 'because we were taught in our earliest days that you must have an association with your villagers'. For Sukhjit Singh in Kapurthala, these morning rides often meant joining his grandfather:

A sort of entourage would accompany my grandfather, because there would be an ADC, there would be the head of the stables, a Pathan gentleman by the name of Wazir Khan who was a tubby little fellow with bow legs, then the commandant of the bodyguard as well as two *sowars* (lancers), so there would be about six or seven people not approaching him too closely. He wanted a little distance between himself and other riders. 'Harold' was a horse that he was very fond of, as well as a lovely Australian Waler, and he rode well and with great ease right up to sixty-six.

These rides also fulfilled an important social purpose: 'I remember instances when somebody would halt my grandfather with an appeal for *dohai*, which really means, "My lord, your attention". So he would ask what it was all about, and his ADC or whoever was with him would take the petition and the matter would be looked into. I saw this on a number of occasions and it struck me that although sometimes nothing could be done for the petitioner, the mere fact that he had come to the palace and met his ruler left him satisfied.'

In the remote and traditionally-inclined Rajput state of Lunawada, learning to ride went hand in hand with other sporting and martial activities. 'Although it was outmoded we were taught how to use a sword,' states Harish Chandra Sinh, half-brother of the present Maharaja:

> We still had to know how to cut a goat in two – although a generation earlier they would try their hand at buffaloes! Then, of course, *shikar* (hunting) was part of our training. As small boys we had to walk ten or twelve miles with a haversack and a gun on our shoulders. This shikar involved game birds at first, but later wild boar, panther and tiger took pride of place because that involved a bit of risk, since we had to stand on the ground and then shoot. We were taught by our elders how to hold our fire, to let the animal come within easy reach and to make sure that you hit him well with one shot – because if it was a panther that got wounded it could turn back on the beaters and a number of them would get mauled.

The skills of shikar were something that girls also learned in many states. In Gwalior, Leela Moolgaokar began by shooting in the state forces rifle range: 'The initial thing was learning how to hold the gun and fire, so they would give us fifty rounds, say, not to see how many birds we shot but to see whether we had bruises on our shoulders, because we had to learn to fire the thing without being afraid of the kick.' This was in keeping with Maharaja Madhav Rao Scindia's belief, set down in detail in his *General Policy Durbar*, that both boys and girls in the royal household should undergo military training, drilling with the state forces and accompanying them on manoeuvres:

> There must have been about fifteen of us who grew up together in the Gwalior palace, including Prince George Jivajirao and Princess

Mary Kamlaraje. We were given military dress – khaki shorts, khaki shirt, a turban with a topknot and a little rifle – and those of us who wanted to could go and live as the ordinary soldiers would live when there were military manoeuvres, which took place every year and lasted for about twenty days. We lived in a tent and we enjoyed marching left, right and doing an 'eyes right' whenever His Highness came along. We also got paid about four annas a month.

Another state where military activities were taken very seriously was Bikaner, where the guardians – 'who were very, very tough' – were often drawn from the Indian Army: 'Grandfather had very strong ideas of what a man should be and one of these was that if you were not an army man and didn't wear a uniform then you were a sissy. So you had to have military training.' One result of this was that when the Second World War came along, seventeen-year-old Karni Singh was taken off by his sixty-year-old grandfather to join the British and Imperial Forces fighting in the Western Desert – an experience that both Ganga Singh and his grandson greatly enjoyed.

Just as important a milestone in the lives of boys from the Brahmin and Kshatriya castes was the Muslim Bismillah ceremony in the lives of boys from the Brahmin and Kshatriya castes was the Hindu sacred thread ceremony. It usually took place at an auspicious time after a boy had entered his seventh year, and marked his formal initiation into his caste and religion. If the boy in question happened to be a Yuvaraj, then no expense was spared in the accompanying celebration. Apasaheb Pant of Aundh was seven when his thread ceremony took place: 'My head was shaved and I felt quite ashamed of myself. But it was celebrated in very grand style and thousands of rupees must have been spent on it.' Guests came from far afield and were put up in luxuriously furnished tents and free meals were provided for the local townspeople. There was no equivalent ceremony for the girls but Princess Padma Lokur remembers the excitement when her younger brother, the Yuvaraj of Bhor State, underwent his thread ceremony:

The religious rituals were performed in the main chamber of the palace and lasted about four or five hours. My brother had to wear only a small strip of cloth around his waist. The thread, which was hung diagonally from his left shoulder, was made of thick solid gold and he also wore a sapphire necklace and some ruby rings on his fingers. Then there was a reception in the Durbar Hall and because he was supposed to ask for alms to support his existence, all his relatives and other guests gave him symbolic alms and the Brahmin priests gave him grain. This was followed by a procession from the main doorway of the palace, which had been decorated with flowers, small banana trees, brass lampstands which we call *samayis* and hanging glass lamps called *handis*. We had two state elephants in Bhor and my brother was seated on the taller one for the ride through the town, which was also lavishly decorated by the people themselves. The roads were thronged with people, all the balconies were crowded and in some places rose petals were showered on my brother – but my strongest memory is seeing tears of joy in my mother's eyes.

The Sikhs also had an initiation ceremony for their boys, which in Sukhjit Singh's case took place in the Kapurthala State *Gurdwara* (Sikh temple) when he was ten:

None of the other members of the family were following the observances of the Sikh religion, which meant keeping hair and beards unshorn and wearing turbans, and my grandfather had really lost his place as one of the premier figures in the Sikh community when he had come back from a trip to Europe clean-shaven. This had had a very profound effect on him and when I was born he had vowed that he would bring me up in the true traditions of the orthodox Sikh. He used to tell me that there was no question of my breaking this vow, I would just have to abide by it – which was rather an onerous responsibility for a ten-year-old boy to take on. So when I was baptised in the Sikh tradition it was something so moving and at the same time so frightening that it has never ever slipped from my memory.

When they were around eight or nine years old, things began to change for both boys and girls. 'Until the age of eight I was living with my mother,' states Iqbal Mohammed Khan of Palanpur. 'Then at the age of nine I moved into the men's quarters, where my father was living. I had separate apartments with a guardian and my own servants and staff to look after me. It was very much a man's world.' For the girls it was a reverse process, as the purdah curtains began to fall. 'I had been more like a tomboy than a girl,' recalls Maharani Rama Kumari of Wankaner, 'riding and driving and playing more boys' than girls' games – until my two elder brothers went off to Princes' College. Then I was barred bit by bit from going out, because this was the tradition. It was not exactly purdah but it was semi-seclusion and for a few days I felt very wretched, but then of course I got used to it.'

For most princesses like Rama Kumari, education beyond the age of eight or nine continued at home under the guidance of tutors and teachers. The majority of boys, however, went to one or other of the four schools set up by the Government of India specifically in order to 'fit the young Chiefs and Nobles of India physically, morally and intellectually for the responsibilities that lay before them', with the idea that instead of being 'solitary suns in petty firmaments' they would become 'co-ordinate atoms in a larger whole'. The first of these Princes' Colleges was Rajkumar College, established in Rajkot in the centre of the Kathiawar peninsula in 1870. This was followed two years later by Mayo College in the centre of Rajasthan at Ajmer and by Aitchison College in Lahore and Daly College, Indore, in 1886 and 1898 respectively.

Like most of the young *Rajkumars* or princes of Kathiawar, the present Nawab of Cambay and the Maharaja of Wankaner went to Rajkumar College at Rajkot, where they were contemporaries, while the Maharajas of Benares and Baria and the Maharana of Mewar were at school together at Mayo College. Some of the younger princes – Dr Karan Singh of Kashmir, the Nawab of Rampur and the Raja of Sawantwadi – broke with this tradition by being sent to the Doon School in the Himalayan foothills, the first of a number of Indian public schools to follow the English boarding-school tradition. A few boys – but only a few, since it was frowned upon by successive Viceroys – were sent to England to go through the preparatory and public school mill. The Maharaja of Dhrangadhara was one: 'In 1935 the entire Palace School – minus the girls – was shipped off to England and an establishment was set up at a place called Millfield in Somerset. I myself was soon packed off elsewhere' – first to a prep school, 'where there was a lot of ragging', and then on to Haileybury, on the theory that 'since the Indian public schools were imitations of the schools in England, why go to an imitation and not to the original?'

Although they had English headmasters and followed English public school codes of discipline, the Princes' Colleges were very different from English boarding-schools. Each pupil had his own quarters where his own staff looked after him. Mayo College, where the present Maharaja of Kotah was sent in 1922, was largely funded by the Rajputana States and every large state had its own house: 'The idea was that all the boys from Kotah would stay in the Kotah House, boys from Jaipur in Jaipur House, boys from Bikaner in Bikaner House. In my case I had a separate bungalow from Kotah House with my guardian and my staff. You had to join in every activity of the college, but then you came away and had your own food and slept in your own house.' At Rajkumar College in Kathiawar both Mirza Hussain of Cambay and Pratapsinghji of Wankaner lived with the Principal, Mr Mayne, and his wife. 'This was in case there was any foul play,' explains the Nawab of Cambay, 'I being the only son of my father. We had English breakfast there with the Principal and in the evening food cooked in Kathiawadi Hindu style. We Muslim students were permitted to say our prayers at the Rajkot *Idgah* (mosque) and we had somebody who brought us *Dinyat* (meat slaughtered according to Islamic practice). The Hindus walked to a small temple nearby and because I was friends with Bhavnagar and a boy from Jasdan I often went with them.'

At Mayo College, too, orthodox Hindus like the present Maharaja of Benares were able to follow their own customs: 'It was a great challenge for a vegetarian to live in this society and keep to the old orthodox traditions. I had my own *Ganga-jal* (water brought from the river Ganges) and would not eat my food from a table but seated on a low stool. The English Principal would say, "How can you compete with the modern world like this?", and I would say, "Why not?" I would go on hikes for the whole day in summer without drinking water and in scout camps I would cook my own food separately.' Having succeeded to the gadi in Benares at the age of eleven, the Maharaja was under the eye of an Administrator named Peters during his minority:

> Mr Peters took a lot of interest in me and tried to develop all the good points that he thought I should have, so he wrote to the Principal, 'Try and make him more modern. Make him give up his old ways.' So the Principal was a little harsh on me and did his best to mould me. We were given Sanscrit classes but there was a bias towards English education. For instance, as small boys in the 7th and 8th classes we were taught auction bridge and the rules of rugby football, even though we didn't know what auction bridge was and never saw rugby football being played in India. They taught these things so that the Indian rulers would not be fishes out of water in English society, but the pity of it was that as a result some rulers felt they had to spend six months of the year in England or spent their time in English clubs.

The purpose of the Princes' College was, in the view of Jaideep Singh of Baria, 'to provide a confluence of Western and our own traditional culture', but the dominant role played by British guardians made it difficult for some to maintain a balance. When Jaideep Singh went to Mayo College in 1938 at the age of nine, he had his own three-bedroomed bungalow in the grounds with its own drawing room and dining room. He also had three cars – two Chevrolets and a French Delage – and a string of polo ponies. To look after him there were more than twenty servants and also his English guardian:

My British guardians were invariably high-ranking retired Army officers. First I had a Major Charlie Law, then a much-decorated Brigadier, Geoffrey Houston, and then a Brigadier Carpendale. All three influenced my life in many ways. I was never given Indian food more often than once a week because they obviously didn't have a taste for it, so I had to eat English food – which is one of the reasons why I hate Irish stew, which we ate almost every day. We wore white *achkans, churidars* and *safa* in class but every evening I had to dress for dinner in dinner jacket or a black *sherwani* and, until my brother joined me at college, there I was as a boy of ten or eleven sitting down to dinner with an old man in a dinner jacket and nobody else. Whenever the Derby or the Grand National were being run, we had to listen to it on the BBC. My guardian had a whole course made out of felt which would be laid on the ground. The horses that were running would be put out and as we heard them going over Beecher's Brook on the commentary, they would be moved forward.

Great emphasis was placed on games and sport. Sundays were often spent going out in open tourers after duck, sand-grouse and black buck, and bird-watching was a compulsory activity. Despite the games and classes and all sorts of arrangements made 'to keep us busy', Jaideep Singh remembers being very lonely: 'We had friends to lunch on Sundays, but if I wanted to invite someone to eat with me I had to write to him days in advance – even if he was right next door – because we were so isolated from one another.'

The Princes' Colleges had their critics. There were those who saw them as one more British wedge being driven between the Indian rulers and their people, where the pupils received 'rather obsolete educations and were conditioned to believe that their relationship with the British was a natural relationship which was likely to endure to their advantage'. Certainly, those who went there were rarely allowed to forget their status. When the minor ruler of Porbandar State was seen by a visiting English Resident to be playing the part of a bard in a school play he was swiftly pulled out of rehearsals because, in the words of the Resident, "You can't turn a maharaja into a bard even on the stage." But there were also those who felt that the education they received gave them the best of both worlds and did no more than recognise the fact of the British presence in India. 'To us England was never another country,' Karni Singh of Bikaner observes. 'When I was a boy we had English officers who were in charge of the police, English principals in charge of schools, the railways were manned by British people, and Indians and British played tennis together. States like Jaipur, Jodhpur and Bikaner were all trying to bring British technology into their states, the English language itself was a very binding force and for three hundred years these two countries had lived together. So to my generation England isn't another country.' Among those who felt that their English-based education did nothing to close the gap between the rulers and the ruled – 'although by my time there was such a distance anyway that it didn't really make all that difference' – was Mayurdhwaj Singhji of Dhrangadhara:

> Being educated abroad wasn't in itself necessarily a bad thing, but if it impaired your communication with your own people it obviously was bad. I remember coming home for a long summer vacation and going on a duck shoot. I said to my picker-up, in my best Gujerati, 'Would you hide behind a bush, your shirt is frightening the birds.' He said, 'I don't know English.' But whether you were educated in India or abroad, the point was really how far you went in adopting alien ways and rejecting your own, in clothes, or ballroom dancing, or your language. Anglicisation brought you closer to the British overlords which in those days was a matter of great moment. There is no greater flattery than imitation. But when it took away your native fervour, others, quite naturally, filled the place. Ultimately that most capable, astute, and winning of negotiators, Mountbatten, hardly gave the Princes a thought. He realised he could play polo with them and deal with them as he wanted – and did.

There was no female equivalent of the Princes' Colleges, but there were a number of schools such as Queen Mary's, Lahore – 'a beautiful school but like a prison, with high, high walls that you couldn't even peep out of' – that were run on public school lines by English headmistresses and catered for high-born Indians. 'Queen Mary's took a lot of girls from our side of India,' recalls Rani Nirvana Devi, who came from Mandi State in the Punjab. 'There were a lot of girls from Patiala, senior and junior, there were girls from the Kangra hill-states, there was one from Ratlam, one from Baroda, one from Bhopal. But we were not the majority and we were treated as any other girl who came there.' Another girls' school of high repute was Huzurpaga School in Puna, which was attended by many of the princesses and daughters of Sardars from the Maratha states. This was where Rani Nirmala Raje of Baroda took her matriculation before going on to complete a degree course in Baroda, and also where Padma Lokur of Bhor and her sister went as day students: 'When we went to school it was either in a car or in a buggy and we were always accompanied – as we were when we returned from school – because we never ever walked on the streets of Poona or of Bhor. In the afternoon a boy used to bring us our tiffin and the moment he saw us he used to start bowing. Then when I had finished my tiffin he would bow, take my tiffin box, and bow again. All my friends used to ridicule me, so whenever I used to see him I would say, "Don't bow! Don't bow!" He did stop after a time but it took a lot of persuasion.'

In some ways the most fortunate of the royal children were those who were educated in their own states and who had the opportunity to watch their fathers or grandfathers going about the business of ruling. Among them was the present Maharao of Kutch, who on his grandfather's orders was educated entirely in the royal palace at Bhuj by English and Indian tutors. In Palanpur State Iqbal Mohammed Khan was also educated at home, as was Raja Lalit Sen of Suket hill-state. Such education had its disadvantages, however, for young princes could come to regard themselves as 'different from other boys' and ran a serious risk of being spoiled. One of the reasons why the Princes' Colleges had been set up was precisely to remove young and impressionable minds from undesirable influences – and one of the consequences was the rapid decline of such time-honoured customs as the initiation into 'worldly affairs' of boys at the age of thirteen or fourteen by what were commonly known as *nautch*-girls. These were 'very dignified ladies and very skilled at their job', which was 'the art of pleasing a man, knowing how to talk, how to make him feel at ease, how to provide him with entertainment'. Apart from teaching the art of sex, these courtesan-dancers also taught the boys courtly etiquette and how to speak Urdu, and in many of the old ruling families they were 'given a place to perfect their arts' and rewarded with jagirs of land. A certain discretion was observed over such activities, but there is no doubt that by the 1920s the custom of amatory initiation was largely a thing of the past.

But if some old customs were on the wane, others continued to flourish – and from these a young Yuvaraj or prince could learn much. In Palanpur State, as in many others, there was the custom known as the *Mashaal-ki-Salaam* or the 'bringing on of light':

We had inherited this old custom from the Mughals and it always took place just when the day ended and the night began. This was when the lights were brought in and it was accompanied by a regular ceremony when people came to salute my father and sit with him in a very informal darbar. People just came and sat. Some didn't talk, others talked or came with problems. Some evenings were spent talking about the events of the day or about news from outside the state. Applications would come with requests for scholarships or with problems over land or property and one of my father's secretaries would collect all their applications and note them down in his register so that orders could be passed against each application the next day. Usually there would be about fifty or sixty people present and I started attending from the age of about nine or ten. I had to be there every evening and I had to go with my turban on because no one could go bareheaded except my father. He was also the only man who sat on a chair. The rest of us sat on the ground, myself and whoever came in from the town, all sitting at the same level. This, too, was part of my education.

7

THE SPORT OF KINGS

Children of both sexes should be taken out shooting once a week without fail, and when they have advanced in years they should, as a rule, be made to spend not less than a couple of weeks annually on tiger-shooting.

Notes on the Education and Upbringing of
the Ruler, from Maharaja Madhav Rao
Scindia of Gwalior's
General Policy Durbar, 1925

I was 10 years and 10 months old when I shot my first panther. There was an old, old *Jamadar* (old soldier), a very, very staunch and reliable Mohammedan called Amir Rathod, who had taught me to shoot. He was sitting next to me and when the panther came, he just touched my shoulder and said, 'Don't lose your nerve, take a very steady aim, wait for one minute, let him present a broadside and then let fly at the heart.' I heard all these things, and that put me in my place. With a completely calm composure I let fly and got him in the heart.

For the youthful ruler of Dungarpur the act of shooting his first panther had something of the significance of an initiation into adulthood, an accomplishment that left him feeling a 'great exhilaration'. It was the same for the Yuvaraj of Kotah who shot his first tiger at the age of eleven, for Iqbal Mohammed Khan of Palanpur who shot his first tiger at fourteen 'with Maharaja Ganga Singh of Bikaner sitting next to me on the *machan* (platform)', and for the young Nawab of Pataudi: 'Because my father had died the Nawab of Bhopal felt sorry for me and asked me what I'd like for a birthday present. So I said, "I'd like to shoot a tiger" – and that was what he gave me as a birthday present at the age of twelve.'

Shooting tiger and other big jungle cats was the prerogative of Indian royalty and because it was an exclusive sport it was the rarest and the most prestigious of the many forms of outdoor exercise indulged in by the Indian Princes. As a group the Princes in the first half of the twentieth century were among the fittest people in India, rivalling the British in their enthusiasm for outdoor games and sports. This was partly the result of their education, in which the British public-school sporting ethic played such a large part, partly because of the unique opportunities provided by their position in Indian society. But local tradition also played its part: 'Hunting and learning to defend oneself was very prevalent among the Rajput rulers particularly during peace time because if they became sedentary in their habits they would be unprepared for war. To hunt an animal like a tiger all your senses have to be sharpened, all your senses have to be honed, you must develop quick reflexes, you must know your escape routes, you must know where and how to hit – and if you don't know this then you cannot protect your people.' Sports also provided a very necessary safety-valve: 'No ruler could go out alone from his state and have a holiday somewhere quiet and enjoy himself in whatever way he liked. It was not possible. So the only way to relax was with your own crowd. You went for sports or you went shooting.'

This intense interest in sporting activities allowed many young princes to develop their skills to a quite remarkable degree. In many cases their fathers or grandfathers extended court patronage to outstanding sportsmen by finding them employment in the state police or military services, or even by employing them as full-time coaches. ADCs were often selected as much on account of their sporting talent as their social graces, and in some cases, outstanding players from Europe and Australia were employed either for a season or for longer terms. 'The basic talent had to be there and the interest, but it had to be groomed,' explains the Nawab of Pataudi, himself an outstanding cricket player who captained the Indian cricket team in the 1960s and 1970s, and whose father played for England in the 1930s after taking up cricket at Aitchison College in Lahore and then developing it at Oxford. Another dominant figure in present-day cricket in India is the Maharaja of Baroda, who as well as being a national junior tennis champion developed his cricketing skills under the eye of such outstanding Indian cricketers as the brothers C. K. and C. S. Naydu and had the advantage of having one of the finest wickets in India as his home ground. The ruling family of Nawanagar was another great cricketing family, producing the great 'Ranji' and then his nephew, Duleepsinghji. Porbandar also developed fine cricketers, with Maharaja Natwarsinhji captaining the first All-India team to visit England in 1932. Dungarpur produced the present Maharawal, who as a young man was admonished by the Viceroy for taking his cricket too seriously:

When the first MCC team came out to India in 1926 I played for Rajputana and Central India combined as a lad of eighteen. It was on a matting wicket and I am glad to say that I made a reasonably decent showing against two of the best bowlers that ever appeared for England, Maurice Tate and George Geary. The Captain, A. E. R. Gilligan, was a thorough gentleman and he said, 'Maharaja, when you come to England come to Brighton and I'll make special arrangements for you to get net practice at Hove, with two or three bowlers bowling at you, especially one old experienced man who knew the redoubtable Ranji.'

Accordingly, when the young Maharawal came to England for administrative training his guardian arranged for him to spend two months in Brighton. 'So I went and had net practice and Arthur Gilligan said – I'll never forget it – "If you come back and play regularly for Sussex, I'll bet you will make 2000 runs in the season."' However, any such plans had to be abandoned when he was accorded his full ruling powers: 'I was thinking of so many wonderful things like playing at Lords for the "Gentlemen of England" against the "Players", which was a great fixture then, but the AGG and the Viceroy both said, "You must be serious about the affairs of your state. Cricket is a game which should form just a pastime. It can't be everything." I bowed and shook hands and walked out, but in my mind I said, "To hell with you!"'

As well as cricket a lot of tennis was played, both competitively and as a social game, and this went down well with the British. Kapurthala State produced a crop of tennis champions from its princes and commoners. One of many visitors who attended the twice-weekly Kapurthala tennis evenings was the French tennis ace Jean Barotra, who professed to be amazed that such a little state should be able to produce so many quality players. Sukhjit Singh recalls that there were two clay courts in the palace grounds:

I still remember the ball boys running out early in the afternoon to apply clay to the surface and mark out the courts, and the chatter that went on as a *shamiana* or marquee without sides was erected, with carpets laid down and tables and chairs dotted around. By about five in the evening everything would be arranged and the players would turn up and my grandfather would arrive from his apartments to greet them. After each game the players would come back to the marquee to sit down and have a cup of tea and if there was any player of special renown he would naturally join my father or my grandfather for tea.

Many of the Princes' sporting endeavours involved horses. The old Maharaja of Rewa grew so attached to his favourite charger that when it died it was given a state funeral and buried in the middle of his parade ground. Jay Singh of Alwar also had a favourite polo pony – but when it stumbled and threw him, he had it doused in petrol and set alight. The Maharajas of Indore, Kolhapur, Morvi and Rajpipla were among those in Central and Western India who maintained racing stables and entered their horses in the Cold Weather race meetings in Bombay. In Bengal the old Maharaja of Cooch Behar was the first ruler to play a prominent role in the Calcutta races and was also a great patron of polo – a connection which led to Princess Gayatri Devi meeting and falling in love with the dashing young Maharaja of Jaipur, probably the most outstanding of a select group of young polo-playing princes in the 1930s that included the Nawab of Bhopal and the Maharaja of Ratlam, all with top handicaps. 'He was a very glamorous figure, this young man of twenty-one,' recalls Gayatri Devi. 'His all-conquering Jaipur team had won the Indian polo championship in 1933, as well as every tournament in England they had played in. The following year when the Calcutta polo season began my mother sent for us and said we'd have to move out of our bedroom and go downstairs in this very large house we had in Calcutta called "Woodlands", because the Maharaja of Jaipur was coming to stay. This young man arrived in his Rolls-Royce with his string of sixty beautiful polo ponies and his turbanned grooms and I was immediately smitten. I used to hope that one day I might be able to be one of his grooms.'

Another equine sport to find a place in the princely sporting calendar was riding to hounds. Some rode with the British hunt at 'Ooty', the South Indian hill-station of Ootacamund, and one ruler, the Nawab of Jaora, hunted with his own pack of imported British hounds against jackals in Central India. Several preferred dogs to horses. The Nawab of Sachin had a dog-racing track built in his capital modelled on the dog-track in Doncaster, complete with electric hare, where race meetings were held every February to coincide with his birthday celebrations. The Maharajas of Junagadh and Darbhanga competed with each other to buy Crufts' champions, while in the Punjab the Maharaja of Jind held a 'Dog Week' every year which not only attracted dog-fanciers from all over India but also numbers of disreputable characters more anxious to enjoy his lavish hospitality than to show their dogs.

Much more in keeping with princely tradition was pig-sticking, which flourished in every state where wild boar came out into open country. Among the greatest exponents of the sport were the nobility of Jodhpur, but Western India also produced many champions who competed annually amongst themselves for the Gujerat Cup and the Salmon Trophy in a sport that demanded considerable daring. 'To hunt a wild boar on a horse over open country you have to ride hard, often on grassy land where you don't know what you are riding on,' maintains the Maharao of Kutch. 'I've had accidents and broken bones but that didn't discourage me. It was my grandfather who encouraged me. He had been taught by a very well-known pig-sticker called Colonel Reay, who was his tutor.' Bhavnagar was one of many parts of Kathiawar where the wild pigs were regarded as a destructive menace, as Rajkumar Dharmakumarsinhji explains:

> They used to breed like hell in the coconut and mango plantations and played havoc with the farmers' crops. So we used to beat them out and either shoot them or pig-stick them. Some of the males were so huge and had such sharp tusks that they were very dangerous to go near. They would menace you and gnash their tusks with their bristles raised in a crest and would even charge without provocation. My brother, the ruler, could kill with one spear-thrust in the heart riding at full speed. A spurt of blood would come out and after 50 or 60 yards the wild boar would roll over dead. But my brother often fell off his horse and was charged by wild boar.

Another sport enjoyed in royal circles in Bhavnagar which was even more in keeping with ancient tradition was the hunting of black buck with cheetahs. By the 1920s, what had once been a widespread sport among the Indian rulers continued only in Kolhapur, Baroda, Bhavnagar and the little non-salute state of Nalaghar, whose ruler owned a pair of cheetahs: 'They were really magnificent, those cheetahs. They would sit in the back of his open tourer as if they were guarding us. Then as soon as the black buck were sighted they would be walked out on their leashes. Once they had seen the animal they would be allowed to run and for a short distance they went like a streak of lightning. No buck could outrun them.' In Bhavnagar, hunting with cheetahs and other trained animals was run on more professional lines:

> We had Muslim trainers who were hereditary keepers of the cheetahs, caracals, falcons and hawks. They originally came from the Punjab and settled down in Bhavnagar, being employed by my grandfather, my father and my brother. In my father's time my elder brother was in charge of the cheetah unit while I was in charge of the falcons. My father had in all thirty-two cheetahs, brought from East Africa because the Indian cheetah had become almost extinct except in

Central India. What I liked about cheetah hunting was that there was no wounding. If the cheetah missed the black buck it would go free and if he caught it the black buck was dead. It was the same thing with falconry and with caracal, a large lynx-like cat which hunted *chinkara* deer, hare or even pigeons. When you released a caracal at a flock of feeding pigeons he would jump up and strike and knock down five or six at a time.

In Bhavnagar, as elsewhere in Kathiawar, there was an enormous variety of wildlife ranging from Asiatic lions to hares and it was this abundance of game in almost every state – 'so abundant that hunting had very little effect on the wildlife' – that provided the princes and nobility with their favourite recreation, which went by the name of shikar. A state such as Palanpur that was not particularly renowned for its jungles or its wildlife could provide its shikaris with 'tigers, panthers, sloth bears and large deer like the *sambur* as well as a lot of smaller game like duck, partridge, quail, snipe, bustard, cranes and rock grouse and seasonal birds like the florican which came from the Deccan jungles in the monsoon and returned when winter started.' All this game was the exclusive preserve of the ruler and the leading nobles of the state, who had rights over the game within their own estates: 'You could rob the state exchequer of fifty thousand rupees and get away with it, but if you poached an animal or cut a bamboo in the tiger preserve or even grazed cattle there, then your life was not worth living.'

It was this exclusivity that made the rulers 'the greatest conservationists of game that ever existed', whose hunting grounds later became India's finest national parks, but at the same time it produced sportsmen obsessed with the notion of running up as many kills as they could – on the theory that 'the bigger the bag, the more important you were'. When Hede Dayal first came to Patiala State, she was disturbed to find that 'all their houses were plastered with heads of dead animals, which I thought was ghastly. But they had shot all their lives – and they were marvellous shots. They could drive a jeep with one hand and shoot with the other and hit every time. What also outraged me was that they drove right through people's fields. Of course, at that time you felt honoured that royalty drove through your fields.' However, not all princes shot to excess: 'Some became trigger-happy and used to go outside the state to hunt – especially after tigers. But at that time people were so engrossed in this shikar that as soon as you got an invitation you went and shot. But we never thought of a large bag as a massacre, because no bird or animal species was really endangered.'

Every state of reasonable size had its own shikar department that kept its reserves in good order and ensured that the ruler and his guests got the best shooting possible. Even in small states like Lunawada, the ruling family could always rely on local tribal people to act as game wardens and as beaters: 'In the good old days you could collect a hundred or two hundred Bhils in about a couple of hours. We sent out word and they all gathered with their tom-toms and drums and bugles to drive the game towards the shikaris.' In great states like Udaipur, the ruler's hunting expeditions were organised on the same lines as those of the old Mughal emperors. 'It was Chittor for tiger in summer and Jaisamudra for panther and pig in winter,' explains the Rao of Bedla:

> Everything was highly organised. One officer was in charge of shikar information, one in charge of the beats, one in charge of transport. Encampments were set up which were like cities of canvas, with two thousand tents varying in size according to status. Supposing the Maharana was camping at Jaisamudra, at about forty or fifty places shooting boxes or *machans* were arranged – for panthers it would be up a tree, for pig on a stone or anywhere with some height and for tiger the platform would be 18 feet off the ground – and in the morning trackers would go out looking for pug or hoof-marks. They had signallers on the tops of hills and they would signal that this hill has so many pigs, panther, tiger or any other animal. Then in camp they would make up a shikar chart and show it to the Maharana who would select where he wanted to go and whether it would be with elephants, lancers or beaters. Only the Maharana decided who would shoot. He would authorise somebody, 'Today you shoot a pig or a sambur.'

Good organisation also lay behind the success of the great duck-shoots that attracted VIPs and foreign visitors to certain well-known states. In Kashmir there was duck shooting in summer and winter, while in the plains states of Patiala, Bharatpur, Dhrangadhara and Wankaner there were isolated lakes on which hundreds of thousands of duck settled for brief periods in the course of their seasonal migrations. Shooting butts were built at carefully chosen points either on the water's edge or on the lake itself on artificial islands, to which guests were driven or boated soon after dawn. Firing began at the sound of a bugle and ended when the bugle call was heard again. 'The bugle was sounded to stop all the guns from firing, so that all the ducks that were ranging round could find a peaceful atmosphere again. Eventually they would realight on the water and the bugle would be sounded to allow the shooting to start again. In places like Wankaner and Dhrangadhara, where the ducks had very little refuge elsewhere, the shoots carried on for days – although the bags could not be compared with those at Bharatpur or Kashmir.'

One of those who witnessed the Kashmir duck shoots was Dr Karan Singh, who as a boy sometimes kept his father company in one of the butts: 'My father was a remarkably good shot and very agile. He used to have two loaders standing behind him and I've seen him drop six birds from one flight, because he'd take two as soon as they came into range, he'd hand his gun over and take the next gun and shoot another two above him, then take the next gun and shoot two more as they were flying away. So he was able to convert his twelve-bores into a sort of machine-gun and it was a very impressive feat to watch.' In Patiala an artificial lake called Bhupinder Sagar, an hour's drive from the capital, was built for the Maharaja by his State Engineer, Dick Bowles' father: 'It had a *bund* or causeway across the middle where His Highness had his butt surrounded by reeds. No one was allowed to shoot until he arrived and he was invariably late, keeping everybody waiting a good hour sometimes, but you'd know he was coming because there'd be a dust-cloud approaching which was a cavalcade of cars. Then His Highness would arrive looking very elegant in his light-weight Rankin plus-fours and go to his butt.' The Maharaja would have the first shot and firing would continue throughout the day, a hydroplane kept on the lake being driven round occasionally to keep the duck off the water. When there was a full moon the shooting would continue after dark: 'You'd hear the squawking of geese high in the sky coming down, huge bar-headed geese. They'd be silhouetted against the moon and fine shots like Patiala and his second son John would shoot them with rifles. You'd hear these great bar-headed geese swirling down and bang-crash onto the water.'

But for duck-shooting on the grand scale, no state could compare with Bharatpur, where the shooting on the ten square miles of marsh known as the Ghana *jheel* was developed by the present Maharaja and his father before him into a thrice-yearly fixture at the beginning and end of the Cold Weather season which no serious sportsman could afford to miss. More shots were fired by British pro-consuls and commanders-in-chief from its famous Viceroy's Bund embankment than from any other comparable site in India: 'The jheel had islands to which I constructed little roads that were wide enough for cars to take VIPs out to their butts,' explains Colonel Sawai Brijendra Singh, the present Maharaja of Bharatpur. 'Each duck-shoot took months to arrange and to see that VIPs were not given bad butts was like making the seating arrangements for a dinner party. At the last moment someone would say, "Sorry, I can't come", and you then had to go through the list seeing who should go into a VIP butt and who could have his place.' There were fifty butts in all dotted round or on the lake and among the many Britons who shot there was Cyril Hancock of the Indian Political Service, who recalls that when the duck rose from the lake at the sound of the first bugle it was 'with a noise like thunder'.

Yet when it came to the largest bags, even Bharatpur had to give way to the imperial sand-grouse shoots at Bikaner. This was also a Cold Weather phenomenon and took place beside 'a little patch of water about four or five acres across' known as Gajner lake. Sited about twenty miles outside Bikaner City, its significance lay in the fact that it was the only stretch of water for many miles around. 'When the Prince of Wales came to shoot in 1905, something like a hundred thousand sand-grouse came to drink from this one lake. They always come within three days of the end of October but over the years they have dwindled in numbers until now only about five thousand come – because all the irrigation systems have drawn them away.'

Like so much else in Bikaner, the Gajner shoot was very much a creation of Maharaja Ganga Singh, who widened its catchment area with drains and had about sixty butts laid out in lines 'as they do on the moors in England, so that you don't shoot each other'. As always, it was the Viceroys and the VIPs who got the best-sited butts, so that fine shots like Lord Linlithgow – who visited Bikaner 'at least twice a year during his Viceroyalty, even though as a rule no Viceroy would visit a state more than once a year' – and Lord Mountbatten were able to down fifty brace of grouse in a morning's shooting. Among the princes who attended a Viceregal shoot at Gajner during Lord Linlithgow's term of office was the young Maharawal of Dungarpur:

The Viceroy came out of his room at 6.15, the Maharaja was waiting to receive him in his Rolls-Royce and as we gathered in the Gajner shooting-lodge courtyard the butler appeared. The Maharaja said, 'Your Excellency, if you listen to the advice of an old man and have some liqueur brandy with me, it's going to put your eye straight and you will shoot a hundred grouse this morning!' So the Viceroy just drained down the liqueur brandy, and off we went. At 7 sharp, the bugle sounded from the top of Gajner Palace, a red flag went up and the shooting started. Within twenty minutes the grouse started coming down to drink water. From 8 o'clock to 9.30, there were literally

20,000 to 30,000 birds coming down to drink at a time, and the entire sky went absolutely black. The Maharaja had told me quietly that if a covey of grouse happened to be flying over me but going straight to the Viceroy's butt I was to leave it alone! So I scrupulously left alone every covey that went past me towards the Viceroy's butt and the Viceroy went on shooting. Every half an hour the Maharaja said, 'Sir, what is the bag like?', and he would say, 'Well, I'm fifty to sixty.' It went on like that until at one o'clock when he was in his nineties the Maharaja said, 'I'm going to wait till Your Excellency shoots a hundred.' Then when he had got his hundred the Maharaja said, 'I'm going to sound the bugle and we'll disperse for lunch.' But the Viceroy said, 'No, next to me is the Maharawal of Dungarpur. Let him have his hundred.' The Viceroy asked me where I was and I replied, 'Sir, I am in my nineties.' So the Viceroy turned round to the Maharaja and asked him if he would mind waiting for ten more minutes, which the Maharaja did. And in those ten minutes I got my hundred. Then we went back to the Gajner Palace to have our lunch. The morning's bag was something like 4000 birds.

Conrad Corfield also attended one of the Gajner shoots as a junior officer in the political service, but did not do so well: 'I was given a butt so far at the end that all the birds I saw seemed to be about 600 feet high!' All the same, from the ruler's point of view such shoots provided an excellent way of maintaining good relations with the British. 'Maharaja Ganga Singh used to get things done for Bikaner by inviting the British to shoots,' asserts M. M. Sapat. 'For instance, when the Government of India took over Bikaner's postal arrangements they paid a subsidy. But how was that subsidy to be raised with the passing of time? The European Postmaster-General was invited to a shoot and the amount was doubled.' According to Lakshman Singh of Dungarpur, inviting political officers to shoots was 'part of the game of the ruler to keep the Political Department on the right side. It pays in the long run and I did it. The Political Agent saw to it that he visited each state twice a year – but I saw to it that he came to my state thrice a year. At Christmas or the New Year when I was out at camp I always sent out a special invitation for him to come along and have a good time.'

However, shikar and sports did provide rulers and Residents or Political Agents with opportunities to meet informally, as Vere Birdwood remembers from her father's time in Udaipur: 'My father and I would be sitting on the floor of one of the shooting towers waiting for the beaters to rustle up a tiger or a panther, waiting sometimes for hours, and it was a wonderful opportunity for my father to do business with the Maharana, who for these shooting expeditions still wore a long Rajput skirt but in khaki drill with a khaki turban.'

The organised shoot also provided the ruler with opportunities to impress his guests, as John Wakefield remembers from the time when his father was managing the estates of the *zamindari* Maharaja of Tikari:

> In 1925 the Governor of Bihar, Sir Henry Wheeler, was retiring and old Tikari said to him at a dinner, 'But, Your Excellency, the finest partridge shoot in India we have in Bhalwar' – even though partridge shoots of that calibre were not known in Bihar. So father got a telegram saying, 'Partridge shoot for Governor three months from now at all costs.' So birds were brought from Calcutta bird market and from the bird market in Lucknow, where you could buy thousands of them although you had to pay the price. They came in huge crates and the old station was nothing but partridges for about a month. There must have been at least five thousand of them, all calling away '*Kain, Kain*' for all they were worth. Then a whole area of forest was set aside, ash baths were laid out, corn fields were sowed, so that when the partridges were let go they stayed there. In a four-hour partridge shoot they fired something like a thousand cartridges and picked up five hundred birds and Sir Henry Wheeler said it was the finest partridge shoot he'd had anywhere.

However, the best means of winning friends in high places was undoubtedly by means of the arranged tiger shoot, a device that was said to have led to fierce competition in the prestige stakes, for 'if a VIP guest came to Baroda and didn't shoot a tiger and went to Gwalior and shot one, then Baroda would be looked upon by the princes as a third-rate state that couldn't produce a tiger for a VIP.' It was also incumbent upon such rulers to produce tigers of suitable size to match the status of the guests, as John Wakefield explains: 'When the Viceroys and Governors General used to shoot, very rarely did they shoot a tiger under 10 feet and I know two or three instances where tape measures used to be specially made with an 11 inch foot instead of a 12 inch foot, so that when these tape measures measured these imperial tigers a 10 foot tiger automatically became an 11 foot tiger in front of everybody and to everybody's satisfaction.' To ensure docility the tethered buffalos used as bait for the kills were sometimes sprinkled with opium. Leela Moolgaokar recalls one such drugged tiger in Gwalior being shot as it snored.

Only in a handful of states were tigers regularly laid on for important visitors, since they were universally regarded as royal beasts and their shooting was very strictly controlled. 'During Maharana Fateh Singh's rule, which lasted for forty-five years, only his nobles were allowed to shoot in their territory,' explains the Mahar-awal of Dungarpur. 'They were sixteen in number but only five had tigers in their territory. So there were five of the nobles plus the Maharana and occasionally the Resident who, if he was in Udaipur for three or four years, would be quite content to shoot one or two tigers with the permission of the Maharana. And that was about it; seven people shooting tigers in an area of 13,000 square miles.' Occasionally, the Maharana allowed other royal visitors to shoot in his state: 'I remember in the summer of 1931 shooting tiger in an area of the Udaipur state where the Maharaja of Jodhpur and his brother had come and shot tigers just before me. They were in camp for about three weeks and they shot fifteen tigers, which I thought was too many. I happened to go there after a week and I saw ten tigers in the same area within ten days and I shot three. Next year when I went back again there were twenty.'

Nowhere were tigers more plentiful than in the equally large state of Rewa, where during the minority of Maharaja Gulab Singh they had been allowed to multiply to a point where they had become a menace to the population. However, upon reaching his majority the Maharaja set about reducing their number with great industry, personally disposing of 481 tigers in the first thirteen years of his rule. 'My father-in-law was a great shikari who shot hundreds of tigers,' recalls Princess Pravinba of Kutch, who married the Yuvaraj of Rewa in 1943. 'But, at the same time, the laws were very rigid. They could only be shot where there was a profusion of tigers. The shikari network would bring news about man-eaters or cattle-lifters and then they would shoot in that particular area, going after that particular tiger as far as possible. I shot three; two tigresses and one tiger.'

Conrad Corfield, who spent two years in Rewa as the Maharaja's Adviser, came to regard the arranged tiger shoot as 'the nadir of shikar' because 'there were occasions when one felt the whole thing was so arranged that there was no sporting element in it.' He also had plenty of opportunities of watching the Maharaja going about his favourite pursuit:

He found the easiest way to bag tigers was to take with him a book and a monkey on a long string. When seated in the machan he would release the monkey, who immediately climbed into the top branches. He would then give the signal for the beat to start and settle down to read. As soon as the tiger approached the monkey would spot him and give the cough with which all monkeys warn the jungle folk that

'Sher Khan' the tiger is on the prowl. His Highness would then quickly put down his book and pick up his rifle.

There were three standard methods of shooting a tiger:

The first was where a tiger had killed the bait. You followed the drag in the middle of the day when the tiger was asleep, you tied up the cot very quietly on a tree above the kill and you sat there until sunset, because the tiger normally came back to its kill between four and six in the afternoon. In the second method you again allowed the tiger to kill and drag away the bait and early in the morning at dawn you surrounded the area with elephants and worked in towards the bait. Then if the tiger was still on the bait, you had a shot at it from the elephant. In the third and most luxurious method you studied the ground and worked out where the tiger was going to lie up and then you would put two machans on a valley ravine going into the hills. You put up sticks on both sides with white flags strung out at hundred yard intervals which not even wild elephants would go through. Then elephants and men would drive the tiger up and hopefully it would come out between your two machans. It was driven out in broad daylight and if it was shot correctly it died a very stupid death like a rabbit.

However, even the best regulated drives did not always go according to plan. 'One of the rules was that you had to wait until it had crossed half the fire line before you pulled the trigger,' John Wakefield recalls. 'Because if you fired too early and did not hit it correctly, it would go back into the beat and maul one of the beaters. I have twice seen the most ghastly sight of a tiger going back and catching a beater and shaking him like a terrier shakes a rat.'

There were those who regarded none of these methods of killing tiger to be truly sporting. The 'cream and the most sporting of sport', according to the Maharawal, was the following-up of tiger in the middle of the day in the hot season:

The tiger may be lying in deep shade close to a pool of water. You approach step by step or crawl on your belly, which may take you half an hour or forty minutes, and then you might see him either in the pool, with just the tips of his ears and his eyes above the surface, or lying in deep shade. You wait until he gets up and gives himself a shake and walks up the bank and when he gives you a broadside you take a careful shot. Then I think you meet the tiger on fairly even terms, about sixty per cent in your favour. Because if he sees you before you take a shot or if you take a hasty shot and wound him then he is going to be an unpleasant customer. With an English

double-barrelled rifle the chances are that eight times out of ten you
will have him before he kills you, but if he mauls you, you're finished.

Despite the fact that the Princes between them accounted for a large
proportion of all the tigers shot in India prior to Independence in
1947, they were not responsible for the rapid decline in numbers.
'History will record that the greatest protectors of tigers in India
were the princes,' maintains the Maharawal. 'The number of tigers
in India in 1930 was 40,000 and in 1946 it was 30,000. But while
in British India the number had gone down, in Princely India the
numbers were the same, so to say that the Princes were responsible
is complete nonsense.'

Indeed, there were quite a number of rulers who resolutely
refused to go in for shikar at all. There were some like the Maharaja
of Dewas Junior who as a young man gave up shooting after killing
a doe that was carrying a fawn: 'The sight of this baby creature dead
because of his bullet finished his shikar,' explains his daughter. 'He
said, "My shooting days are over. Here are my guns, here are the
best of instructors, you learn from them." And he never accompanied
us on a shooting party again.' Another ruler who gave up shikar was
Maharaj Rana Sir Udai Bhan Singh of Dholpur who, according to
Conrad Corfield, was 'the finest game shot in India but learned to
love wildlife so much that he never handled a gun again'. He had
the area round his country estate made into a game reserve where
'you could take a launch round the lake and see tigers yawning in
your face from the bank ten yards away'. As a young boy, Lalit Sen
of Suket was taken to see the Maharaj Rana whom he remembers
as 'one of the most polished, most suave, most learned rulers I ever
came across. I sat beside him in the evening when he drove through
his sanctuary. He had food with him and he'd stop the car, call an
animal by name and it would come rushing up to feed from his own
hands. He had a name for the stag, for the tiger, for the kite. I saw
that with my own eyes as a boy and it had a lasting effect on me.'

Another youngster who was greatly influenced by personal
example was the present Maharaja of Bikaner, Karni Singh, who in
later years became India's top clay-pigeon champion and represented India in five Olympics:

My father, Maharaja Sadul Singh, was an exceptional shot – at least
six times as good as I am. But my mother came from Rewa and in
the eastern parts of our country people are very old-fashioned. She
didn't believe in eating meat or drinking alcohol and she didn't like
to shoot, so consequently when my father tried to bring me up in the

usual tradition of shikar and meat-eating and drinking alcohol her influence cancelled his out. The net result is that my brother, my sister and I are all vegetarians, we are all teetotallers and I hardly ever shoot except clay-pigeon. When my father first took me out to shoot partridges and I shot three I was so miserable I couldn't sleep all night. I'd come back from shooting and my mother would say, 'But didn't you know today was *Ekadashi* (eleventh day of the month)? You shouldn't have shot today.' Or, 'Today was *Amavasya* (new moon). You shouldn't have shot today.' So that atmosphere was always there.

Even Lakshman Singh of Dungarpur, who remains a keen and active sportsman in his old age, found it difficult to enjoy his shooting when he returned to Gajner lake a second time: 'After about an hour and forty-five minutes I stopped shooting and just sat in my chair and watched others shooting. The first time I had shot with gusto, but this time I said, "*Bas*, that's enough", because it was a pity to see these birds just drop down on the water. This was not in Ganga Singh's time, because he would have been very annoyed, but Maharaja Sadul Singh was a friend and belonged to my generation and I knew he would not mind.'

Another son who found it difficult to follow his father's example was Dr Karan Singh of Kashmir:

Daddy was determined that I should become a good rider and a great polo player, but perhaps it wasn't in my *karma* because I was more interested in the world of books and ideas. So that whole ethos of hunting and shooting and fishing and riding was something that I fairly decisively and successfully rejected. What is interesting is that my elder son has reverted. He's tremendously fond of riding and polo and fishing and shooting – so maybe it was just a normal psychological reaction.

8

ROYAL PROGRESS

As we neared the capital of the Haras, clouds of dust, gradually obscuring the atmosphere, were the first signal of the Raja's approach: soon the sound of drums, the clangour of trumpets and tramping of steeds became audible, and at length the sadni-aswars, *or camel-messengers, announced the Raja's presence. As my friend twirled his lance in the midst of about eight hundred cavaliers and fifteen hundred foot, I thought of the deeds his ancestors had performed when leading such a* gole, *to maintain their reputation for fealty.*

Lt.-Col. James Tod describing
a visit to Bundi in *Annals and Antiquities
of Rajasthan*, 1829

The days were long past when the rulers of the Indian states went on their journeys with all the panoply and accoutrements of a medieval army on the march – but the journeys themselves continued and they were still performed in style. When John Wakefield's uncle went to Patiala as a Dewan in the early years of the century he found 'Gladstone bags specially built for elephants. One Gladstone bag carried all the furniture for the camp dining room and the other for the drawing room.' These camps were no mean affairs: 'Some tents covered an area of about half an acre of land and were made for the ruler to his own design with perhaps four bedrooms and a combined drawing-dining room. Your junior staff knew exactly what to do when you went camping or on tour. You said you wanted so many VIP tents and so many ordinary tents and it was all laid on. In Jind State I have even seen a double-storeyed tent with a ground floor and a first floor.'

Camping out in the districts away from the state capital was an annual fixture in most states. The more responsible rulers made it a point to spend a good proportion of their time touring their land and in a small state like Dewas Junior, consisting of 419 square miles of territory, it was possible to keep in touch with even the most remote corners. 'Daddy tried to visit all his villages during the year,' recalls Shashi Wallia. 'He would take the car as far as he could and then go in a bullock cart on the jungle roads into the interior – which was a much better way of travelling and more fun. He took a doctor with him and he personally checked everything once a year; whether a tank (reservoir) had to be built or how they had utilised money they had been given; whether they had squandered it or built a good road, fenced their fields properly or attended to the sickness among their cattle.'

In a state like Kotah that was thirteen times as large as Dewas Junior, it was impossible for a single person to visit every area within the year. Instead, the state was divided into two regions which were toured by the ruler in alternate years – a system that the present Maharaja inherited from his father:

> My father used to go with all his ministers and some of his clerical staff and camp in tents that were transported on camel-back, elephants and bullock-carts. They used to move by regular stages and they had two sets of tents, one set being pitched about seven or eight miles beyond the other. His Highness would stay one or two nights, according to the importance of the place, and then move on horseback or camel to the next. And as soon as one camp was vacated it was taken down and put up again on the far side of the other camp on the same route. On this touring His Highness would inspect the different district headquarters and if he found any judicial file which had lain there for six months or more then the fellow in charge was taken to task – with the result that normally we never found more than two or three files in any year that had been around for that long. His Highness would also listen to petitions in the afternoon which were read to him and his ministers – and because it had come to the notice of the ruler nobody would have the courage to oppose the petition going forward through the proper channels. In those days, of course, there was a lot of jungle round about in Kotah so if the camp was in a place where there was good shikar you stayed there for two or three days. You got the paperwork finished and then for two days you enjoyed your shooting.

In Kotah they toured in winter, but a hundred miles to the south in the slightly larger state of Bhopal the touring was done in summer – 'to see if the farmers had suffered or not in the harvest, to see what their problems were and to keep in touch'. The present Begum often accompanied her father, sleeping in tents which were kept cool in the traditional way by wickerwork thorn-bush *tatties* that were kept wetted and fanned by hand-pulled *pankahs* (fans): 'These camps were usually in a grove of mango trees and at night we slept out in the open, although the Bhopal region did not get very hot in those days. If it reached a temperature of 39 degrees in the daytime we thought the world would fall in!'

Even in a large state like Gwalior, almost five times as large as Bhopal, both Madhavrao Scindia's father and grandfather believed strongly in 'the principle of accessibility – and the only way to achieve that in a large state like Gwalior was to constantly live in inspection bungalows or tents'. Dotted about the state were eleven such bungalows that served as bases for touring: 'My father didn't tour as much as my grandfather did, but that was because he was only just getting into his stride when the merger of the states came about. However, I know that on these tours he gave special attention to what were known as the Scheduled Castes and Tribes. I was told that at one such village they had a welcome prepared for him and they offered him milk – and to drink milk offered by a *Harijan* ('Untouchable') or someone from the scheduled castes was to pollute oneself. But the moment they offered him the milk, he got down off his horse and sat down with them and drank it, with the result that all his officers had to drink that milk, too.'

It was the railways that first began to alter long-established patterns of behaviour by putting the states in closer contact with the outside world – although without seriously weakening local loyalties. 'Most of the Deccan states were adjacent to each other, but each one liked to maintain its own separate identity,' asserts the Rajmata of Sangli. 'I remember when any member of the Miraj royal family visited us they were asked about the weather in Miraj – and Miraj was just five miles away! We used to feel that Kolhapur was very far away – but that was only thirty miles distant. It was a bit like Lilliput in *Gulliver's Travels*.' The railways brought the Indian states and British India closer together, but with the British firmly in control: 'They were not very keen on giving railways to the rulers, and they always insisted that the rulers should have only the metre gauge line and not the broad gauge – for strategic and military reasons. They never allowed parallel roads to be built either, so that you had to go by the railway and you had to trans-ship everything from one gauge to the other.' Where the major railway lines across the subcontinent ran through state territory, the land was leased to the Government of India by treaty, allowing its jurisdiction to extend over what were known as the 'Railway Lands of the Indian States'. However, a state could levy customs duties on goods being carried by rail through its territories and a coastal state with deep-water harbours like Bhavnagar, which had more than 400 miles of railway track on its land, did extremely well out of such levies: 'In the pre-war days we used to earn about a crore of rupees every year from customs revenue, which helped to make Bhavnagar the richest state in India for its size.' Like many much larger states, Bhavnagar had its own

State Railway, always run by an English General Manager, and its own rolling stock, including a number of state carriages and saloons: 'One saloon was for the Maharaja and was very well furnished with a bedroom, sitting room, kitchen and the usual services. The other also had three main compartments which were for the Dewan and the Secretary. Those two were eight-wheelers, but we also had several six-wheel carriages with only one or two compartments in each, some of which were for the railway officers.' Indore also had its state saloon – 'a marvellous thing,' according to Richard Shivaji Rao Holkar. 'A broad-gauge coach not meant for Indore State but for travelling to Bombay and Delhi and to give my father a place to stay without his having to go to a hotel. It had a very modern body of some white metal like aluminium with mirror-glass windows that you could look out of without others looking in. Inside it was air-conditioned, with light wood panelling and all 1930s furniture. It was a marvellous way to travel.' Suket State, by contrast, possessed a state saloon built at the turn of the century and so 'ancient and awkward' that it was rarely used in later years.

Impressive and useful as these state railways and saloons were, they never excited the interest of the Princes in quite the same way as the motor car: 'There was a passion for what we called pedigree. The era of pedigree horses had gone and so cars took over.' From the moment that the first automobile was driven through the streets of Bombay, it was recognised as an ornament fit for a prince. The Maharaja of Cooch Behar and the Sixth Nizam were among the first to possess one and every ruler who could afford to indulge himself followed suit. 'We had a Didion first in 1906, which I don't remember,' states Apasaheb Pant of Aundh. 'But I well remember the magnificent Mercedes that my father bought in 1911, which had a top speed of 15 miles an hour.'

Rolls-Royces soon came to be regarded as the most regal of motor cars – 'having one meant that you were somebody in British eyes' – and during the next forty years over eight hundred found their way into the princely states. The first was bought by Madhav Rao Scindia of Gwalior in 1908 and was known as the 'Pearl of the East', while Rolls-Royce's best customer was probably Bhupinder Singh of Patiala, who owned twenty-seven various models as well as some one hundred other cars. The ever-different Jay Singh of Alwar championed Hispano-Suizas, always finished in blue and bought in threes. It was said that when their owner tired of them, he had them ceremonially interred in the hills around his palace. Jay Singh's fastidiousness also demanded that no leather be used either in or on his cars: 'The upholstery was invariably in single-point

French tapestry and even the usual leather "boots" that protected sections of the suspension were made of other material.' But the pride of the Alwar collection was a magnificent custom-built 1924 Lanchester that was half car and half royal coach. It had two seats at the front and a throne at the back, flanked by wide running-boards on either side and with room for two postillions at the back.

Another ruler with a catholic collection of cars was Jagatjit Singh, who had a large circular structure known as the *Elysées Curées* built in the palace grounds at Kapurthala to house them. 'The outer circle contained the household and bodyguard's stables and the inner circle contained the motor garage.' explains Sukhjit Singh. 'My sister and I used to cycle over there with carrots and go round feeding all the horses. After that we'd walk into the inner circle and see all the cars lined up. Whenever I get a whiff of that genuine smell of leather it takes me back to my grandfather's Hispano-Suiza, a lovely old thing which had a telephone in the back seat. You pressed a button and spoke into the telephone and told the driver where to go because there was a partition between the driver and passenger. Then there was a more modern Buick which had two jump seats beautifully lined in velvet that fell out from the front seat's back-rest, which was where the ADCs usually sat.' Rulers also went in for more practical vehicles: 'cars for the zanana ladies with smoked-glass windows' and 'converted Fords and Dodges that were used for hunting, with spotlamps and gun racks and which were used very roughly'. Much to the distress of the manufacturers, the father of the present Maharaja of Bharatpur had a number of his Rolls-Royces converted into shooting brakes and used them to transport guests to and from his famous duck-shoots.

In the late 1920s, air travel began to capture the imagination of some of the more Westernised Princes. One of the first to try the newly-opened overland air route to London in the early thirties was the Maharaja of Jodhpur. A few years later, the Maharaja of Bhavnagar bought a single-engined plane in which he and his brother, Prince Dharmakumarsinhji, often flew to Bombay: 'It was a three-seater plane named "The Eagle" and it took about two-and-a-quarter hours to reach Bombay. It was piloted by an Englishman called Fowler who wore a monocle and while we stayed at the Taj Mahal Hotel he stayed at Greens next door, where he would drink gimlets, or gin and bitters, up to 2 or 3 am without showing any change. Normally he didn't drink before he took us back to Bhavnagar.' Apasaheb Pant of Aundh took up flying as a young man in 1930 and was among the first Indians to gain a flying licence. On one memorable occasion he borrowed a friend's Puss Moth and flew from Karachi to his home state:

> I didn't know whether there was a place for an aeroplane to land in Aundh, but when I reached Pune I sent a telegram to my father saying that I was arriving at such and such a time and to clear a place about five hundred feet long and two hundred feet wide. When I flew in I found the state band and the state constabulary turned out with camels, elephants, horses and trumpets, so there was hardly any space for me to land. But they had done a good job filling up the holes in a field and I landed safely.

The aeroplane, however, would always be an intruder on the Indian scene. Within the confines of the state motor-cars, camels, elephants, horses and even bullock-carts continued to provide the main means of transport, while beyond its boundaries the Indian railway system kept rulers in touch with one another and with the Paramount Power in New Delhi, also allowing them and their families to make their seasonal migrations to cooler climes in the summer months.

In the early decades of this century it became fashionable in a number of states to follow the British habit of making an exodus to the hills as the hot weather months approached. The smartest of the British hill-stations was Simla, summer capital of the Government of India, but close proximity to the Paramount Power in the person of the Viceroy and his staff was not something that many rulers desired. 'It was nice and cool but it was very, very formal in Simla and we were restricted in every way,' declares Shashi Wallia, who twice accompanied her father when he went up on official business connected with the Chamber of Princes. 'We loathed it if we had to go and pay a formal visit, because we never knew if we were saying the right thing or not. We were always being told that this person was from that state and so you had to give way to him.' Simla had formerly been part of Patiala State and although it had been ceded to the British in the nineteenth century the Patiala rulers continued to regard it as a second home until Maharaja Bhupinder Singh, a prominent and colourful participant in the Simla Season, overstepped the mark:

> Bhupinder Singh's penchant for beautiful women led him to have an association with one of the Viceroy's daughters and he was banned from Simla. So he built a second Simla nearby in Chail, which had its palace with probably the world's highest cricket pitch, tennis courts, swimming pools, shoots and rides. Everything you wanted

was at Chail so everybody from Simla started coming down to Chail
for weekends, including the Viceroys.

For young Dick Bowles it was the cricket ground – 'where you could
look across and down onto the lights of Simla' – that was one of
the chief attractions of Chail:

> It was sawn off the top of a mountain and had a concrete batting area
> with a matting surface and the ball used to fairly whistle off that
> matting. We had some wonderful matches there. I remember a
> cricket match where we all had to dress up in fancy dress and this
> vast figure of Bhupinder Singh emerged dressed as a nun, looking
> marvellous with his black habit and black beard. Everyone was
> dressed in some female outfit. I went as a European bride and found
> it very difficult to bat in a long dress with pads on underneath.

More popular among the princes than Simla was the more relaxed
Himalayan hill-station of Mussoorie, where a number of rulers had
their own houses or rented them for the summer. Its grandest private
residence was undoubtedly Maharaja Jagatjit Singh's Chateau Kapurthala, the most prominent landmark on Mussoorie Ridge: 'As
you were carried up the hill in your *dandi* (sedan chair) you saw this
magnificent vista with the turreted roof-tops glistening in the sun,
four turrets and a steep-sloping roof typical of an old French
chateau. Then as you got closer you saw the coat of arms emblazoned
on the central masonry and you entered through magnificent
wrought-iron portals.'

The moves to and from Mussoorie were always major operations,
as Sukhjit Singh recalls:

> Virtually the seat of governance of the state shifted, like the move of
> the government from Delhi to Simla but in miniature. First of all the
> Comptroller of the Household would come up to make sure that
> everything was ready, because other houses would sometimes have
> to be rented to take the overflow from Chateau Kapurthala. Then
> the Maharanis would move en bloc with a special train. The Senior
> Maharani would go in my grandfather's saloon and they would reserve
> two or three first class carriages for the others and their entourages.
> The baggage, the dogs and the horses would also go up and even
> some of my grandfather's more delicate birds who couldn't stand the
> heat of the plains, such as the Japanese pheasants and the *monals*.
> They went in their travelling-cages with their keeper and were housed
> for the summer in a specially constructed aviary.
>
> Before we moved up my sister and I would have to pay our respects
> to our various grandmothers, who always insisted that we couldn't

leave until we had taken a little curd, a little sugar and a little money, which was auspicious for a journey. Then we would disembark from the train at Dehra Dun and go on horseback or in a dandi to Kincraig, where a rickshaw would take you on up to the house.

In Mussoorie there were no cars, the road traffic consisting entirely of horses, rickshaws and pedestrians: 'Anyone of any status had his own rickshaw pulled by four or five men known as *jhampanis* who dressed in the livery of their employer. It was a unique sight to see the number of liveried rickshaws on the Mall in those days.'

Another popular Himalayan hill-station was Darjeeling, where many of the rulers and zamindars of Bengal and the Eastern states had summer bungalows, among them the ruling family of Cooch Behar – although they also patronised the longer-established British hill-station of Ootacamund, situated many hundreds of miles away to the south in the Nilgiri hills between Cochin and Mysore. 'Ooty' was especially popular among those princes who liked riding 'because there was hunting and polo, a racecourse and horse-shows'. The young Maharaja Sawai Man Singh of Jaipur went there 'for the hunting season' with his brothers under the care of his English guardian, and it was here that Princess Gayatri Devi first met him when he was thirteen years old and she five:

> This guardian was trying to get him a bit slimmer because he had been fed so much by the ladies of the zanana in Jaipur and so he had put him on a strict English diet. Now all the princes used to invite each other to meals and one day he sneaked up to my mother and said, 'You've invited me to lunch. Please see that I have a huge *thali* of Indian food, because I'm not allowed to eat Indian food at home.' So she did that for him and although the guardian couldn't say anything in front of her he wrote afterwards to my mother, 'Your Highness, next time the Maharaja of Jaipur is invited to your house please don't give him this Indian food.'

For the Maratha states along the Western Ghats there was the lesser hill-station of Mahabaleshwar, a summer retreat for British officials from Pune and Bombay, but for the Kathiawar states and Baroda there was no local refuge from the heat and humidity of the summer months. Their nearest hill-station was Mount Abu, a small British enclave in Rajputana where the AGG for Rajputana had his summer Residency and combined his political office with the post of local Chief Commissioner. One of a number of rulers who maintained a house in Mount Abu was the Nawab of Palanpur, whose state was barely two hours' drive away to the south:

It's a beautiful hill-station standing about four thousand feet above
the surrounding plains, full of greenery and with the most magnificent
Jain temples, over a thousand years old and covered with marble
carving of outstanding workmanship. Quite a number of princes
besides ourselves – Alwar, Bikaner, Jaipur, Jodhpur, Tonk and
Dholpur – had houses there beside a nice lake. We generally went
during the months of May and June when the temperatures in
Palanpur soar up to 115 degrees and more. We got very good tennis
and cricket and a little bit of golf on the 'browns', and every evening
there was a very nice get-together at the Club, with dances once a
fortnight.

The club was the Rajputana Club, whose membership was confined
to the Political Agents of Rajasthan, Central India and Kathiawar
but with an honorary membership that was extended to all visiting
Indian princes and their families as well as members of the Indian
nobility. This was where the Nawab's son, Muzaffer Khan, first
came into contact with British India as a small boy: 'The Club was
where we played with English children and got to see their customs
– how they dressed and behaved – and because our elders and the
British mixed freely and were very friendly with each other there
was no feeling of being different in any way. So Mount Abu was
"Little England" for us, where we stayed for two months every
year.' One of Muzaffer Khan' s most vivid memories as a child was
of a fête held at the British Residency 'with its very English garden'
at Mount Abu during wartime, when the children threw tennis balls
at cardboard figures: 'There was Hitler, Himmler, Goering and
Goebbels. Himmler was the closest, then Goering and Goebbels
and Hitler was the farthest. None of the children were able to knock
Hitler over, so in the end I took a tennis ball, ran very close to Hitler
and knocked him over from about two feet away – for which I got
a prize!'

Some of the larger states had their own summer retreats. In
Gwalior the entire administration retired to Shikoli seventy miles
south of the state capital in the Shivpuri hills, where it was slightly
cooler than in the plains. In many other states it was a question of
staying put and making the best of the two enervating months before
the coming of the rains in July and August.

The temperate six months of the Indian Cold Weather were the
season of travel. Most weddings took place during this period, being
confined among Hindus to certain auspicious periods of the year,
and given the degree of intermarriage which existed between states
every wedding was also a family reunion. Gayatri Devi remembers
one such wedding that she attended in Dewas, where she and her

elder brother were briefly reunited with a younger sister who had been informally adopted by a childless aunt: 'There was a terrible moment when she appeared wearing emerald earrings and an emerald necklace. She was dying to come over but was looking so grand and aloof in all her finery and jewellery that my brother and I just looked at each other. But at that wedding they threw a lot of yellow powder at each other, which is what they do at Maharashtrian weddings, and naturally when the colour started being thrown we made a bee-line for our little sister and in the end she didn't want to go back to her new home.'

The Cold Weather was also the time when formal visits between states were made. Protocol decreed that the visiting prince should be met by a guard of honour either at the state boundary or at a certain designated distance from the palace as befitting his status vis-à-vis his host, together with the firing of an appropriate number of gun salutes – about which the princes were quite as fussy as the British. Not all rulers enjoyed what they regarded as unnecessary ceremony. Sahibzada Ata Muhamed Khan of Palanpur remembers the occasion in the late 1930s when Maharaja Hari Singh of Jammu and Kashmir attempted to pay an unannounced visit on the ruler of Palanpur, Nawab Taley Mohamed Khan: 'My uncle got a message from one of his stations to say that His Highness of Jammu and Kashmir's saloon was attached to the mail train so we all rushed down to the station. I still remember how when the saloon came in and he opened the door and saw us all there he shrieked like a little child. He then opened the door on the other side, jumped down onto the railway lines and ran towards the palace, with all the people watching.' This was also the time when informal visits were made for shikar or for holidays. Bapa Dhrangadhara remembers the visits he made during his childhood to his mother's home state of Jodhpur, 'a magical world full of intrigues but which we loved. We really were spoiled because your *nana* and *nani* (maternal grandparents) will always look after you better than your father's parents since it is a rare occurrence for them to see you. So love was lavished on us and I gained about fifteen pounds every fortnight with ghee (clarified butter) almost coming out of my ears.' A less happy visit was once paid by a certain ruler from a Central Indian state to Alwar when Jay Singh was still on the gadi:

My father was surprised to find when he got there that, instead of old and young courtiers which was what most rulers have, this gentleman was only attended by extremely good-looking young men, all dressed in the same *churidars* and *achkans* as His Highness and with *safas* (turbans) of the same type and colour. Then there were boys ranged between ten and twenty years of age lining the steps of the marble staircase and as His Highness passed up the staircase with my father he would either pinch their cheeks or tweak their ears, which my father found very peculiar. In the evening there was a lot of *nautch* (dancing) and *tamasha* (fuss) with dancing girls and eventually my father excused himself and went to his room. He washed and said his prayers and then climbed into bed where, to his horror, he felt somebody next to him. He had a candle and lit it and found it was a nude young boy of about 10 or 11 who said, 'Your Highness, I have been sent by my lord to entertain you.' 'Entertain me?' said my father. 'Look, Your Highness, I am clean,' said this little boy – and pulled a silk handkerchief out of his bottom! 'That's it!' said my father and threw him out of the room.

Alwar, it must be said, was viewed by many of his fellow-princes with respect for his quite brilliant intellect, mingled with alarm and even pity because 'he was quite clearly deranged'. To some he was a great Hindu patriot, to others a psychopath who did much to bring the Princes into disrepute. His fear of losing caste caused him to always don gloves before shaking hands with a European and he avoided leather like the plague. 'He came to Palanpur for a wedding when I was a chubby boy of four years,' recalls Sahibzada Ata Muhamed Khan. 'He picked me up and put me in his lap but the moment he saw my leather shoes he pushed me off and I fell down.' Alwar's neighbour, the Maharaja of Bharatpur once upset him deeply by inviting him to the state and making him inspect a guard of honour 'fitted out with leather jackets, leather boots and leather leggings'.

For some rulers getting out of their state was as much a necessity as anything else. Mansur Ali Khan of Pataudi remembers how his grandfather, the Nawab of Bhopal, felt under constant pressure when he was in the state: 'My grandfather always used to say that the atmosphere of a state was such that unless he could escape to England or abroad for three months in the year he felt he would go insane, because as a ruler you were always on show, and with everybody saying, "Yes, sir" and "No, sir" and "Whatever you want sir", it does tend to drive even the sanest man a little bit bonkers.'

Every journey was accompanied by taboos of one sort or another. Departures might have to be delayed for several hours or even postponed until more auspicious days had been found and the blessings of the family deity sought with prayers and offerings both before leaving the state and after returning. In Sangli State there was a strong prohibition that forbade any member of the ruling family from setting out on any enterprise by the southern gate of the palace, because long ago 'when the bravest of the Sangli rulers, Parshuram Rao Bhausaheb, went south there was treachery and he never returned'.

As travelling increased, so the need for accommodation outside the state grew. In New Delhi, houses were needed to accommodate the rulers and their Dewans, who after 1921 were increasingly being drawn to the capital for political discussions and debates in the Chamber of Princes. In Bombay, too, there were less formal political sessions that took place from time to time behind closed doors in the Princes' Room at the Taj. Quite a few rulers solved the problem by building mansions for themselves in New Delhi and Bombay. One exception was Dhrangadhara, 'because one of our ancestors had given a command that as the ruler was the first servant of the state he was not to buy any property outside the state. This was an ancient edict that we respected, although we had a small house in Rajkot, where the British Residency for our area was situated, in which the ruler or his Dewan could stay whenever he was seeing the Resident.' The Maharaja of Dhrangadhara, like the majority of his fellow-princes, had to make do with the Imperial or Maiden's Hotel in New Delhi and the Taj in Bombay. Palatial in size and Indian-owned, but run on Western lines, the Bombay Taj was uniquely suited to accommodate royal visitors and their entourages. 'The Taj became a second home for us,' explains Dharmakumar-sinhji of Bhavnagar. 'It had a very cosmopolitan atmosphere like a huge club where it wasn't necessary to have yourself introduced. Having been brought up in England we couldn't take Indian spices, so we preferred the English-style menus and because Bhavnagar was a "dry" state with prohibition enforced we did all our drinking in the privacy of the Taj. Its hairdressing saloon was also very popular because getting a good haircut was a problem in those days in India.'

The Taj was also able to provide facilities for shopping for the ladies, since 'all the sariwallas, banglewallas and jewellers would come to the hotel', and Arab horse-traders were a familiar sight in its corridors, especially when a sporting prince was known to be in residence. Its princely guests could also entertain royally. One of the liveliest in the late 1930s was the dashing Nawab of Sachin, Secretary of the Chamber of Princes for a time and a great party-giver, as Shashi Wallia remembers:

His Highness always had a very convivial crowd around him made up of painters, writers, artists and beautiful women. We would meet in his suite and His Highness would always be very well groomed, dressed in white jodhpurs and white jodhpur coat. We would have drinks and then go down to the dining room where there was always a little gift for each lady at the table, accompanied by a posy of flowers – a lipstick, a bottle of perfume, a powder compact or a cigarette case. His dinners were always lavish and there was always champagne. He would encourage us to get up and go on the dance floor but His Highness never danced himself. Maybe he thought it was beneath his dignity to dance in public.

Sited on the sea-front close to the Gateway of India, the Taj was the first and last stopping-place for travellers either coming from or bound for Europe – among them the ever-increasing number of princes and their families who regarded England as a natural part of their heritage. For them foreign travel presented few of the difficulties that had faced their fathers and grandfathers in the late nineteenth century, when travelling over the *kala pani* or 'black water' to Europe was fraught with difficulties, not least because caste-conscious travellers insisted on drinking only Ganges water. One of the first rulers to take the plunge had been Maharaja Takhatsinhji, Kumar Dharmakumarsinhji's grandfather:

My grandfather chartered a whole boat to go to England at the invitation of Queen Victoria. He took his own water, he took his own buffaloes, his own barbers, his own staff and servants and even his own musician, Rahim Khan, who was one of the best-known musicians in India and who, after he had played in front of Queen Victoria, got such a swollen head that when after his return to India he was asked by the ordinary gentry to play he would say, 'But don't you understand? I have played in front of Queen Victoria. Who are you to ask me to play?' My grandfather also took his own cook, of course, to make Indian food and chappatties for himself and the staff because they weren't used to eating English food and ate from thalis in the Indian style. He could use a knife and fork but it is said that at a banquet at Buckingham Palace my grandfather, instead of drinking from his glass, drank from the finger-bowl because he wasn't used to finger-bowls. The Queen realised that he could have been placed in an embarrassing position, so she herself took up her finger-bowl and drank from it.

By the turn of the century all princely inhibitions had disappeared and Indian royalty had become a familiar if exotic part of the social scene both in England and on the Continent. A number of rulers bought country houses in England and in France the Maharaja of Kapurthala was often to be seen 'striding along the *plage* at Dieppe or one of the other seaside resorts being followed by his four sons in their turbans'. A European Grand Tour, if not a spell in an English university, came to be regarded by a number of the more Anglicised states as a necessary part of a growing prince's education. One young man who went on just such a Grand Tour was the Nawab of Cambay State in 1928:

> I was taken to Europe by Mr R. M. S. Pasley, the Vice-Principal of Rajkumar College. We lived in a house in Reading and toured important places in England, Scotland and Wales. I shook hands with His Majesty King George V and Queen Mary at a garden party and met the Duke and Duchess of York. I went to the Derby, Hendon Air Show, Richmond Horse Show and the Aldershot Tattoo. Then we went to Europe and visited Rome, Paris, Geneva, Heidelberg, Cologne, Strasburg, Nice and Monte Carlo – where I was not allowed to gamble because I was under age. We returned to India in May 1929 and I then went on an Indian tour with Major Lee Harrison, visiting all the larger Indian States from Travancore to Kashmir, and ending with three weeks in the offices of the Collector in Pune.

A decade later Princess Nirmala Raje Bhonsle came over to England with her mother to visit her elder brother at Cambridge. They then travelled round Europe, where 'people showed a lot of respect for the Baroda family name and made a great hullabaloo over us', although there were occasional brushes with the popular press: 'We had a rather small maid with us whose nickname was "*Thengni*" (short) and one day when we were in Sweden her picture appeared in the newspapers with the caption "Royal Family Members and the Little Princess". "Look, your photo has been published," we said. "Oh, those horrid people," she replied and cursed. "Don't talk like that," I said. "They've called you a princess." "*Murkh lok ahet*," she said. "Foolish people."'

The Coronation of King George VI in 1937 drew many visitors from India, both official and private. Among them was the young Princess Padma Lokur of Bhor, who stayed with her grandfather and his entourage at the Kensington Palace Hotel, 'where we first came into contact with the telephone, so every five minutes we were ringing downstairs for a steward or a maid – until eventually they complained to my grandfather'. They also came into contact with the British public:

> Wherever we went we were accompanied by five *huzras* who acted as a sort of bodyguard. They wore very traditional Indian dress of *churidar* pyjamas with *angarkha* (waistcoat) and *safa* while my

grandfather, father and uncles all wore English suits. All these girls used to chase them for their autographs, thinking that our servants were the rajas. Our servants were ashamed because they didn't know how to sign their names, so my aunt and uncle and I taught them and after that they used to sign autographs.

Among the official guests at the Coronation was Iqbal Mohammed Khan of Palanpur, whose father was one of four Indian rulers who acted as honorary ADCs to the King:

It was my first trip out of India and very exciting but the Coronation itself was particularly interesting because coming from a ruling family with its own customs and ceremonies it was fascinating to see that their traditions were more or less the same as ours; the way Their Majesties walked in procession with the various types of heralds and stick-bearers. As for the actual Coronation Service itself, I was there in the Abbey with my father and it was beautifully organised but afterwards the arrangements completely broke down and no one could reach their cars. It was raining and we were all dressed up in our brocade *shervanis* (long coats) and coloured turbans and wearing jewellery and swords so it was impossible to walk to St James's Palace where we were staying. My father's ADC and I eventually got a lift from a passing MP while my father commandeered the Maharaja of Cooch Behar's car. But I remember Lord Willingdon, the Viceroy, turning to my father and saying, 'Taley, don't you think we do things better in India than they do here?'

9
ROYAL ALLIANCES

The selection of a bride or bridegroom for their children or for the Ruler of a State is, as a rule, made by their parents or guardians. Even though a boy may have attained his majority the selection of a bride for him, according to the usage of our country, generally rests with the parents. In the case of grown-up boys however, it would be advisable to consult them before nominating a bride for them.

Notes on the Education and
Upbringing of the Ruler, from
Maharaja Madhav Rao Scindia of
Gwalior's *General Policy Durbar*, 1925

'You were brought up and betrothed and married as part of the whole feudal system – and for the main actors, at least, that system was not really conducive to happiness.' Rarely was marriage within princely circles a matter of individual choice, it being accepted that the duty of a son or daughter was to obey the wishes of parents or grandparents. 'Youngsters like myself had no choice,' remembers the Maharao of Kutch. 'I was told that my betrothal would take place and that my marriage would follow. I didn't have to say yes or no, because I had no choice. I *was* shown a picture of my bride – but my bride didn't look like her picture at all!'

This was entirely in keeping with the value placed on the family in India: 'Society didn't consist of individuals but of houses and it was important for houses to maintain alliances. This applied tenfold among royal houses, where a matrimonial alliance was the next best thing to a military alliance.' As the need to make political alliances diminished, so other considerations assumed great importance – economic factors, the preferences of parents and rulers and, above all, the need to marry within princely circles. 'Our make-up was such that you could not marry an ordinary boy,' reflects Nirmala Raje Bhonsle. 'We were used only to the idea of marrying somebody from a royal family. That idea was dinned into us and so we had to keep to that. "My Akka is not going to marry anyone except a ruler," my grandmother would say.'

Although there were many princely families, the choice of brides or bridegrooms was often limited. Brahmins could only marry Brahmins, Rajputs did not marry Marathas, Muslims would not think of marrying Hindus and vice-versa. And within each social group further taboos narrowed down the field considerably. 'The whole Rajput community is very close-knit,' observes the Maharani of Wankaner. 'We are all relatives in different forms and so we have to hunt for suitable matches. My father was a Sisodia, so I could not marry a Sisodia. I married into the Jhala clan whose members cannot marry other Jhalas.' Among some Rajput families there were also special relationships that were maintained by marriages, such as the ancient alliance between Jaipur and Jodhpur, which meant that when the last ruling Maharaja of Jaipur, Sawai Man Singh, was adopted as Yuvaraj, he was married off as a boy of twelve to a Jodhpur princess considerably older than himself – as well as being betrothed to a second Jodhpur princess whom he married nine years later. Friendship between parents was also an important consideration. The marriage of the present Maharao and Maharani of Kotah in 1930 came about because their fathers were very old friends and wanted an alliance between Kotah and Bikaner – notwithstanding the fact that the Maharani was only seven at the time of their betrothal.

One unusual marriage ceremony that combined both love and duty was that which took place between Maharani Pravinba's grandfather, Maharao Khengarji III of Kutch, and two Rajput princesses:

My grandmother's father had some squabble with his elder brother in Dhrangadhara and came and took shelter in Kutch. As a little girl my grandmother used to come to the palace to help around, although they had been given accommodation outside the palace, and my grandfather and she used to play together as children. This developed into a love affair, but when my grandfather said that he would marry Gangabai – that was her name – my great-grandfather told him that he had arranged his marriage to a girl from Sailana. So my grandfather said, 'I shall marry both the girls. One for your sake, one for my sake' – and his father agreed. Now in those days you could send your *khanda* – your sword – to your bride's house instead of going yourself. She would then marry the khanda and return to your place where further ceremonies would take place. So the khanda was sent to Sailana, while he himself married the Dhrangadhara girl who was his love. He used to be very nice to both wives and both had children, but he was extremely fond of my grandmother and that love affair of theirs which had started when they were children lasted until the last moment of their lives.

Among the few Sikh princely families, alliances had to be sought outside their own small circle. 'It would be wrong to assume that a Sikh could only marry into a Sikh family,' declares Maharaja Sukhjit Singh. 'Many Sikh states married into the old Sardar families which were powerful enough to muster political clout or had achieved a certain status of their own, but a lot also married into very high-caste Rajput families from the hills, as did Kapurthala. Both my grand-mother and my mother were Hindu Rajputs from the Kangra hills.' Among the Muslim royal houses choice was more restricted, partly because of their widely differing origins, partly because of the sectarian divide between rulers such as the Nizams of Hyderabad who belonged to the Sunni Muslim sect and those, like the rulers of Rampur, who were Shiahs. An almost unbridgeable social gulf separated a family like that of the state of Cambay, who were Shiah Muslims of Persian Moghul origin, from their near neighbours of Sachin State who were Shiahs of part African descent. Muslim families of Afghan or Pathan origins solved the problem by turning to their ancestral homes for brides. For the sons of the rulers of the pre-eminent Muslim state of Hyderabad, princesses had sometimes to be found as far afield as Turkey.

To assist them in their alliance-building rulers employed their own match-makers, Charans or priests whose job it was to find suitable husbands for the daughters of the ruling house and to check with the clan Raj-barot and the royal astrologer that the potential bridegroom's genealogical tree was unsullied by marriages outside caste and that his horoscope matched that of the bride-to-be. In Lunawada State this was one of the duties performed by the Nagar Brahmins, priests and physicians to the royal family: 'We were so trusted that we were deputed to find good matches and empowered to state in writing on behalf of the ruler that so much would be given over if the other party accepted the match, because a ruler would always try to give his daughter to a boy one level higher than himself.' It was then up to the father of the bridegroom to send his own emissary to ask for a dowry that was in inverse proportion to the girl's good looks and status. If he wished to escape from the proposed match, he would ask for an impossibly large dowry. In the not-so-distant past these marriage ambassadors travelled in style: 'We have a letter dated 23 January 1859 issued by the ruler to my grandfather which gave him authority to pass through other native states like Baroda. He was empowered to go with an armed escort of soldiers and *nagara* and *danka* – two drums carried on horseback and trumpets to announce his arrival.'

Dowry – 'it would be lakhs and even crores of rupees, both in cash and kind, jewellery, silver and gold, clothes and household things, even your cooking utensils, even the pipes used for blowing on the embers of the fire, everything except items like needles and soap about which there were superstitions' – took up a large part of every marriage contract and many a match foundered on the inability or the unwillingness of a potential bride's father to meet the expectations of his opposite number. Originally a dowry had some practical value when 'parents saw to it that their daughter was well provided for before she went into the *sasural* (home of her in-laws), so that she was not embarrassed to ask for each and every little thing'. But over the centuries its original purpose had been obscured to the point where dowry became 'a status symbol, with the practical side neglected', and because it touched so deeply on family honour the eradication of the dowry system proved well-nigh impossible. A brave effort in the 1730s by the great Jai Singh, founder of Jaipur State and City, to ban excessive dowries from his kingdom was frustrated by the richest of his nobles who proceeded to lavish a king's ransom on his daughter's dowry in a deliberate gesture of defiance – and to this day it remains a burden of pride that affects rich and poor alike.

Princely squabbles over dowry threatened many a marriage. In Dhrangadhara there was the case many generations ago of a bride who was to marry a prince of Jaisalmer: 'The custom is that when a bridegroom arrives at the bride's home he touches the *toran* (floral bunting) hanging down from the entrance with his sword, but this the prince refused to do because he wanted an elephant as additional dowry on top of the agreed dowry. This the bride's family was very reluctant to give because they knew an elephant couldn't possibly survive in the sands of Jaisalmer. Ultimately they had to give in because it was a question of *izzat* (prestige) and the guests were already assembled – but the elephant died en route and the wife herself six months later.'

Marriage or betrothal at a tender age was also an inevitable part of the business. In the case of the present Maharana of Mewar, this meant marriage 'before I even knew what marriage meant and, after a year and a half, a child while I was still virtually a child myself'. For his fellow-clansman, the Maharawal of Dungarpur, marriage came even earlier:

My first marriage was, I think, for money. The treasury of the state was practically empty because my poor father had done so much for the 1914–18 war effort. So he contracted this alliance and in the *tikka* (arrangement) took two lakhs of rupees which he thought would rehabilitate the finances of the state to some extent. I was betrothed to marry this lady in 1917, during my father's lifetime, and I married in 1919 as a lad of eleven, my wife being one year older than me. This was after my father's death and the Political Officer said, 'The minor Maharawal can't live with his wife till he is nineteen' – and that was that. So my wife used to live at her mother's place in Benares until I returned from England, when the Political Officer said, 'You can now go and sleep with your wife!'

In such circumstances it was not surprising that a number of arranged first marriages failed to work. But for the men at least, there was always the chance for a second or third marriage: 'The first marriage would be when you were young and therefore very much in awe of your papa and less likely to argue about things. But since plural marriages were allowed to Hindus you could marry of your own choice when your parents were no longer there, although you had to treat these ladies with great respect and honour.'

The Maharawal of Dungarpur married for a second time in 1928, shortly after being invested with his full ruling powers:

Although we lived together, my first wife and myself, my mother and some of my nobles felt that I was none too happy in life. There was no ban on a second marriage then and my mother knew the Maharaja of Kishengarh well, because he happened to be her kinsman and the Maharaja gladly offered one of his daughters to me. But before the marriage I implored my mother that I must be allowed to see my would-be wife. That was very unusual in those days, but the Maharaja of Kishengarh regarded my mother as a sister, so a tea-party was arranged and seven or eight people invited and it was made to look as if the Maharaja of Kishengarh had just turned up accidentally. This young girl was brought along with the Maharaja and he never looked at me but just said to my mother, 'This is my daughter – your child.' Then he sat down and had a cup of tea and stayed for about fifteen minutes and went away. My mother said, 'What about it?' So I said, 'It's all right. We'll get married.'

Once a prince had acquired full ruling powers he could exercise much greater freedom in his choice of bride or brides, although direct access to high-born women from other families besides his own remained extremely limited. Princess Shashi Wallia's parents met in 1910 in a doctor's surgery in Bombay where there was no purdah. 'Daddy was sitting on one side and mummy and her mother on the other and apparently they fell in love at first sight. Daddy made discreet enquiries and then invited them to Dewas but my grandmother was not in favour of this. "If you want to make her your mistress then I am not willing," she told him. "Statewallahs are always like that!" It took a lot of haggling and correspondence but eventually she gave in and they were married.' However, due to the fact that Princess Shashi Wallia's mother came from Goa and belonged to a different caste, this was one of a number of marriages contracted by rulers that was deemed to be morganatic by the Paramount Power. As a result, the line of succession passed on her father's death not to her brother but to her uncle.

The British were strongly opposed to the Indian Princes marrying outside their usual spheres. An alarming precedent had been created early in the century when the Maharaja of the Madras state of Pudukottai married an Australian lady. The marriage was declared to be a morganatic alliance and after the Maharaja's death in self-imposed exile in Europe in 1928 a collateral relative rather than his son was chosen to succeed him. Another controversial marriage was that of the Sikh ruler Jagatjit Singh to the dancer Anita Delgrada in 1910. As a junior officer in the Indian Civil Service, Conrad Corfield was once given the task of organising affairs at a Governor's Durbar for the Punjab Princes so as to obscure the 'Spanish Maharani' from gubernatorial view: 'There were a number of alcoves in the Durbar Hall so I had a lot of potted palms put in one alcove so that she would be shrouded from view. But when she arrived she took one look at this and went into another alcove. When the Governor's wife came in she was so interested to see her that she bowed in public and Anita was delighted.'

There was even stronger opposition to Maharaja Yeshwant Rao Holkar's marriage in 1943 to an American lady, which became the subject of no fewer than six files of correspondence at the India Office, much of it taken up with deliberations as to how the lady was to be addressed. It was finally decreed that she was to be known as 'Maharani Holkar' without the prefix of 'Highness' accorded to other senior rulers' wives. Their son, Richard Shivaji Rao Holkar, was later to be denied the title of Maharaja by the Government of India after the death of his father in 1961. One foreign wife who finally succeeded in circumventing the Foreign and Political Department was the Australian second wife of the late Nawab of Palanpur. He and Lord Mountbatten were old friends and the final act of the last British Viceroy of India before handing over power at midnight on 14 August 1947 was to draw up and sign an instrument conferring upon her the title of 'Highness'.

There were other foreign wives who so wholeheartedly adapted themselves to the customs of their husbands' states that they won total acceptance from the princes' relatives and subjects, most notably the English wife of one of the leading rulers of Kathiawar. This was no easy matter, as even sixteen-year-old Princess Nirvana Devi of Mandi discovered when she became the bride of the ruler of Bilkha State:

> On my arrival in Bilkha I was faced with a nightmare! The Bilkha Chiefs are Vala Rajputs who intermarried with the local Kathi tribe, who were professional mercenaries and very powerful. Now the Bilkhas never married into a princely state; they married local girls and it was customary for the son-in-law to move in with the bride's family, so there was a lot of opposition when my husband married me because I was a Rajput. When we reached Bilkha I was just whizzed off from the station to the palace because some distant family members were sitting in the trees with rifles in their hands. I really thought I had landed among barbarians! The immediate family members greeted me very warmly but my mother-in-law was very particular about not letting me meet anyone from the community till the whole thing had died down. Now I can laugh about it but at the time it was terrifying.

Even though the subordinate role of women in Indian society – 'Your husband was your lord and master, that is what you were taught' – changed dramatically during the last decades of British rule in India, old traditions died hard. The Rajput attitude towards women was not universally admired, even among some of the Rajput princes themselves:

> Unfortunately, we were permitted to marry as often as we liked, unlike the Muslims who could only marry four times. Because there was no bar there was an element of thinking that if you aren't happy with her or if she just says boo to you then you just marry again – and that did take away a lot from the normal bonds of what love and marriage ought to be. The Rajputs' attitude towards women covered a vast gamut of emotions, from regarding them merely as child-bearers to great love – even to the point of fighting battles over women. But there were many marriages of alliance in the past where somebody gave you his daughter saying, 'Don't attack me next week', and Rajput girls were very often given away without much thought beyond prestige and the right kind of home.

It was to prevent this sort of abuse that the present Maharani of Wankaner's father, the late Maharawal of Dungarpur, had laid down in his will that his daughter was on no account to be given as a second or third wife – and that she was only to marry a ruler whose personal qualities had been most carefully vetted. This was duly done by her mother, who also offered her daughter practical advice on how to make a success of her marriage: '"A Rajput girl works to make others happy, not herself," my mother told me. "You should make the whole house happy, your husband's family and your children – and never think of your own personal happiness. Against all odds, never be disobedient to your husband, to your mother-in-law, to your elders." My mother's last words to me before my marriage were that even if someone from my father's home was abused by someone from my husband's place I was not to take it ill.'

This was not an easy code to live by, and although there was great love in many royal marriages there was also great unhappiness in others. 'Sometimes you were lucky,' declares one Maharani. Another had hoped to train as a doctor but was married as a teenager: 'My life has just withered away. It has been wasted.' 'Love,' according to Princess Padma Lokur of Bhor, 'was never the issue in royal families. After my brother was born my father told my mother, "I have done my duty. Now our relations are finished." This was when she was twenty-five years old, having got married when she was thirteen. So my mother's life was completely ruined. I saw the same situation with other rulers where the wives lived in luxury but their husbands had so many mistresses. Three members of my mother's family had been given to rajas and all were unhappy marriages.'

Padma Lokur's turn came in the 1940s, by which time attitudes had begun to change:

We went to Kurundwad Senior State for the coronation of the Raja and there were many princes present. My mother asked me to look at a particular boy who was sitting in the gallery and asked me what I thought of him. When I asked her why she was asking me she replied, 'Well, how would you like to marry him?' I said, 'Nothing doing! I'm not going to marry any prince, not even a jagirdar or sardar. Look at your own plight. What have you achieved by marrying a prince?' I later became the first person in my family to marry a commoner.

Thirty years earlier such an attitude was almost unheard of – until Sayajirao's only daughter, Indira, broke with convention. In 1910 she was informed by her parents that they had arranged for her to marry forty-year-old Maharaja Madhav Rao Scindia of Gwalior as his second wife. Indira Gaekwad, then eighteen years old, acquiesced, but in the following year met the handsome second son of the ruler of Cooch Behar at the Delhi Durbar and fell in love with him. Shortly before her marriage was due to take place she wrote to Maharaja Scindia, asking him to break off the engagement. Enlightened as they were, her parents were horrified, as much at the loss of face suffered by the ruler of Gwalior as at the shame brought upon their own house by their daughter's behaviour in going against her parents' wishes. Their daughter, however, proved to be as strong-willed as her parents and was eventually allowed to marry the man of her choice. Three weeks after the marriage her husband became the new Maharaja of Cooch Behar. His elder brother had earlier been refused permission by his parents to marry an English actress and had virtually drunk himself to death.

The impact of this break with tradition was still being felt a generation later when Indira Cooch Behar's third daughter, Gayatri Devi, was asked by Maharaja Sawai Man Singh of Jaipur to become his third wife, a prospect that provoked as much disquiet in the emancipated Cooch Behar household as disapproval in traditionally-minded Jaipur at the prospect of a non-Rajput alliance. In Gwalior, too, there were reverberations when in 1941 the engagement of Madhav Rao's son – Maharaja George Jivaji Rao Scindia – to a Tripura princess fell through. The young Maharaja thereupon decided to find a wife from among his own largely Rajput subjects and chose the beautiful Lekha Divyeshwari Devi, the part-Nepalese daughter of a Deputy Collector. 'My uncle had been given the task of finding eligible girls for the Maharaja and my other maternal uncle proposed my name and sent in my photograph,' explains the woman who is now Rajmata Vijayaraje Scindia, mother of the present Maharaja of Gwalior. 'It was just luck because my husband was attracted and said he'd like to meet this girl.' A meeting between the two families took place in one of the private rooms of the Taj Mahal Hotel in Bombay, which had by then become a recognised place of rendezvous where parents and potential spouses could meet unofficially and in private before either party committed themselves. 'Because the parents never knew if the girl would be accepted or rejected it had to be a central place like Bombay and it had to be a very private affair which nobody knew was being arranged. Otherwise everybody would come to know if a boy didn't like a girl and her chances of getting married to somebody else would have been affected.' In the case of Vijayaraje and the Maharaja of Gwalior the meeting passed off almost without incident:

> I met him in January and in February I was married. He was a fully-fledged ruler when we met, but I was very impressed because he was a very friendly, outgoing sort of person who made everybody

feel quite at home within a short time, so that my aunt and uncle were freely chatting with him all the time. I didn't have a very high opinion of princes but this was a very different prince, not a proud, stuck-up person as I had imagined all the princely order to be. I was keeping very quiet and my maternal aunt who was with me felt that I shouldn't be too shy so she kept on telling me, 'Talk, talk about something'. There was some talk about Gwalior coins with the Maharaja's head on them, so I just happened to break in with one sentence, 'Your Highness, your coins come right up to Lalitpur.' Instead of replying to me he replied to my aunt, like a good Hindu bridegroom. He used to joke with me about that later on, because after marriage, too, we are not supposed to speak to each other in front of our elders as newly-married bride and bridegroom, so we never used to speak to each other when any of his aunts or my aunt or grandmother were present. We would speak only through somebody.

A similar meeting in that same year preceded the betrothal of Princess Vijayadevi of Mysore to the ruler of Kotda-Sangani. Her husband-to-be was one of a number of princes sent to this model state for a period of administrative training: 'My father met him and liked him so he introduced us to each other and we agreed to get married.'

Yet even in the early days there were states where princesses had some say in whom they should marry. One was Bhopal, where the engagement of the present Begum of Bhopal to her late husband, the cricketing Nawab of Pataudi, was a case in point: 'It was I who chose the alliance. I met Pat in England and that was that. There was a lot of opposition but we managed to get through.' And in Travancore State, where women enjoyed a freedom that was then almost without parallel in the Princely States, there was no opposition when the ten-year-old Princess Setu Lakshmibai made her choice of husband – even if the choice was somewhat limited. 'The story is quite romantic,' remembers the lady who is now Senior Maharani of Travancore, recalling an event that took place in 1906. 'Two brothers had been selected from the Haripads, a branch of the Kilimanoor family of high Kshatriya caste from which bridegrooms are usually taken for all the Travancore princesses. My mother told me to look through an upstairs window of the palace and down below in the courtyard were the two brothers, who didn't know I was looking at them. My mother told me, "Now look carefully and tell me which one of the two you like." They were all saying I should marry the older one because he was more experienced but I chose the younger one.' Forty years later it was the turn of her fourteen-year-old daughter to choose her husband, as Rukmini Varma, the Senior Maharani's granddaughter, relates:

> We have these annual temple festivals which last for about twelve days and on the last day there is the *aarattu* procession with all the men in *lungis* (sarongs), carrying swords and shields and wearing a red head-dress that looks rather like an Arab head-dress. All the men of the royal household have to walk to show humility, because they are following the God to the sea. Now the ladies watch from a palace roof-top and mother saw somebody in the procession and fell in love with him and came and told my grandmother that she wanted to marry this man. Grandfather was very upset and said, 'No, no, we don't do things like this!' And grandmother said, 'What are you saying? You're only fourteen years old. You have no mind of your own.' But mother stuck to her guns and said, 'If I can't marry him then I'll jump from the balcony and commit suicide.' Then it just happened that this young man she had seen came with his uncle to the palace and they then found that not only was he unmarried but he also came from Kilimanoor, so that even my grandmother could not have picked anybody better.

Marriage was an extremely costly business, because custom dictated that rulers should spend vast sums of money on their daughters' weddings. Before privy purses were settled at a certain percentage of the state's income, it was not unusual for a ruler to spend over half the state's entire annual revenue on one wedding alone. Much of this went on the dowry as agreed upon in the negotiations prior to betrothal, but a great deal was spent on the celebrations and ceremonies surrounding the wedding itself, which in earlier days could last for a fortnight or more. Big spending was a matter of prestige, but it was also a recognition of the fact that for Hindu women the wedding ceremony was regarded as the most important religious event of their lives. In marked contrast, marriage according to the rites of Islam was short and simple and centred on the ten-minute *nikaah* or contract ceremony at which bride and bridegroom signed a marriage contract in the presence of a *pir* and three witnesses.

Among Hindus the proceedings began with the issuing of invitations, which had to be delivered by hand and in due ceremonial style:

> An auspicious date is found on which invitations can be issued, first by the fathers of the bride and bridegroom to their family deities and to other local deities. Rice and coconut are laid in front of the deity and the priest recites and says that this is an invitation to a marriage

that is to take place at such and such a time. Then invitations to other people are delivered by a deputation consisting of a sardar of the state accompanied by a clerk and an attendant. He would deliver this invitation personally in the form of a *kharita* or manuscript.

It was customary for the wedding to take place in the bride's home state. After an elaborate send-off the bridegroom and his party – known as the *barat* and consisting of several hundred relatives, nobles and retainers – would be met at the border or at the local railway station by a reception committee and escorted in the first of many processions to their accommodation, which usually took the form of a tented camp in the grounds of the palace. The bridegroom's feet were washed – 'the girl's mother is supposed to do it but in Gwalior, at least, she never did. It was always one of the senior sardar's wives' – and if no formal engagement had previously taken place, the proceedings opened with a troth-plighting:

> The bridegroom's father goes along with members of his family and selected sardars to the bride's house. The bride is brought out, her father sits by her side and offers her in marriage. Sugar is then put in her mouth to signify acceptance and she is given jewellery and clothes, which she changes into. Then a reverse ceremony is gone through. The bride's father comes to the bridegroom's house or camp and applies a *tilak* mark to his forehead. Then the family priest reads out the bridegroom's horoscope and announces the most auspicious time and date for the marriage.

Other ceremonies and processions followed. Family deities had to be set up in temporary residence in the camp and the *mandap* or marriage pavilion had to be ceremonially erected. Then on the evening of the third day the cleansing and anointing rituals known in the Deccan states as the *haldi* (turmeric) ceremonies took place:

> At least five married ladies would go along with a lot of unmarried girls and they would make the bridegroom-to-be sit and apply turmeric paste on his ankles, knees, shoulders, cheeks and head which was then rubbed on with mango leaves because that is supposed to be auspicious. A lot of jokes and banter used to go on while this was being done and it was great fun. Then five married women would come from the bridegroom's side to rub *haldi* on the girl. She had to be bathed by these five married women each using five *lotas* (water pots) of water.

The cleansing and anointing of the bride had a very practical reason behind it, 'because the groom's family wants to have a good look at her whole body to find out if there are any defects, no moles in the wrong place or concealed birthmarks. If that were found then someone would come running to say, "Cancel the whole thing!"' Outfits for the wedding ceremony were also exchanged at this point, the groom's family presenting the bride with a *shela* or brocade shawl with which to cover her head during the marriage ceremony.

Hindu brides traditionally wore red- or gold-coloured saris of Benares silk, but there were many local variations. In Palitana royal brides wore green petticoats and blouses with long red scarves rather than saris. In Travancore a long strip of white pleated cloth like a sarong, called a *mundu*, was worn tucked between the legs. In Rajasthan brides wore saris of red or saffron, the colour of the sacrificial flame. 'Saffron and red are the two Rajput colours,' explains the Maharani of Wankaner. 'Saffron is the colour that ascetics wear and I found it awe-inspiring having to wear this saffron sari, which I had to do every day, as well as all the jewellery that was put on me, including my husband's jewellery from Wankaner, part of which was an ivory bangle that you must always wear and which means that your husband is so brave that he'll kill an elephant. In the old days these bangles were worn from above the elbow down to the wrist.' Every bride was required to wear five essential articles of jewellery:

> A *tikka* for the forehead, worn in the parting of the hair, signifying 'walk on the straight path', earrings to remind you not to have weak ears and listen to gossip, a necklace so that your head is always bowed down in humility, bangles to tell you that your hand must always go forward for giving charity and anklets so that you put the right foot forward – and the nose-ring of which it was said that the pearl should not be heavier than the nose, meaning you should not spend more than what your husband could afford. So every bride was given these and told the significance and she had to wear them throughout her married life.

The actual wedding ceremony itself, the *kanyadan* or 'giving away', usually took place on the fourth or fifth day in the courtyard of the City Palace, and was concentrated round the sacred fire lit under the marriage pavilion, culminating in the *saptapadi* or seven steps taken by bride and bridegroom round the fire. A wedding that is still remembered in Dungarpur and Wankaner was that between the present Maharaja and Maharani of Wankaner in 1929:

> The marriage ceremony started in the evening with my husband-to-be coming in procession on an elephant with bodyguards, policemen,

infantry, band, jagirdars on horseback and dancing girls. Money was thrown on him throughout the four mile procession which took about two or three hours to reach the palace. On his arrival he was made to stand on a silver *patla* (platform), he had to remove his socks and shoes and then my brother washed his feet and put *kum-kum* (red powder) on them. I don't know whether this custom is unique to Dungarpur but I was then dragged outside and given cow's milk and sugar. I was supposed to see my husband for the first time but I felt so shy that I never opened my eyes! After that we were made to sit with a curtain in between us with all the religious chants and ceremonies going on. My brother performed the kanyadan, or the giving away of the bride – and with what words! A beautiful recitation: 'Daughter of so-and-so, granddaughter, great-granddaughter, coming from the illustrious house of Chittor'. He named five generations of our ancestors and then, 'Maharajadhiraj Maharawal Shri Lakshman Singhji is giving away the bride to Yuvaraj Maharajkumar Shri Pratap Sinhji of Wankaner', and then *his* family history was given by the Charan. The ceremonies and the *havan* – the rituals performed before the sacred fire – went on for about two or three hours. Prior to the ceremonies I had been smeared with a paste made of *kesar* and sandalwood oil and turmeric, all over the body. All the jewellery that had been given to me had been put on me and I felt terribly laden down by it and so uncomfortable! Instead of having any pleasure it was really a bit of a torture, but in those days the girls were so subdued and so obedient that they never opened their mouths or stirred, whereas a bride today would revolt!

Not everyone who went through the marriage ceremony did so without protest. Rajmata Gayatri Devi recalls her husband growing increasingly impatient during the 'hours and hours' of ritual and finally calling out to the Brahmin priests to hurry up. Earlier she had been carried to the *mandap* on a silver tray by her relatives, a custom peculiar to Bengal, where 'the bride does not touch the ground on her wedding day'.

Once the wedding ceremony was over the bride followed her husband in a closed palanquin in a torchlight procession to his parents' residence, but this was by no means the end of the festivities. The following morning there would be music and dancing and, in the Maratha states, the playing of a game called *bashi haldi*, in which people threw turmeric powder at each other, as well as other marriage games that often involved the townspeople and local schools taking part in races and sports. For the important guests there would be shikar during the day and musical recitals, dancing and feasting in the evening. In a large state like Baroda which had its own arena in the town there were gladiatorial games that included wrestling, combats between fighting rams and buffaloes and, as the climax, a fight between a pair of bull elephants on rut. The women would watch from behind *chik* blinds in the purdah enclosure: 'The elephant fights were more for show than anything else. People would wave strips of cloth and push them at each other but only rarely did they really fight, so it wasn't very frightful.' Prisoners also benefited from the marriage celebrations. In some states all were released, in others only a token number of the less serious offenders were pardoned.

Once the festivities were over a suitably auspicious moment had to be found for the departure of the newly-weds together with their barat, now swelled not only by the bride's dowry but by the maidservants from her father's state who would be accompanying her to her new home, together with all their families, chattels and livestock. Their departure to the local railway station was once again done in great style, although in some parts of Rajasthan the bride was taken away in secret – a relic of the uncertain days of the past.

Not all brides left their parents' homes. Those not yet of age, like ten-year-old Setu Lakshmibai of Travancore, were able to enjoy a few more years of childhood:

> My husband lived in a different house and came to see me every evening for an hour. We used to have great fun. We played a game called 'four corners' like hopscotch, then we would sit together on the swing and he would tell me stories or read me fairy tales like Red Riding Hood. My mother was always there or my guardian, the old Maharani's husband, as a chaperone. He would never allow my husband to be with me for a minute longer than an hour. We only began to live together when I was fourteen.

But for other brides there was no such period of transition. Marriage meant a total break from one way of life and the start of another. Upon their arrival at their new homes there would be more ordeals for them to undergo: the ceremony of their acceptance into their husband's household by the women of his family and, in many cases, the assumption of their married names which, by tradition, were chosen by their in-laws and whispered into their ears by their new husbands. There would be other rituals to be performed relating to their monthly cycles until finally, after one more marriage feast, the new bride would be carried in her husband's arms into their nuptial chamber and the marriage consummated.

Like many another newly-wedded bride, Maharani Rama Kumari of Wankaner was full of doubts as she said goodbye to her old home: 'I was sad at the thought of leaving my family. I was full of apprehension about what was going to happen to me, about what the future held in store for me.' As the third wife of the Maharaja of Jaipur, Gayatri Devi also left her home full of apprehension, although in her case there was to be a Western-style honeymoon in Ootacamund before she entered Jaipur:

> We left by train down to Calcutta and that's where I got my first taste of purdah, because when we arrived a silver screen was put round the door of the compartment. There was a car inside it complete with curtains and I was told to get into this. This depressed me a lot because I hadn't expected it. One of my brothers who was just going to join his first regiment came in the car with me and all the way he kept nudging me, saying, 'Hey, I hope you're not going to live like this all the time.'

10

WITHIN THE ZANANA

*Those were the days which the Rajpoot yet loves to talk of, when
three things alone occupied him: his horse, his lance and his
mistress; for she is but the third in his estimation. After all, to
the two first he owed her.*

Lt.-Col. James Tod, *Annals and
Antiquities of Rajasthan*, 1829

*The Purdah system has its advantages and disadvantages, but
when a thing goes beyond its proper limits it becomes productive
of disadvantages only and one is forced to look small in the eyes
of others. I feel and would readily affirm that the non-observance
of the Purdah system is more advantageous than the observance
thereof, but while we do away with the system we must not allow
the women to assume an undue measure of liberty, which has
become a common spectacle of the present times.*

Notes on the Education and Upbringing
of the Ruler, from Maharaja Madhav
Rao Scindia of Gwalior's *General
Policy Durbar*, 1925

'I was rather nervous coming to Jaipur as a bride because I wasn't
sure what reception I'd get.' Even though some of the trappings
were modern, Gayatri Devi's reception in Jaipur as the new bride
of the Maharaja was fully in accord with local custom:

> The train was taken into what was called the Biman Bhavan, a house
> with a railway track running into it and a platform on either side
> where there were reception rooms. There were ten or twelve ladies
> waiting all dressed in their *ghagras*, the Rajasthani skirt with the big
> shawl over it, worn with a lot of jewellery. Following my husband I
> got out with my face covered with the end of my sari and paid my
> respects to my sisters-in-law. I was then taken into a room where I
> bathed and changed into Rajasthani costume before being driven in
> a purdah car with curtained windows to Rambagh Palace where we
> went through almost the same ceremony again at the zanana porch.

Rambagh Palace was a modern building 'all white and pink and
surrounded by beautiful gardens and lovely trees. There were guards

ABOVE Leading princes in the 1920s: from left to right, the rulers of Kalsia, Loharu, Mandi, Nawanagar, Jammu and Kashmir, Kapurthala, Alwar, Patiala, Bikaner, Bharatpur and Palanpur. A photograph taken at the Silver Jubilee of Maharaja Jagatjit Singh of Kapurthala. (Popperfoto)

BELOW The lower end of the princely scale: the ruler of a minor state in the Western Deccan, photographed with his courtiers in the late 1880s. (*Charles Allen*)

A prince on parade: four-year-old Maharajkumar Sadul Singh, *yuvaraj* or heir-apparent of the royal house of Bikaner, mounted on his pony, 1906. He was to become the last ruling Maharaja of Bikaner, succeeding his father, Maharaja Ganga Singh, in 1943.
(*Royal Commonwealth Society*)

ABOVE The last ruling Maharaja of Baroda, Pratap Singh Gaekwad, with his family in 1939. The present Maharaja, Lt. Col. Fatehsinghrao Gaekwad, stands at his mother's shoulder on the right. (*Maharajah of Baroda*)

BELOW Sayaji Rao of Baroda with family and senior staff, Indian and European. On the Maharaja's left is his eldest daughter, Indira, later to become Maharani of Cooch Behar. (*BBC Hulton Picture Library*)

ABOVE LEFT Young Rajput princes from Pratapgarh, Shahpura and Banswara in their drilling uniforms. All four were sent to Dhrangadhara for their early education. The present Maharawat of Pratapgarh is third from the left. (*Maharajah of Pratapgarh*)

ABOVE RIGHT The young Princess Rajkumari Setu Lakshmibai of Travancore in 1902, when she was seven years old. (*Sharada Dwivedi*)

BELOW Practising the martial arts: the young *walihad* of Hyderabad, Osman Ali Pasha, cuts a goat in half at the gallop, *c.* 1904. (*Times of India*)

LEFT Rajput warrior-princes of the Mid-Victorian era: two Maharao Rajas of Bundi, Maharao Raja Ram Singh (1812-1889) and Maharao Raja Raghubir Singh (1889-1927) (far left, above and below), and Maharaja Jai Singh Pal of Karauli (left, above). (*BBC Hulton Picture Library*)
BELOW LEFT Servant of the deity: Maharaja Raghuraj Singh of Rewa, photographed shortly before his death in 1880. (Copyright Reserved – reproduced by gracious permission of Her Majesty the Queen)

A panther shot in the hills of Palanpur by the young *walihad*, Iqbal Muhammed Khan, with his father, the Nawab, at his elbow, *c.* 1934. (*A.L. Syed*)

RIGHT
ABOVE A dead tiger shot in Kotah is ferried across the river to the palace, late 1930s. (*A.L. Syed*)

BELOW Maharaja Ganga Singh of Bikaner prepares to go on an elephant drive through swamp country in the United Provinces, 1939. (*A.L. Syed*)

ABOVE The Nawanagar State chariot, *c.* 1890. (*Popperfoto*)

BELOW Maharaja Umaid Singh of Jodhpur and his sons depart from Croydon airport for the Continent, 1932. The Maharaja's eldest son, who succeeded him, was killed while flying his own plane in 1952. (*BBC Hulton Picture Library*)

ABOVE The entrance to the City Palace, Kotah, originally built as a fort in 1264. It is now a museum. (*India Office Library*)

BELOW Kapurthala: the state drawing room in Jagatjit Palace. (*Popperfoto*)

Royal wedding: the Maharaja and Maharani of Jaipur after their marriage at Cooch Behar.
(*Rajmata of Jaipur*)

ABOVE The dowry of a princess of Dhrangadhara laid out in the Darbar Hall. (*Maharaja of Dhrangadhara*)

BELOW The *barat* or bridgegroom's procession sets out: the present Maharaja of Bikaner leaves Junagadh Fort for Dungarpur, 1944. (*A.L. Syed*)

The 'Spanish Maharani': Maharani Anita Delgrada, whose marriage to Maharaja Jagatjit Singh of Kapurthala caused much disquiet in British official circles. Photograph by Raja Deen Dayal, 1909. (*Hemlata Jain*)

ABOVE Hidden under her familiar pale blue *burqa*, the Begum of Bhopal welcomes the Prince of Wales to her state in February 1922. (*Illustrated London News Picture Library*)

BELOW Palace women behind chick bamboo screens watch *nautch* dancers and singers entertaining in a palace courtyard below. Jaipur *c.* 1875. (*Copyright Reserved – reproduced by gracious permission of Her Majesty the Queen*)

ABOVE The Resident of the Rajputana States Agency, Major Battye, and colleagues at the investiture of the new Maharao Raja of Bundi. Major Bahadur Singhhi succeeded his father in April 1945 and in the same month won the Military Cross for gallantry while serving with Probyn's Horse in Burma. (*A.L. Syed*)

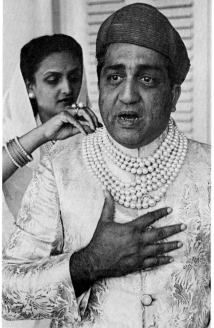

LEFT The late Maharaja Pratap Singh of Baroda, wearing the famous seven-string Baroda pearl necklace, 1948. (*Henri Cartier-Bresson/Magnum/John Hillelson Agency*)

RIGHT The Resident of the Rajputana States rides in procession through the streets of Bundi on his way to pay a formal call on the Maharao Raja in his ancient palace-fort, 1945. (*A.L. Syed*)

ABOVE Last rites for a prince: the funeral pyre of a ruler, Western India *c.* 1890. (*Penwick Collection*

BELOW One of the last gatherings of the ruling princes: India's Governor-General Lord Mountbatten attends Maharaja Sawai Man Singh's Silver Jubilee in Jaipur in October 1947, two months after Independence. (*Times of India*)

at seven different gates, all very smartly turned out, and the building itself had four different wings. One was for the Maharaja, one for the guests, one was the nursery and the other was the zanana in which the Maharaja's two other wives were living and where we used to go to have lunch and dinner with the two Maharanis.' Everything was done to make the new Maharani feel at home: 'In the evening of my arrival there was a ladies' reception for me on a terrace in the zanana garden, given by my eldest sister-in-law, and another party on the next evening given by my second sister-in-law. On the third day another lady gave a party and so it went on for about a week.'

On a suitably auspicious day Maharani Gayatri Devi was driven in style to the City Palace for the ceremony known as the *griha pravesh*, the coming into the home:

> This entailed a procession with my husband's personal mounted bodyguard round my car, then having to sit in a palanquin to be carried into the temple of Govindevji where I had to perform certain pujas. This was followed by a Durbar in the women's quarters, where I had to sit quietly with my face covered while all the ladies of the zanana and the Jaipur nobility came in turn to lift my veil and drop a present on my lap. When they looked at you they made all sorts of personal remarks about what you looked like, which was pretty off-putting, but I had been told not to look up. Out of curiosity I did look up at one of the women and my husband's second wife, who was already a friend of mine by then, told me afterwards that I shouldn't have.

For Gayatri Devi, used to the freer atmosphere of Baroda and Cooch Behar, coming to terms with purdah or even semi-purdah was not easy: 'My first few months in Jaipur should have been very happy because I was very much in love with my husband, but I wasn't quite sure of what I could do and what the limits were. Because of the war my husband had a lot of work on his hands and so I hardly saw him during the day – but it was thanks to the war that I kind of came out of purdah, because I started to organise the Women's Red Cross Movement.'

A contemporary of Gayatri Devi of Jaipur was the present Rajmata of Kishengarh, who faced similar difficulties of adjustment when she married:

> In Palitana life had been more free and to adjust to sitting in one room with strict purdah was quite difficult. Whereas in Palitana we used to eat our meals on tables and chairs, in Kishengarh we had to

eat off silver thalis placed on the ground – all the ladies together. I lived in the palace, but my mother-in-law was in the old fort, so I had to go there in the morning and spend the whole day with her. There were no sofas – so we had to sit on a mattress on the floor. Initially I felt quite miserable sitting down there with my head and face covered with a *ghunghat* (sari worn with its border pulled down over the face).

By the 1940s plural marriage had become a rarity in princely circles, but in the 1920s and 1930s it was still commonplace and the newest bride had to learn to accept her place in the pecking order of the zanana. Yet there was surprisingly little friction or jealousy in these plural marriages, 'because the women of that time knew that this was the established norm and they accepted it as a way of life'. Sometimes a new wife was also required to accept the presence of concubines, as the present Rajmata of Patiala had to do when she married the Maharaja in 1933. 'She was just a kid who had come straight from school,' recalls Hede Dayal. 'She was dumped in the palace and had no idea who these nine *ammajis*, living in a separate wing of the palace, were. Her Highness told me that the Maharaja said to her, "I will send these ladies away." But she objected and said, "Then with whom shall I play cards?"'

What lasted for longer than plural marriage in royal circles was purdah, which was maintained in all but a handful of Indian states right up to 1947, the year of India's Independence, and beyond. 'The zanana system was only given up in Kutch after Independence,' states the Maharao. 'Until then we had strict purdah. My grandmother never went anywhere. My mother did go to Bombay with my father, but that was all arranged with the ladies' compartment on the train and motor cars with blackened windows. She never came out of purdah – although my wife came out in 1948.'

The purdah system, originally devised for the protection and defence of women, had been extended throughout India during the eight centuries of Muslim influence and was deeply entrenched among the upper classes of society in both British India and the Indian States. Sahibzada Ata Muhamed Khan remembers how in the 1930s he accompanied his uncle, the Nawab of Palanpur, to a town just on the borders of the state, where the wives of the local jagirdars expressed a wish to look upon the princes of Palanpur: 'We were sitting like idiots on these chairs wondering how these women in purdah were going to see us, when suddenly we saw this big *shatranji* (carpet) with holes in it coming towards us. The carpet stopped about six feet away from us and we could see eyes at all these holes! We didn't know where to look! Then after ten minutes or so the carpet went back.'

Within the states themselves purdah was enforced with varying degrees of severity. In some households male relatives of the royal family, court officials of long standing and trusted servants came and went at will; in others, armed guards saw to it that only the ruler or his sons had access. Even in the more emancipated states such as Gondal and Bhavnagar, where there were no zanana quarters in the palaces, purdah was still observed whenever royal ladies went outside the palace grounds. Nowhere was it more rigorously enforced than in Hyderabad where, as in all the stricter Muslim states, girls went 'behind the curtain' from the time of their Bismillah ceremony. Here even the nobility employed African or Arab guards to stand at the zanana entrances, while at the Nizam's King Kothi Palace both were used – African soldiers to guard his treasury; Arabs to guard his official wives, the numerous ladies of his harem, their own close relatives and the scores of women attendants who looked after them all.

Because it was regarded throughout India as virtually inviolate, the zanana was also a place of sanctuary – not only for women but even on rare occasions for men – as the Maharani of Rewa remembers of her childhood home in Kutch: 'If, for example, someone has committed a murder and runs away and comes into the *Deori* or the main gate of the zanana palace and takes shelter of the Maharani, nobody can take him away. She has the right to give him sanctuary. I remember my grandmother did that once when somebody who had been accused of murder came and took shelter. He gave all the facts of the case in writing to her and after making a lot of enquiries she gave him shelter and my grandfather had to release him.'

The newly-married bride never came to her husband's home alone. To add to the staff already provided by her husband, she brought a retinue of her own servant women who had attended her as a young girl and with whom she had close bonds. 'My mother had hundreds of maids, mostly from Osian where she came from,' recalls Padmavatidevi of Jodhpur, Maharani of Baroda. 'Since there were umpteen relatives each with umpteen members of their retinues and then the retinues' umpteen staff, there were hundreds of women in the Jodhpur zanana, but it was like one big happy family. They were all fantastically dressed and because they used to keep ghunghats you sometimes mistook the maid for the mistress – I mean, how many ghunghats are you going to lift to see who it is?' If they were unmarried these maids or *bais* were generally found husbands from among the *dadas* or male staff of the *mardana*, and since they had come as part of a bride's dowry they were widely regarded as a ruler's property, with few rights of their own, as also were their children. According to the census of 1921 there were 48,000 such *Darogas*, as they were known, in Jodhpur alone; a community built up over many generations that remained entirely dependent on the rulers and nobles who, to all intents and purposes, owned them.

One such attendant was Chichibai, who came from Dhrangadhara to Pratapgarh with her mistress in the 1920s: 'I used to get a salary of 5 rupees a month and clothes, with four outfits a year at Divali, Dassera, Holi and on the Maharaja's birthday. We used to get *dal* (lentils) and vegetables from the palace kitchen and we could buy one *maund* (about 42 lbs) of wheat for a rupee, while *jowar* and *bajra* (varieties of millet) were about 12 *annas*. Pure ghee was one rupee for 3 *seers* (about 6 lbs), so everything was very cheap and we managed very well. The Raj also paid for all the expenses at the time of marriages and deaths.'

Accompanying the new bride's retinue there would also be a *kamdar* or clerk who looked after her accounts – 'the idea was to see that your daughter was properly looked after by her husband'. These kamdars 'created a tremendous lot of friction in the palaces' because of their mixed loyalties and their positions of influence over the Maharanis, as Chichibai confirms:

> In the old days the Kamdars used to rule the ladies in the zanana; they were the power behind the women, and ultimately destroyed the rulers of Pratapgarh and the Yuvarajs by taking over everything. Legend has it that years ago there was one kamdar who cheated the then Maharaja Raghunathji, who punished him by making him carry a pot of hot live coals in his bare hands from Devgarh to Pratapgarh. His hands were completely burnt and before dying he cursed the house of Pratapgarh, declaring that all future Maharajas of Pratapgarh would be destroyed by their kamdars.

The bais themselves – and their mistresses – were another obvious source of dissension in the zanana. 'The influence of the women was not always a good one, I'm sorry to say,' declares the Rajmata of Porbandar. 'Quite often their loyalty was not to the state into which they had married, but to the state from which they came, so there was a lot of friction, particularly if the ruler had more than one wife and the wives had children. The result was a lot of intrigue and disloyalty – the word for it was *khatpat* – which disturbed the peace of many of the ruling houses. I have seen it over and over again, the survival of the craftiest and the most cunning.'

Chichibai had come to Pratapgarh as an attendant of the Yuvaraj's second wife:

> My mistress was at the fort while the first wife lived in the palace bungalow. In the fort zanana there must have been about fifty of us, including seven or eight very old women, all for one Rani Saheb. She would wake up at six and we would help her to bathe, which meant bringing hot water heated over a log fire, and then dress her in a sari, a Gujerati ghagra. Then she used to do her puja, for which we prepared the ingredients, and afterwards we would serve her food – all Gujerati food – which she ate seated not on a chair at a table but on a low stool. Every day she had to pay her respects to her mother-in-law. She would go and touch her feet and for this she wore Rajasthani clothes, because her mother-in-law had forbidden her to wear her Gujerati dress from Dhrangadhara.

The mother-in-law was a dominant and often forbidding figure in every Indian household, but when she was also the Senior Maharani or Senior Begum then her position within the confines of the zanana was all-powerful. When Maharani Pravinba came to Rewa as the new *Yuvarani*, or wife of the heir-apparent, she found her in-laws to be no exception:

> Rewa was beautiful, with lots of jungles, but it was very backward and its people did not seem as nice as Gujerat people. Although my mother-in-law and grandmother-in-law were very nice to me, they didn't like a Kutchi girl walking into their house at the beginning, because I didn't know their customs or their language, which was Baghelkhandi. I didn't know a word of Hindi, but fortunately my mother-in-law and my husband spoke English, so I could communicate with them but not with other people and within a couple of years I was speaking Baghelkhandi.

By comparison with her home state of Kutch the purdah in Rewa was 'terrible' and caused the new Yuvarani considerable distress:

> My husband was very purdah-minded and never permitted me to come out of purdah. Even when walking from a car to the railway coach you had to go into a chhatri, which was a burqa-like umbrella thing. They made you walk in that with somebody holding it for you so that you could not see anything. My husband was very strict: he told me that if my hand or foot was seen, they would cut it off! So I said, 'All right, I'll make a fool of you one day!' Now there used to be lady-guards who would put you into this chhatri and lead you to the train. So I told my maid how I was going to trick these guards. I

said, 'As soon as the car door is opened, I will get out of the other
door and you quickly get into that purdah as soon as they open it and
I will walk behind you.' So they led my maid as the Yuvarani right
up to the saloon and as she was being put inside they saw who she
was and were horrified and started looking around for me. But before
they could say Jack Robinson I was also inside the saloon! I was
fighting the system all the time. I used to threaten my maids that if
they talked about all this to my mother-in-law I'd deal with them
somehow. They were all terrified of me because I was a foreigner
and a person whom they could not fathom.

Purdah did not prevent many royal ladies from travelling extensively,
but it required special arrangements and particular apparatus or
articles of clothing such as the burqas worn by Muslim women or
the 'little umbrella with brocade curtains reaching right down to the
ground with slits and little windows at the front' that Shashi Wallia's
mother always carried when she went out into a public place in
Dewas. Shahvar Sultan of Cambay remembers as a child leaping
up to try to see beyond the 'suffocating' red curtains between which
they were required to pass on railway platforms; Nirmala Bhonsle
of Baroda recalls jumping into small palanquins or walking inside
box-like curtained frames on wheels as they were pushed up to
cars or railway compartments; Leela Moolgaokar of Gwalior has
memories of visiting local sardars' daughters in the *shigram*, a
'bullock-cart with a curtained canopy on top with two small domes,
the bells round the bullocks' necks making a lovely jangling sound
as we went along'.

For special occasions such as processions or festivals many states
had their own enclosures for the purdah women, such as the
justifiably famous Hawa Mahal or 'hall of wind' overlooking the
main street in Jaipur which was connected to the City Palace zanana
by a series of passages. Some states even had movable enclosures
on a grand scale and in Rewa there were two magnificent elephant-
drawn chariots: one for the mardana, the other for the zanana, each
of which could accommodate over a hundred spectators. Their
principal use was for the Dassera festival, when the palace women
would be transported out to the site where the demon Ravana was
annually burnt in effigy amidst a blaze of fireworks.

Going out to public places was never a simple business, and Leela
Moolgaokar recalls how when she accompanied her mother to a
'picture house' in Gwalior or to see a Marathi drama at the theatre
'we'd go along in the car, the huzras would hold up a sheet and we
would walk into the theatre and up into a special box with curtains
that were drawn when the lights went on'. Hede Dayal remembers

similar arrangements involving curtained rickshaws and bamboo chik screens in Simla, and recalls the first time she accompanied some of the Patiala royal children and their mothers on a walk in the surrounding hills above the nearby hill-station of Chail: 'I got so irritated because some idiotic chap in front of us kept blowing a shrill whistle. I said to my eldest charge, "Kuku, can't you stop that man's whistling?" And she said, "Oh, you've still got a lot to learn!" Because we were out in the open this chap had a whistle and when he blew it any man on the path had either to disappear or to practically dig his nose into the hill-side.'

The whole system was full of paradoxes. In a big city like Calcutta or Bombay, or when the princes took their wives and daughters abroad, purdah was either ignored altogether or reduced to a symbolic gesture. Many royal ladies managed to enjoy a vigorous outdoor life as shikaris, shooting tigers and camping out of doors alongside their husbands without in this way compromising their official seclusion. By her own choice the Maharani of Lunawada remains in strict seclusion to this day, but while her husband was away fighting on the Italian Front during the Second World War she acted as his Regent: 'When a cholera epidemic broke out in a part of the state, without hesitation Her Highness went to that area to organise medical aid and mass inoculation. While she was moving from one place to another in the car she was in purdah, but when she got down she did away with it and visited all quarters. She considered herself to be a trustee of the state for His Highness so she mingled purdah with non-purdah – and within about three days the situation was under control.'

As an institution, purdah had long outlived its usefulness and there were many, particularly among the British, who saw the zanana as a place where a young prince or princess could be dominated by ignorant and superstitious mothers and grandmothers, counteracting the best efforts of tutors and guardians. Yet, as was so often the case in these pre-Independence years, there was no strong challenge to a system which was by no means confined to the Indian States. Even today many still believe purdah to have been a beneficial rather than a repressive system, especially where 'there was only one Maharani and she was a woman of character'. There are ladies who recall – and, indeed, still enjoy – zanana life as 'a wonderful and unique life such as no other country had, highly civilised and with an ancient tradition behind it'. Its greatest virtue was companionship, albeit of the same sex, for 'there was no such thing as loneliness in the purdah system. Your mother-in-law was there, your aunties-in-law were there; if there were children other than your own they too were there. They all helped each other and if there was discipline then it was an excellent system.'

Zanana quarters were rarely unfriendly or silent places. 'They rang with sounds of life and laughter and if people weren't happy they seemed full of good cheer,' contends the Rajmata of Porbandar. 'You can't hear our women walking because they're barefooted, but what you hear is the jingle-jangle of their jewellery because all the maidservants in their anklets and bangles and earrings made a most wonderful sound.' Music of one sort or another was always to be heard:

> The young princes and princesses were taught music, so one could always hear soft music from the *tablas* (small drums) or from the harmonium which was very popular. And along with the harmonium, of course, they were taught to sing and so one always had soft music in the background. My husband was very fond of European classical music and composed music and there were younger members of the family who liked jazz, while the very old orthodox people played religious music. Then perhaps in the courtyard you might hear the women doing what we call *gurbas*, dancing with the sticks. In the evenings when the sun went down the women and maids – the whole household – would get together and sing devotional songs known as *bhajans*. Every woman must have a room kept apart for prayers and devotions and here we would sit down and sing these bhajans, the most famous being the ones that Mirabai sang in front of Lord Krishna.

Yet however relaxed the atmosphere might be, 'all chatter and laughter stopped the moment His Highness appeared'. At least, that was Hede Dayal's experience in Patiala State, where she often used to reflect on how lonely Maharaja Yadavendra Singh must be when 'every circle of laughter and fun he wanted to join turned absolutely silent with his appearance'.

As well as music and cheerful sounds the zanana was also filled with colour. Many states – most notably the Rajputana states of Kishengarh, Bundi and Kotah and the Punjab hill states – had their own long-established schools of art patronised and encouraged by their rulers, whose palace walls were richly decorated with wall-hangings, frescoes and miniatures portraying both religious and secular scenes. Every state also had its own local art forms and crafts. In Kathiawar and Kutch many a zanana wall was decorated with embroidered or beadwork hangings made by local womenfolk. Adding further colour were the clothes of the occupants themselves; saris or skirts, blouses and shawls worn by both the privileged and by their attendants – 'reds and blues and greens and silver and gold'.

Much time and attention was also devoted to bathing and toilette in the women's quarters. In Travancore this occupied the first two hours of the Maharani's day:

> We used no soap in those days. instead there were three silver bowls, each with a different oil for the face, the body and the hair and four copper vessels filled with four kinds of fragrant herbal waters. Your hair was washed first, using green *thali* paste made from freshly-plucked leaves, then washed and oiled with coconut oil and dried with a thin porous material called *tortu*. Then your body was washed, powder *gram* (chick peas) was applied and removed with a circular sort of sponge called *incha* made from a fibrous bark, and you were washed again with warm *Nalpamaravellam* water, absolutely red in colour and made by boiling the bark of forty different trees. Your body was oiled and massaged and your face, taking great care that the oil did not get on the hair because it contained saffron which prevented hair growth. Finally, your hair was slowly dried over fragrant smoke from a *karandi*, an iron pot filled with live coals with all sorts of herbs in it. After your hair had been combed a powdered herb was rubbed down the parting in the middle, which was to prevent colds.

After her bath the Maharani would put on the heavy anklets of solid gold, each 2–2½ inches thick, that only women of royal blood could wear. She would then proceed to the temple where, in common with many millions of Hindu women all over India, she would perform her daily puja and present offerings of flowers and coconuts to the image before her.

Periodically there was also dancing and celebrations to be enjoyed, particularly during the women's festivals. Among the Rajputs these were traditionally said to begin with Teej, marking the arrival of the summer rains, and ending in the following March with the Gangaur festival, celebrating the ideal marriage as represented by Shiva and his consort, Parvati. At Teej, a day early in the month was set aside to be enjoyed by daughters of the house and a second later in the month for daughters-in-law. All women except widows participated in the Gangaur festival, while newly-weds were required to observe the occasion more conscientiously by praying and making offerings throughout its eighteen-day course. Dancing was a common feature of such festivals. In Rajasthan this took the form of the popular *ghoomar* dances, in Gujerat it was the *garba*, both communal dances performed by any number of women linking hands and dancing in a circle. In Kutch the dance known as the *hinjh and dandia* took place in the palace at the start of the new year and also whenever there was a royal wedding. 'It was a beautiful dance,' remembers the Maharani of Rewa. 'It was arranged in the same manner as the darbar in the zanana, with about a hundred ladies dancing – the royal ladies, noblemen's wives, the jagirdars' ladies, ladies from the zanana and from the town. When my brother got married his wife had to learn the dance within ten days and then dance on the eleventh day with all of us. That palace was meant for music. My father and his forefathers before him had all been interested in music, so the Darbar Hall was perfectly made both for music and dancing, without echoes and with excellent acoustics.'

As well as music and dancing, games also played an important role in the lives of the zanana women. In Sangli State the Mangala-gaur festival in honour of the goddess Devi was always linked with newly-married women and Rajmata Padmini Raje remembers how when she first came to Sangli as a bride the occasion was celebrated 'in great style' by her mother-in-law:

> The idea is that for the first five years after marriage brides do puja to Devi on the four Tuesdays of the month of Shravan (August). The monsoons are in full swing and the trees in full bloom, so you collect leaves of several varieties of trees and offer them to Devi, which is a way of bringing awareness to the bride that there is such a profusion of variety in nature. On all the four Tuesdays the young girls and brides of Sangli were invited for the puja and played the typical games which are associated with Mangalagaur all through the night. One of the games played was *nam ghene* which is taking your husband's name in rhyme. In the old days a wife never addressed her husband by name and the only time she did was in this way, usually during a ladies' function. It had its own charm and romance and it also gave the women a chance to compose in rhyme. It was also a good way of enabling the bride to meet the women of the town and a great opportunity for her to wear all her new clothes and jewellery and to try out new recipes.

The fact that the zanana was officially out of bounds to the male sex did not mean that it was inaccessible to visitors, female or male, even if the latter might have to conduct their business from the far side of a curtain or a chik screen. The visits of traders or sellers of wares were always particularly welcome, as Leela Moolgaokar remembers:

> The *attarwalla* (perfume-seller) would come and the *bangriwalli* with her bangles, and in Gwalior there used to be these very thin bangles which were made in Czechoslovakia and fitted you so tightly that it

was a feat getting them over your wrist. Then, of course, the *rangari* (dyer) would come and you would order the colour for your saris of Number 26 Dacca muslin. Another thing was that just before the cold weather, a man would come with his wife carrying a big *matka* (earthen pot). They would put a charcoal fire underneath it and make the matka really hot. Then there used to be a special type of material in cotton but like taffeta, which he would put on the matka, fold it and then press it in a particular way with his fingernails, fold it again and pinch it, and then fold it another way and pinch it again. We would have our waistcoats and *chughas* (coats) made out of this material with the design which was done by the nails, and that would be lined with thin cotton wool and Dacca muslin Number 26. Even the Sardars' wives would get this done. They did it so quickly and we'd all sit around and watch them.

Local women from the town were also frequent visitors during the day, for just as the ruler received male petitioners in the mardana so his consort received requests and complaints from the women. 'Courtiers' wives came and the commoners,' states Shashi Wallia of Dewas Junior. 'Some would complain of their husbands beating them. They would not have dared to go to my father so they came to her and she would give her decisions – whether the wife should stay with her husband or perhaps go to her father's house for some time.' In Travancore, too, petitioners were welcome at all times except during meals: 'A lot of women would come to see my grandmother after she had come out of her bath. They would line the pathway that led from the bathing house to the palace with documents and petitions; her secretary or whoever followed her would receive them all and then she would look at them when she got back.'

Many evenings were spent in informal darbars when both zanana women and their visitors would gather round the senior figure present: 'All used to sit there and talk, with a lot of exchanging of ideas or to hear music or to take part in a *katha* (religious discourse).' On a limited number of occasions during the year there would also be formal darbars in the zanana which complemented the main state darbars being held in the City Palace Darbar Hall, as well as special women's darbars. In Dewas Junior there were two such darbars held every year – 'once on April *Purnima* (full moon) and once on *Lalita Panchami*, just before Dassera, when my mother used also to go in procession on an elephant'. In Porbandar, women's darbars were held on the Maharaja's birthday and again at Dassera and were comparatively informal affairs:

We would sit there and all the ladies would come – wives of officials and many people from the town, as well as other people who had come perhaps for the celebrations – and we would have something to drink and some sweetmeats because one never had any celebration without having trays and trays of sweetmeats, huge round silver thalis covered with magnificent velvet satin cloth in red and orange with silver tassels and braid and the state coat of arms embroidered in gold and silver thread. When these great round bowls were uncovered you saw these magnificent sweetmeats that looked like gold and silver bars, because they were covered either with gold or silver paper rolled ever so thinly. It was very good for you, of course, and a lot of our ruling houses in the olden days used also to have tiny seed pearls crushed in a silver bowl and taken with honey, which was excellent for one!

In Baroda, by contrast, Maharani Chimnabai's darbars that Nirmala Raje Bhonsle attended as a young girl were very formal and splendid affairs:

A special hall was constructed for my grandmother to hold her darbars in, with a big platform that was curtained off with chiks. My grandmother sat in a chair and there were other chairs on a lower level for my mother and myself and a senior aunt and there we sat all dressed up in our jewellery. There was a table placed beyond the screen in the hall with a gold tray on which were sesame seeds. The *Khangi Karbhari* who looked after the personal expenditure of His Highness stood there and poured this sesame seed into the hands of the people as they came up in turn to make their salute to my grandmother behind these chik curtains. The chik was very thin and you could see through it, so it was only a form of purdah.

The ceremony was followed by enormous luncheon parties attended by three or four hundred women which lasted for a couple of hours: 'You had to sit down on a silver *paat* (low stool) with a gold thali in front of you and my grandmother used to say to me, "*Savkash jewra* – Eat very slowly*", because if you stopped eating then all the other women stopped, so you had to pretend to be eating from this dish or that.'

In Baroda, as in nearly every Hindu state, the royal ladies' food was prepared by Brahmin palace cooks. Many households had very strict taboos governing the cooking and handling of food, particularly if the ruling family was itself of high caste. In Mysore the royal family paid for the upkeep of a number of temples, so whenever there was a religious festival special food known as *prasadam* or offerings from the gods, consisting of 'various types of rice and *payasam*, all the South Indian delicacies', was cooked by the temple priests and sent up to the palace. In Travancore the food was prepared by Brahmin women: 'It always had to be cooked by Brahmins and served by Brahmins, but after you had finished eating they wouldn't touch the plates, which had to be removed by lower-caste Nair ladies.' The meals themselves also followed a set pattern. 'My grandmother's meals were always quite a ritual,' explains Rukmini Varma:

> She had to have a certain number of dishes in front of her. For lunch she would have two curries cooked in a certain manner with curds as the base, one dal curry, two vegetable curries with gravy and one dry vegetable, plus a silver bowl with rice in it from which she would help herself. For tea there had to be ten things, six salty and four sweet. For sweets there was *apam*, made of bananas and rice flour fried in ghee, and a kind of *halwa* made of arrowroot, sweet but very bland. Among the salty dishes there was a variety of *bhajiyas* and *pakoras* (types of fritters) fried in batter and varieties of *dosas* (savoury pancakes) and *idlis* (steamed rice-cakes). The whole family would assemble for this ritual, but not the *Amachis* (the wives of the men of the royal family). They couldn't come anywhere near us when a meal was being eaten and if by accident they did, then the whole meal had to be sent back – because if anyone below caste set foot in the room while the meal was in progress it would all have to be cooked again. Dinner was always a bit more relaxed because that was after sunset, when everything is more relaxed.

In some wealthier states the women and children of the ruling family ate off plates or thalis of gold. When Gayatri Devi had visited Baroda as a child this had caused her some embarrassment, 'because I had a little girl-friend who was also at the table but while I had a gold plate she only had a silver one'. It was only when she grew older that she learned the conventions governing the use of gold and silver among Indian royalty: 'Every Indian woman in India, however poor she may have been, had a bit of gold on her because a woman is supposed to be Lakshmi, the goddess of wealth, and gold represents wealth. Because they respected gold ordinary women did not wear gold on their feet. Only if you were of royal blood did you wear gold on your feet and if you were of that class you never put on silver.' Yet even gold by itself was considered vulgar in some states. 'For us gold was only the metal in which precious stones were set,' declares Padma Lokur of Bhor. 'We never wore full gold bangles on our wrists, only pearl ones. It was our servants and courtiers' wives who wore gold jewellery.'

Every married princess had her jewellery given to her at the time of her marriage by her husband and other relatives, but in addition there was also the state jewellery and the personal jewellery belonging to her husband's family. This was kept in a strong-room known as the *Toshakhana* and looked after by a *khazanchi* or state treasurer, which like so many occupations in the state was a hereditary profession handed down from father to son. In every state a distinction was drawn between personal jewellery bought by rulers out of their privy purses and state jewellery, which usually took the form of ancient family heirlooms and regalia going back in some cases many hundreds of years. Jewellery worn on state and public occasions nearly always belonged to the state and was jealously guarded and zealously rationed in use by its guardians. In Baroda, the state treasurer was known as the *Jamdar* and possessed a book 'that was ten feet long giving the description of every piece down to the minutest detail'. Every time an item of state jewellery was worn a prescribed routine had to be followed:

> In the morning there were cotton saris worn, because we had to encourage the Indian handloom industry, but in the evening you could wear georgette with a golden border – and jewellery was compulsory. The Jamdar would take it out and hand it to the maid who had to sign for it by putting her thumb-mark in the book. She brought it to us on silver thalis. There was no 'I'd like this' or 'I'll wear that'. You had to wear all these things from the Jamdar khana according to turn; one group of earrings, necklace and bangles one evening, the next evening another set. Then after dinner you removed your jewellery and next morning the maid took it back to the Jamdar.

Nirmala Raje was always drawn to a particularly magnificent emerald necklace in the Toshakhana that belonged to her grandfather: 'My grandmother would sometimes say, "Akka, what would you like to wear?" And I would say, "I want the emerald necklace, Ma." But of course it never came. Nobody wore it, because my grandfather had practically given up wearing jewellery. Even for his Golden Jubilee he only wore a single necklace. To compensate, my grandmother had some very good personal jewellery bought from Russian grand dukes after the Revolution, mostly big emeralds.'

As might have been expected, Maharani Chimnabai of Baroda became a leading proponent for the ending of purdah. 'My grandfather was rather hesitant at first, being an Indian man, but my grandmother argued, "You talk about the emancipation of women and this and that and yet we are all put in this purdah. Whether you allow me or not I am going to give it up." And she did give it up, although she always insisted that unmarried girls were not to be taken into public places and that when men came – particularly Maratha men – we should cover our heads with our saris.'

The real change did not begin until after the end of the Second World War. In Patiala the purdah revolution was led by the Maharani, albeit a little reluctantly at first and only after the encouragement of her friends, among them Sardar H. S. Malik, the State's Dewan, and his wife:

Although the Maharani rode and shot she did everything in purdah and purdah meant that when she came along the road they used to shout, 'Bandobast! Bandobast!,' and all the people on the road had to get off or look the other way. But there were a lot of Americans in Delhi in 1945 and we knew some of them and invited them to Chail. During one of these visits I said to the Maharaja, 'It's a great pity that none of these people can ever meet your wife, because she is such a charming person and would create such a tremendous impression.' So finally he agreed and she came out of purdah – and soon afterwards all the Sardarnis (wives of Sardars) came out of purdah, too.

In Jaipur, also, the lead came from the top. 'My husband was trying to get the other women out of purdah,' Gayatri Devi explains. 'We would give receptions in Rambagh when my husband would ask some of the nobles to come with their wives – but very few would do so. After that he said, "We must do something about breaking purdah." But I was only twenty or twenty-one at that time. "Nobody's going to follow me," I said, "but give me a school and I promise you within ten years purdah will be broken." And that is how the Maharani Gayatri Devi School, which is now one of the premier schools in India, began in Jaipur.'

11
DARBAR

Please to imagine the Viceroy and His Highness to have taken their seats, the great hall aglow with colour, the throbbing of the Indian drum, and the nasal, but not unbeautiful, voice of a singing girl alone breaking the stillness. Then at a signal advancing, rank upon rank, an army of perfectly drilled retainers, dressed in dark blue velvet and gold and bearing golden trays of jewels, of pearls, of diamonds, of emeralds; trays of silks and of cloth of gold. At the gates of the palace stand six elephants and six horses in all their state trappings, necklaces of gold mohurs round their necks, anklets of gold and jewels, and draperies of velvet, silk and gold; these, too, form part of the Durbar's offerings to the Viceroy. The trays are laid at his feet, the servants retire, and with a gesture His Excellency conveys to the assembled company that he gratefully accepts the spirit of the gift – only. With the same stately ceremonial the trays are removed, and then the Sardars and Chiefs are in turn presented; Itr and Pan is brought in, a great golden garland is hung round the Viceroy's neck by his host, and the Durbar is over.

Yvonne Fitzroy,
Courts and Camps in India, 1926

The word *Darbar* – or Durbar, as the British wrote it – was of Persian origin, introduced to India by the Mughals. It could be used to describe a ruler's court, the formal and informal levees held there, his executive government and even the ruler himself, who might be referred to as the Darbar-Saheb. The British applied the same word to the great imperial assemblies which they organised from time to time in British India, the first of which was held in 1877, when Queen Victoria was proclaimed Empress of India, and the last and most magnificent in 1911 in the presence of King George V and Queen Mary. The tentage on that memorable occasion spread over 25 square miles of the Delhi plain and was made up by 233 camps, the King's camp alone occupying 85 acres. Among those who paid homage to the King-Emperor was Shashi Wallia's father, the Maharaja of Dewas Junior. Despite a minor catastrophe when a raja's elephant ran amok through the Durbar Camp an hour before the main ceremony, the presentation of *nazar* by each of the princes in turn made a lasting impression on all those who witnessed the scene:

> The various princes advanced according to protocol to the dais where the king and queen were seated and did their *mujras* (salutes). 'I of course was small fry,' daddy said, 'so I came at the latter end of the procession.' First was the Nizam, who gave the king a ruby necklace in which each ruby was as big as a pigeon's egg. Then the other princes followed – Baroda, Gwalior, Mysore, Kashmir – each presenting the king with other items of jewellery which must have been lying in their coffers for centuries but were unearthed and brought to light for this great occasion. His Highness of Panna presented the king with an umbrella for his throne which was at least twelve inches in diameter, carved out of a single piece of emerald from his emerald mines. Sir Tukoji Rao of Indore, dressed in gold and silver brocade clothes, walked up to the dais twirling a gold stick with jewelled engravings and with a hilt carved out of a single ruby. Unfortunately he slipped on the polished wooden floor, put his weight on the stick to retain his balance and it fell and shattered, so he was very put out. 'I couldn't give very much compared with all these,' daddy told me, 'but I also had something which had been with us for a long time.' He gave the king a silver box engraved with various scenes from the *Ramayana* and *Mahabharata*, which had originally been captured by a Peshwa from one of the kings they had conquered, so old that in places the faces on the figures had been rubbed smooth.

The imperial durbar followed Indian tradition. 'We innovated nothing,' maintains a former British Political Officer, John Cotton. 'The institutions, titles, customs, ceremonials were all part and parcel of what the British had inherited from the former masters of India, the Emperors of Delhi. The ceremonies by which a Maharaja or Nawab was installed, the meticulous exchange of official presents as between the subordinate ruler and the representative of the paramount government, the seating at these ceremonies and the order of precedence – all this was not something invented by the British or even by the ruler, but a survival of a state of affairs that had existed long before the British ever came to rule these parts.'

The order of precedence was taken most seriously by both the British and the princes, because 'when you go back to Mughal times or even earlier it was your place in court, and where you sat in court or where you were greeted on arrival that showed the world what your position was. It affected your prestige and it was on that prestige and influence that the ruler's power depended.' Constant attempts by princes to improve their position in the established order of precedence created many headaches for the members of the Foreign and Political Department of the Government of India. Put in charge of arrangements for a Government Durbar in Lahore in the 1920s, Conrad Corfield had to go to great lengths to ensure that the local order of precedence was observed: 'The Punjab princes would always try to get in just ahead of somebody more senior. I knew this, so by using a map of the city I worked out different routes for every ruler to get to the Durbar Hall and then an officer with a map was posted to each ruler to bring him to the durbar. Some of the princes were amazed as to why they had to go round all the streets before coming to the durbar, but I think they realised why when they got there one after the other in the right order.'

The British contribution to princely protocol was the gun-salutes that reinforced a ruler's public standing. They, too, provoked much inter-state rivalry, which successive Viceroys only fuelled by awarding personal salutes to favoured rulers that gave them an additional 2-gun salute on top of the state salute. One ruler in the 1930s who was notorious in the Political Department for 'always pushing himself forward' in an attempt to increase his gun salute from 13 to 15 guns was the Jam-Saheb of Nawanagar, who believed he should be placed higher on the table than his near neighbours Junagadh, Bhavnagar, Porbandar, Dhrangadhara and Palanpur. There was good reason behind such ambitions, for 'if you were a prince with no gun salute, then every twopenny-halfpenny Political Agent could come and visit you every three months and ask to see the accounts. Whereas if you had a high enough gun salute, then the Political Agent could only come to you like a *chaprassi* (messenger), and if you had a 19-gun salute then you were left alone, because only the Viceroy could come and bother you. So the higher the gun salute, the less trouble you had – and this was the attraction.'

Another form of public recognition that 'touched the princes to the quick' was the awarding of titles and decorations. Many were hereditary and went with the job, appellations such as *Rais-ud-Daula* (Chief of the Kingdom), *Sipar-i-Saltanat* (Shield of the Kingdom), *Farzand-i-Khas* (Privileged Son) or *Lokendra* (Protector of the World), either given in the days of the Mughals or self-awarded by ancestors to bolster their prestige – part of a process of aggrandisement that saw plain *raja* develop into such superlatives as *Maharajad-hiraja* (great king of kings), or even *Sawai Maharaja*, a title conferred on the rulers of Jaipur by Emperor Aurangzeb and meaning 'one and a quarter Maharaja'. To these the British added their own honours, notably the KCSI, KCIE, GCIE and the much-coveted GCSI. The end result was that a ruler such as the Seventh Nizam had a title that ran on for several lines and could be translated as:

'Lieutenant-General His Exalted Highness Seventh in Line Equal to the rank of Asaf Jah, Victor of the Realm and the World, Regulator of the Realm, Regulator of the State, Viceroy Sir the Honourable Osman Ali Khan, the Brave, Victorious in Battle, Faithful Ally of the British, Grand Commander of the Star of India, Knight Grand Cross of the British Empire, Nizam of Hyderabad and Berar.'

Physical symbols of kingship – the *Raj-chinnha* – were equally important outward signs: the royal *chhatri* or umbrella that was held over the ruler's head when he walked or rode in procession; the *chamars* or *chaoris* made of yaks' tails set in silver handles that originally served as fly-whisks; the gold *morchals* and silver *abdagaris* in the form of fishes and pear-shaped discs on the end of long poles that were carried as standards; the fans of peacocks' feathers and the great gold and silver maces carried by the court heralds and mace-bearers; and, above all, the *gadi* or raised cushion 'synonymous with power' upon which the ruler sat cross-legged or with his feet tucked under him. Adding weight to this royal regalia were the various declarations of sovereign authority made on all formal occasions by the royal bards, poets, singers and heralds.

Not every state ran to resident singers and poet laureates to extol the virtues of the ruler and his clan in music and words, but every formal Darbar would have its *chobdars*, *bhaldars*, *chamardars* and *chhadidars* in attendance. It was the duty of these last two to carry the state regalia, in particular the silver-handled fans and fly-whisks: 'These people were normally Muslims who in the old days functioned as bodyguards and you can see their importance when you go into a temple. On both sides of the idol there are often statues of "Jai" and "Vijay", the two bodyguards.' In Sangli State they 'dressed in red with gold embroidery and gold turbans, with a waistcloth or belt made of Paithani cloth'. In larger states the more important members of the nobility might also be given the privilege of having their own mace-bearers, so that in Bikaner there were as many as fifteen attending the ruler's court.

The roles of court criers and heralds were filled by the chobdars and bhaldars, armed with their rods and maces of office. The most senior acted as Master of Ceremonies during Darbars, while the others gave notice of the ruler's approach and progress. Their announcements varied according to the occasion, but the manner in which they were made was very much the same everywhere. In Kapurthala the chobdars 'lined the steps of the Darbar Hall and would take up the chant of the ruler's titles and official designations as accorded to him by the British. These would be repeated from chobdar to chobdar all the way into the Darbar Hall, with the final title being recited as he got to the dais.' '"*Ba-adab Ba-Mulaija Hoshiar*" was said as the ruler approached, meaning "Be prepared to receive the ruler with respect". Then it was "*Daulat zyada*" which meant "May you have plenty of wealth" and as the ruler sat down "*Madade Parvar Digar* – May God be of help".' The chobdar performed two functions, as Muzaffer Khan remembers from his childhood in Palanpur – and always to great effect:

> There were four of them, spaced out so that the senior-most was about three feet away from my grandfather, one at the entrance to the Darbar Hall and two in between. The one closest to my grandfather was the noisiest and the most raucous because he only had this opportunity two or three times a year to shout into my grandfather's ear. He was doing two things simultaneously, asking whoever came forward to bow and respectfully pay his homage to my grandfather while periodically and in the same stentorian voice he would be shouting at my grandfather, telling him that he had to keep an eye on everyone that came in and to return their *salaams* (salutes). This returning of the salaam was the only Islamic bit that came into it, because the rest was what would be said in a Hindu court. But returning the salaam was based on an injunction in the Koran which states that whenever someone salaams you, you are bound by religion to return the salaam. The chobdar would also be there in a parade, shouting at my grandfather during the procession to look to both sides and to return the salaams.

Surrounded by pomp and circumstance – the Hindi word for it was *dhoom-dham* – a ruler could not be other than acutely conscious of his regal status, especially since kingship was widely believed to carry with it divine powers. Divyabhanusinhji Chavda of Mansa recalls how villagers would come to his father expecting to be healed of certain types of illnesses: 'They would come with short pieces of string which my father would tie with seven knots. It was believed that if this string was tied round an ailing part of the body such as the knee or ankle, then the pain from that part would disappear.' This semi-divine status meant that the ruler was always accorded the greatest respect. When Maharani Lakshmibai was Regent of the State of Travancore during the minority of her nephew in the 1920s, visitors would 'bow and give her fruit and flowers, placing them in a bowl at her feet because they could not touch her'. And whenever she appeared in public she was greeted with the most elaborate salutations: 'Even her brothers and sisters had to address her as "Your Highness" and pay her all due respect. All her younger brothers would greet her after removing their shirts, putting their sacred threads over one ear and then doing first a *namaste* (salutation with palms pressed together), then moving both hands outwards and in again in a fast motion, meaning "Many, many greetings".'

The Regent responded by playing her part as custom demanded: 'They say when she walked into a hall it was like Lakshmi come alive. They say she was so regal and gracious, that every step she took was a queenly step. It came naturally to her, maybe because she had trained for this since she was just four years old.' But regal authority was acquired at some cost: 'You had to accept that you could not behave like an ordinary citizen. You were always accompanied by people and you were always being watched. Even when you met another ruler it was always very formal, because that was the tradition that had been established.'

Kingship in the Indian states found its most splendid expression in the great darbars held on such notable occasions as the ruler's birthday or at the culmination of the most important festivals of the year. Their chief purpose was the public declaration of allegiance by the ruler's chief subjects in an act of homage known as *nazar* that took place in the Darbar Halls of the City Palace – itself widely referred to as the *Darbar-Griha* or Darbar House. Every old palace had two such darbar halls; an inner room known by the Mughal appellation of *Dewan-e-Khas*, reserved for private audiences, and the larger *Dewan-e-Am*, frequently a pillared loggia opening onto the central courtyard of the palace. The exceptions were big states like Mysore and Gwalior, where the modern palaces provided the setting for the darbars. The Amba Vilas palace in Mysore, rebuilt at the turn of the century after the old building had been destroyed by fire, was a quite extraordinary confection of Indo-Saracenic, European Baroque and South Indian temple architecture. At its heart was a *Dewan-e-Khas* lit by a skylight of stained glass and with walls thickly encrusted with Mughal-style decorations in amber, lapis lazuli and gold, but its outstanding feature was the majestic *Dewan-e-Am*, a pillared Darbar Hall capable of accommodating more than a thousand persons and supported by scores of thick stone columns after the manner of South Indian temple interiors. Equally magnificent but more consciously European was the great Darbar Hall in Gwalior's Jai Vilas Palace, designed and built by a Neapolitan named Filose who entered Maharaja Jayaji Rao's service at the time of the 1857 Indian Mutiny and became a Sardar of the state. Since the hall was built on the first storey and had to carry the weight of perhaps a thousand persons, its floor was laid on huge stone beams: 'These were tested by elephants walking on them and one which cracked is now in the public park, a solid seventy-foot block of stone.' Elephants were also hoisted up to the roof to test whether or not the ceiling was strong enough to support the weight of the Darbar Hall's main feature: two three-ton glass and crystal chandeliers, each carrying 250 candles.

The dhoom-dham of the Darbar commenced with the donning of ceremonial finery by everyone from rajas and nawabs down to the humblest minion who wore the state's uniform or livery. All those attending the darbar itself were expected to wear traditional court attire or formal clothes. While employed by Maharaja Yadavendra Singh as Patiala State Dewan, Sardar H. S. Malik had to wear costumes sent over by the Maharaja. 'One was a brocade *achkan* of pink with gold all over,' recalls Mrs Malik. 'Another was saffron coloured with gold, worn with a belt and decorations. When our daughter saw him all dolled-up like that, she said he looked like a *darwan* (doorkeeper).' To attend the darbar 'you had to wear a *pagri* or turban and a *kamarband* (waistcloth) and those who had the privilege of wearing a *talwar* (scimitar) wore them,' remembers M.M. Sapat from his years of service in Bikaner. 'As well as the royal family there would be the Sardars, who were the Rajput chiefs and nobles of Bikaner, and the officers of the state – the dewan and his ministers, the heads of department and their assistants. Then there were the *seths* and *sahukars* who made up the business community and even some of the artisans – the *tamboli* who supplied *betel, paan* and *supari* (nuts, lime and leaves chewed as a savoury), the *pinjara* who thrashed cotton, the *darzi* (tailor), the *guzdar* or mason in charge of stone carving. They all had their place in the Darbar Hall.'

Other than the ruler and his family, none would be so magnificently turned out as the nobility of the state. In Gwalior their court dress consisted of the long coat known as the *angarkha* with gold epaulettes on the shoulders, together with the arms that a warrior was required to carry when he left his house: 'The Sardar must have his *panch hatyars* (five weapons) – the *dhal* (circular shield), *talwar* (sword), *katyar* (dagger), *bhala* (spear) and *bichwa*, which literally means a scorpion and is a small throwing knife hidden in the back of your *angarkha*.' On their heads they carried the distinctive boat-shaped Maratha *Shindeshahi pagri* worn at a jaunty angle. In Hyderabad the *paigah* nawabs who made up the powerful nobility of the state – so called on account of the cavalry paigahs or squadrons that each was supposed to maintain – wore equally distinctive mitre-like hats called *dastars*. Other states had their own characteristic headgear, which in every Hindu state north of Mysore consisted of a turban of specific length and width tied in a special way so as to immediately identify its wearer's home locality or caste. One of the longest turbans was the Mewar *pug*, 'about six inches wide and yards and yards long', which Mahendra Singh of Udaipur was taught to tie for himself by an old palace retainer: 'Because the number seven is considered a significant number it was seven times round to cover one side of the head and seven times round on the other side, with the last part coming up in very neat symmetrical folds over the forehead. It could be tied and kept ready for use on a dummy and you could wear it for a couple of times but after that it had to be retied.'

Turbans worn by state employees had to be of uniform shape and colour. In Porbandar it was 'a sort of wine colour', in Kapurthala it varied according to the whim of the ruler: 'Orders used to go out that everybody would wear either light blue or a blue and white striped turban. These would be uniformly dyed so that everybody wore the same colour.' The ruler and the male members of his family exercised greater freedom in their choice of colours with saffron and salmon pink being accepted as exclusively royal colours. The colours also varied according to the seasons – 'usually the light colours like pale shell pink in summer and the brighter colours to match a particular festival, so that at the *Kajalya Teej* function during the monsoon it would be a bright colour with a lot of black in it, because *kajal* means black.' Another royal prerogative was the wearing of the safa, a medium-sized turban with a *kalgi* or plumed aigrette pinned to the front, which among commoners was worn only by bridegrooms during their marriage ceremonies when they were popularly regarded as being 'kings for a day'.

It was for such occasions as the darbar that the state jewellery kept in the toshakhana was reserved, to be worn by all members of the royal family, irrespective of age or sex. 'The jewellery that the princes wore on these occasions was quite magnificent,' declares Conrad Corfield, 'but one has to remember that the wonderful pearls and emeralds they wore on their *pagris* and round their necks were mostly state jewellery drawn from the state treasury and that in some cases their actual private jewellery was negligible.' This state jewellery was even spoken of as '*hamara* – ours' by the populace: 'At a marriage or darbar they'd say "Look at our jewels", rather as they referred to the ruler as "*hamara Raj*".'

Some rulers enjoyed dressing for the occasion; others did not and there were always rulers like Maharaja Natwarsinghji of Porbandar who dressed for state occasions in a plain homespun achkan worn with decorations but without jewellery. Some took the opportunity to display not only themselves but also the majesty of the state in its most dazzling form. Two rulers who always presented 'resplendent figures' on all public occasions were Bhupinder Singh of Patiala and his son Yadavendra Singh – whom Sardar H. S. Malik had many opportunities to observe at close hand while attending his darbars:

> Several strings of pearls festooned his silken turban, which was crowned with a delicate diadem. Around his neck he wore a great collar of diamonds set in platinum along with four or five other massive and beautifully set necklaces of diamonds and emeralds. Another necklace with exquisite diamonds hung from his waist, with more diamonds on bracelets round his arms and wrists. He also wore diamond buttons on his achkan and around his waist was a gold lamé scarf held in place by the clasp of a single emerald, about four inches by two and a half. Also at his waist was a sword in a jewelled scabbard, its hilt sparkling with gems. With his height and good looks, he carried it off very well.

To Mrs Malik, Yadavendra Singh in such attire appeared 'a splendid medieval figure', but when her daughter attended her first darbar and saw the ruler she 'gave a wolf-whistle. The Maharaja was stupefied but took it sportingly and grinned!'

As on every important occasion, the darbar ceremonies began for Hindus with visits to the state temples, beginning at the Ganesh temple because 'anything you start you start with Ganesh, the god who will remove all obstacles and so has first priority among Indian gods'. Music would also be heard at an early stage in the proceedings. 'I don't remember any function, formal or informal, of which music did not form an integral part,' declares Rani Vijaya Devi of Mysore, a state renowned for the calibre of its musicians and the patronage extended to them by its rulers. 'In Mysore every ceremony or festival was always heralded by the *nagaswaram* (clarinet-like wind instrument). Even during the daily religious puja it was customary for one of the palace *Vidwans* (learned men) to perform. There was also a Western band and orchestra directed by Mr Otto Schmidt, a German national, with a wind and brass section which played during the Dassera Darbar and parades.'

Not every state had a military or police band, but even the humblest could organise a band of drummers or *dhol* and *shahnai* players to lead off the procession that escorted the ruler to the Darbar Hall. 'The ruler was always the last in the procession,' states Dr Karni Singh of Bikaner. 'In front of him were his nearest kin, so that in my father's time it was my brother and I ahead of him, with the next nearest relations ahead of us, and so on until finally you got to the chobdar at the front who would be warning everybody to prepare for the coming of the Maharaja.'

As the ruler's procession made its way slowly through the streets of the state capital, the Darbar Hall itself filled up under the supervision of a Master of Ceremonies who directed commoners to one side of the hall and courtiers and nobility to the other. The places closest to the gadi were occupied in strict order of precedence, with the most important Sardars of the state filling the front row on the right. 'Everybody had a seat at the darbar according to their status,' explains Maj.-General Rao Manohar Sinhji of Bedla, head of one of Udaipur's most distinguished Sardar families. 'It was first, second, third, fourth on the right, all with fixed seats on the floor, then on the left and then at the back of the gadi. My family seat was just about in the middle on the right.' In Gwalior arrangements were more complex, as Sardar Sitole describes:

> In our court there were three degrees of Sardar. First there were *neem tajim* or First Class Sardars, like ourselves who had *toda* and *gashia* rights. When we went to court the ruler had to get up to receive our respects. There were the Second Class Sardars, to whom the ruler also made a gesture of showing respect, and then there was the Third Class from whom the ruler received *mujras* (salutes) without either getting up or returning the gesture. Our protocol was that the first five Sardars on either side of the gadi were the First Class Sardars, who also had the gashia, which meant that they were entitled to sit on a special carpet, whereas the rest all sat on the *bichhayat* or white cloth.

Outside the Darbar Hall chobdars lined the palace steps and a guard of honour would be drawn up to await the arrival of the ruler. In Kapurthala they wore 'a strikingly attractive uniform of a very dark royal blue with white facings and spats and pom-poms and whether they were Sikhs, Muslims or Hindus all wore turbans in the same regimental colours'. The approach of the ruler's procession was signalled by trumpet calls, which in Dhrangadhara State were the same as the British Army call known as the 'Approach':

> This was sounded as your carriage entered through the outer gates of the palace under mounted escort, having done the rounds of the temples, and it was prolonged until the moment you alighted and the guard of honour presented arms. You were then escorted by your ministers and your ADCs up the aisle to the gadi and precisely as you sat down the first of the guns was fired off. The gun salutes used to be shot off from the promontory on the lake in Dhrangadhara. It was as if there was a button under the gadi, because the moment you sat down the first gun would go off. It must have been done by heliograph, I suspect.

Once the proceedings of the darbar got under way all traces of a
British influence disappeared. The *nazarana* ceremony in Dewas
Junior during the reign of Maharaja Malhar Rao was typical of
many:

> All the courtiers would be massed on one side of the Darbar Hall
> with the *ryots* or ordinary people on the other. Of course, it was fully
> carpeted, with the gadi covered in gold and silver and with a golden
> canopy over it. Daddy would come up the aisle and first he would
> *mujra karo* (salute) the gadi himself three times and then mount it.
> Each one of the courtiers would then come along with a gold *mohur*
> (coin) and present it in a silk handkerchief to my father, who would
> just touch it and pass it on. Then the poorer people would come with
> their offerings, whatever they were. Sometimes it would be sugar,
> sometimes garlands of flowers, sometimes wheat or rice from their
> farms or even a little heifer. Whatever they could spare to give to
> their king they would bring.

Every man of consequence in the state from the Yuvaraj or Walihad
downwards was required to perform this public act of homage.
Those rulers who conformed most closely with Mughal custom
required their nazar to be a tribute in the form of a gold mohur or
sovereign, and nowhere was this convention more strictly enforced
than in Muslim Hyderabad – 'where even before you opened your
mouth you had to come in with a nazar'. Instead of gold mohurs
the state used its own currency of *ashrafis* which were given as nazar
according to status:

> Maharaja Sir Kishen Pershad had to give eighteen ashrafis and four
> rupees. Salar Jung had to give sixteen and four rupees and all the
> Mughal men and senior people of the state had to give at least one
> ashrafi, and the richer the Jagirdar the more he had to give. So it
> went on down the line until it came to the officers of the state, some
> of whom gave four rupees but were not expected to give an ashrafi.
> This nazar was presented on a handkerchief to the Nizam who had
> two safe boxes called *haramdars* beside him, one for silver and one
> for gold. 'When he takes the gold off your handkerchief you don't
> even feel the weight of his hand,' my father told me once. 'He seems
> to magnetise the thing to put it into the boxes.'

As a young boy of eight, V. K. Reddy had occasion to test this
lightness of touch for himself when his grandfather took him to the
King Kothi Palace to be presented to the Nizam:

> The Nizam was sitting in a very rickety chair by an uncovered table
> and after saying a few words to my grandfather about some day-to-day

business he turned to me and said, 'Is this your grandson? Let him come to me.' At that moment I was given four bright shiny new silver rupees in a handkerchief, which a servant had been carrying because my grandfather thought I would drop them. I rather hoped this would be just a token presentation and that he would put his palm on them and return them to me. But to my disgust he did no such thing and took them. However, I gave a very deep *adaab* or salaam and walked out backwards when it was over, because you couldn't turn your back on the Nizam.

All this was in complete contrast to the presentation of nazar in another Muslim state, Palanpur, where the handing over of money was all but abandoned during the reign of the present Nawab's grandfather – 'although if anybody wished to offer money my father could not turn it down, but there was no question of gold mohurs. It had to be rupees.' Similar compromises could be found in many other states and in Porbandar, instead of money being offered to the ruler, it was waved over his head two or three times and then left on the ground to be collected by an ADC:

This was meant for the ruler's valets or, if it was offered to the maharani, for her maidservants. An account was kept and at the end of the year it was divided up among the valets and maidservants. If money was offered to you directly you didn't take it. You returned it and a little more, so if my husband was given a hundred rupees then a hundred and fifty was given back immediately. But the only person who received money directly from the ruler was the *purohit* who put him on the gadi at his coronation. When he came round on my husband's birthday – or on mine – so much was put into an envelope and given to him personally.

A similar ritual of passing money over the ruler's head as a gesture to ward off evil spirits was found in Gwalior, where 'certain families who were considered as equals or the ruler's kith and kin had the privilege of not paying nazar. Instead they did *nachhawar*, which meant that you took five rupees or whatever it was, passed it over the head of the ruler, and then threw it on the ground. It was supposed to go to the menial staff.' Nazar did not always take the form of money. In Gwalior there were certain festival darbars where *apta* leaves symbolising gold replaced the real mohurs and what were known as *poshaks* or outfits of clothes were presented:

There were ready-made poshaks for weddings and darbars that you had to take from the *khajina* (treasury) and then come along and offer to the Maharaja. He would touch it and it would be left there to go back into the khajina for the next darbar. For a man it would be a shawl or a safa, for a lady a sari, blouse or piece of jewellery depending on her status – because the women's side also had these poshaks, which meant that they didn't have to spend money.

Officers of the state forces might also offer their allegiance in their own way. In Kapurthala, 'officers in their magnificent uniforms with silver facings and Wellington boots would present the hilts of their swords. They would draw the sword partially from the scabbard and the ruler would touch it as if to accept their fealty.'

These proceedings were often observed by hidden spectators: the women of the palace and their children watching from galleries or from behind chiks and curtains in alcoves or side-rooms. In Baroda, Nirmala Raje witnessed her grandfather's darbars from 'high up in a gallery that had nice wooden carvings. Mattresses were laid down to sit on so that you could see very nicely from up there. You were not supposed to put your head out of the windows, but of course the people below must have seen us.' In Patiala, Hede Dayal remembers, the women observed the darbars from behind decorated screens. 'Sometimes we behaved so badly, making fun of whatever we saw. Once they even had to come and say, "You can't behave like this. We can hear you from outside."'

The presentation of nazar in whatever form it took could last for an hour or more and might be followed by the ruler presenting honours in his turn: 'Soldiers who had distinguished themselves had to be given awards, or deserving students would come up and be presented with prizes and medals'. The ruler might make a speech 'concerning an administrative change or some improvement for the agriculturalists or on the medical front'. But once these official proceedings were over the atmosphere tended to become more informal. The ruler might move among his subjects or receive favoured guests in private audience. While this was going on music would be played and *paan-supari* distributed to the guests – a pungent concoction of betel-nut, lime and spices folded in an aromatic leaf intended to 'convey respect to the person to whom it was offered as well as being very auspicious', and on such occasions often coated in thin gold leaf.

The music played frequently provided an accompaniment to dances performed by the palace courtesan-dancers, known in the Rajput states as *tawaifs*: 'They were hereditary dancing girls really, so they had the right to be at the darbar where they danced in all their jewellery to the accompaniment of a band.' In Hyderabad there were transvestites called *hijras* who dressed, danced and sang as women.

Another auspicious offering sometimes consumed on these occasions was opium, taken much diluted in water, and occasionally *bhang* or Indian hemp, but a universal feature of all darbar ceremonies was the offering to guests of *ittar* or perfume sprinkled on handkerchiefs or handed round on trays, an indication that the proceedings were drawing to a close. If there were important guests present, they would be garlanded by the ruler or by one of his sons with garlands of gold and silver tinsel and then to the accompaniment of a further gun salute the ruler would take his leave – preceded as before by chobdars, guards, ministers, ADCs and family: 'It was an unforgettably colourful spectacle and so moving in its own way – to see how this mass of humanity would receive one individual who was their father-figure, their *Ma-Baap*.'

12

SERVANTS OF THE STATE

Allegiance is as hereditary as the land: 'I am your child; my head and sword are yours, my service is at your command.' Fidelity to the chief is the climax of all virtues. The Rajpoot is taught from his infancy, in the song of the bard, to regard it as the source of honour here and of happiness hereafter.

Lt.-Col. James Tod,
Annals and Antiquities of Rajasthan, 1829

'My father used to tell us how when he and other rulers went hunting together their servants would all sit together and gossip, telling each other tales about how good at shikar their own rulers were. One would say "My Nawab can shoot at such a distance", another, "My Raja can shoot from an even greater distance" and then his own servant would say "*Hamare Khambat ke Nawab* – Our ruler of Cambay – he is such an accurate shot that once on shikar he saw this *nilgai* (blue bull) miles and miles off and racing away, but he took aim and shot and although the nilgai was racing ahead at terrific speed it was chased by my master's bullet until it connected."'

Loyalty to the ruler was absolute and unquestioning among the ryots and aboriginal agriculturalists who made up more than ninety per cent of the population of every state. Loyalty was 'enshrined in the culture of the Dungarpur people', explains the Maharawal of Dungarpur. It was 'that ma-baap feeling between the ruler and the ruled. I had the Maharaja of Bikaner with me once on a beat for pig, nilgai and panther and we had collected about 500 beaters. I noticed that they were heading in the wrong direction and I shouted that they should turn and come towards me. Five or six heard my voice and a hundred stood up with folded hands and said, "Ma-baap." I had never taught them; it was just that inborn feeling.'

Even in the face of extreme provocation such as in Alwar in the 1920s, where Maharaja Jay Singh claimed half of the state's revenue for himself, taxed his ryots almost to the point of beggary and was even rumoured to tie up old widows as tiger-bait, open revolt by the peasantry against their ruler was almost unheard of. Opposition only came from those who had the power to threaten the stability of the kingdom; the thakurs, sardars and big jagirdars who owed the sovereign their allegiance but were powerful men in their own right with vested interests. While they provided a useful 'internal check' against despotism, these landowning nobles were never slow to dominate a ruler who was weak or inexperienced. Every state could provide examples from the recent past of 'wicked uncles', overlooked sons or ambitious nobles attempting to seize power. In Palanpur State there was a notorious instance in its past history of regicide by a group of jamadars who hoped to rule the state through the murdered Nawab's fourteen-year-old son:

> Nawab Feroze Khan was taken out shooting in one of those silver bullock carts called shigrams. A man called Taj Mohammed shot him, threw out the driver and the two bullocks took the shigram back to camp with the dead body of the ruler. But fourteen-year-old Fateh Khan's mother was very clever and she broke the jamadars' power by getting help from other jagirdars, because at that time they were all intriguing, younger brother against elder brother. So Fateh Khan ruled but he was such a serious man that they say he only laughed once in his life-time, when some jesters came to the palace – but even then it was just a smile.

Nevertheless Palanpur also had its share of strong rulers who had their own ways of keeping their jagirdars under control, particularly Nawab Sher Khan who once summoned a troublesome jagirdar to dine with him alone: 'While they were eating Sher Khan called the cook and, as prearranged, said, "Why have you made such bad food today?" The cook said, "What's wrong with the food? Look, I'm a human being after all", and when he heard this insolence the jagirdar picked up his talwar to chastise the cook – whereupon the Nawab picked up his own talwar and sliced off the jagirdar's head, which fell into the silver thali before him.'

Even after the umbrella of British protection had been erected over the gadis of the Indian princes in 1858, the feudal nobility still remained a force to be reckoned with. In Hyderabad the *paigahs* and the four ranks of noblemen from *Jah* to *Jung* created by the Nizams drew incomes from their jagirs that were far in excess of an average salute state. The state's Hindu prime minister, Maharaja Sir Kishen Pershad, had an estate that provided an annual income of 22 lakhs of rupees, which put him higher in the revenue league than all but two of the 15-gun salute states. Nobles like Salar Jung and the leading paigahs had their own courts and private armies three and four thousand strong, while a score of others maintained large palaces and establishments which would have been the envy of any ruler in Kathiawar.

The Sardars of Gwalior State were hardly less powerful. The Sitoles had a jagir of 600 square miles encompassing 250 villages. Much of it was jungle and the income was no more than three or four lakhs of rupees a year, but the authority of the head of the family was on a par with that of the ruler of a minor state:

> Within the jagir territory we had our own jurisdictional rights. I had my own police, my own *tehsildar* who collected taxes, my own powers of revenue settlement and my own shikar rights. I even had my own sub-jagirdars, eight jagirdars to whom I issued jagirs and who sat at my court, as well as my own *takedars* (lessees of land) and zamindars. When the Viceroy came to Gwalior or the Governor called he was supposed to make a courtesy call on my family, during which I had the right to offer him *beeda* (betel nut) and he would give the poshak (robes) in return, which was an acceptance of each other's status.

In return for these privileges, jagirdars like Sardar Sitole were required to contribute to the state in a number of ways:

> There was a lot of social binding on both sides. The jagirdar's sons were supposed to serve the state according to their qualifications and there was always a job for them, provided they were qualified for it. Up in Gwalior Fort there was a school known as the Sardars' School, meant for the education of the sons of the Gwalior sardars, where as well as the normal curriculum up to matriculation standard there was a special jagirdar class in which we were taught the administration of a Tehsildar or of a Collector, so that when we went into the state service or went to administer our own jagirs we had the basic knowledge. My father, for instance, started his career in the Third Lancers of the Gwalior Cavalry and was then taken into the administration, where he served under Maharaja Madhav Rao before becoming a minister under His late Highness. But even as a minister he took no pay because we were jagirdars.

The First Class Sardars of Gwalior expected to play leading roles in affairs of state. As late as the early 1940s, one of their number made a bid to secure power over the still inexperienced 'George' Jivaji Rao Scindia, father of the present Maharaja. 'The ruler was all-powerful in Gwalior and the nobility had to fall in line,' explains Madhavrao Scindia. 'But of course as in every traditional court there is intrigue and there certainly was a big conspiracy in my father's time. He had a council of which the chairman or president was the ruler. The vice-chairman happened to be a leading Sardar named

Angré who tried to intrigue with the British to see that the chairman became more or less like a constitutional monarch while the real power was exercised by the vice-chairman. Unfortunately for him, some letters came to my father's hand in time and as a result he was stripped of all his commissions and his jagir was put under court award.'

It was the duty of a nobleman to attend his ruler at court as and when requested, often to play an important role as official or unofficial adviser to the ruler. In Hyderabad, V. K. Reddy's grand-father was for many years *Kotwal* or commissioner of police in the city, a job that 'involved much more than just being a policeman, because he was much closer to the Nizam than any of his ministers. He used to report to the Nizam at eight in the morning and then again at five in the evening, every single day, come rain or shine, and I have a letter from my grandfather to the minister of police saying that he hadn't had any leave for thirty-eight years and could he please take a day off as his wife wasn't very well.' Raja Bahadur Venkat Rama Reddy saw to it that 'there was no problem in the city or the state' with the help of a secret police of Turkish origin known as the *Khofia*:

> It came with the Mughals and whereas in the rest of India it dissolved under British influence into a regular police CID, in Hyderabad it remained the Khofia, so that Hyderabad was the last place in the world that had the grapevine system for information run by my grandfather from police headquarters. Each police area had a circle inspector and under him fifteen to twenty-five informers, each re-sponsible for a particular street. So if the Nizam wanted to know what a particular family had had for lunch and who had come, he would have the answer in fifteen minutes. If a Congress party member came into Hyderabad my grandfather would know about it within minutes, because nothing happened without my grandfather knowing about it. As a result there was very little crime in Hyderabad because everybody knew they were under watch.

Just as Hyderabad had two Hindus in influential positions in govern-ment, so the Sikh state of Patiala in the 1930s had two very able and experienced outsiders in authority: a Muslim prime minister in the person of Liaquat Khan and a Brahmin foreign minister from Kerala, K. M. Pannikar. But surrounding the ruler's gadi was a very powerful group of Sikh Sardars upon whom Maharaja Bhupinder Singh also relied very heavily for support, a courtly cabal whose members made a strong impression on a young Englishman at court named Dick Bowles:

The power who ran the works machine was the Military Secretary, one of the greatest and most charming men I've ever met. That was Colonel Gujial Singh Dillon, a huge chap of six foot four who'd been trained as a policeman and always accompanied His Highness, organising all state occasions. He looked after me like a father his son, but he had his problems because in court circles you could be in and out of favour in no time. However, he seemed to know who was going to throw the arrows into his back even before they let them fly and he weathered the storms very well. There were lots of other close advisers and friends, among them two very senior and respected ADCs, General Joginder Singh and Colonel Jaswant Singh, who had really grown up with His Highness from childhood and like him were magnificent polo players who had played in the Patiala Tigers in the 1920s, unbeaten with a maximum handicap of forty goals, ten each. They too had weathered many storms and had been in and out of favour many times. Then there was another great man, even more senior, General Chunder Singh, a magnificent Sikh of the old school with a fantastic white beard. Another close associate was Raja Mohinder Singh. All were men of great stature who drank like fishes.

In addition to the 'close circle of intrigue' that often formed itself round a ruler, the court frequently had its minor circles in which the ruler's brothers or his older sons were the central figures. In Patiala Dick Bowles observed that the young Yuvaraj, Yadavendra Singh, made the mistake of 'surrounding himself with weak characters – Captain Mubarak Khan, an alcoholic and a most ghastly person, and a couple of ADCs who were hillbillies from some hill state, but whose sisters were of value to one household or another and who were really a couple of goons'.

After Bhupinder's death in 1938 it was this new circle of courtiers that came to power, with the result that when Sardar H. S. Malik came to Patiala as Dewan on loan from the ICS six years later, he found Maharaja Yadavendra totally isolated from his subjects by those close to him, 'his feudal sardars, who didn't want him to get close to the people'. Of these, 'some were good men but many were thoroughly bad, wicked and corrupt and not interested in anything except making themselves rich. They wanted to get hold of the Maharaja and get him to support them against their occupancy tenants who had been on their land for generations but had not owned it. They were often bad landowners and because they had the state administration behind them the result was a lot of trouble in the villages.'

On becoming Dewan, Malik learned that he too was expected to form his own little group of intriguers, for 'the custom there was that whoever was the Prime Minister at the time had a party of his own in the State. So the moment I arrived in Patiala, I was approached by people to form the Prime Minister's party, to have the Prime Minister more or less intriguing against the Maharaja. I refused. I said, "For me there is no party, there is only the Maharaja and the State, and I have come to serve them both and I am not interested in money, funds or any party."'

Whereas Maharaja Bhupinder Singh had been able to dominate his court by the strength of his personality, his less forceful son was not so successful:

> Despite all the reforms there was still a remnant of feudalism and an illustration of that was when a *Sardarni* and her son came to see me in Simla. When the chaprassi (office bearer) announced that they were there I refused to see her because I couldn't have people saying that I had seen Sardarni so-and-so, but I saw her son and heard his story, which was that he had married the daughter of one of the old generals who was a favourite of the Maharaja. This marriage had failed and the girl had gone back to her family, which was considered a disgrace. So this family had concocted false cases against the young man and he was convicted by the lower courts only to be declared innocent by the high court. Despite this final verdict the Maharaja by personal order had taken away all this man's property and confined him to his village – from which he had now escaped to tell me the whole story. I checked up on this and found that it was a true story, so when I was convinced I went to Chail and told the Maharaja what had happened, adding that I couldn't believe that this had happened after a man had been acquitted by the highest court established by the Maharaja himself. But the Maharaja said, 'No, it's true. I couldn't let this very loyal family down that had been dishonoured so I gave this order.' This was very unlike the Maharaja's usual actions, but he justified it on the grounds of loyalty to some old servants, not realising what injustice had been done.

In an effort to break the power of the landowners and bring about necessary reforms, Sardar Malik encouraged the ruler to get out and meet the tenant farmers of the state:

> The simplest way was to have big public meetings in the villages, where the Maharaja could have direct contact with the village elders and the headmen, because they knew very little about him. It had not been done before and I had to persuade the Maharaja first of all to agree to it. So these village darbars were then organised and they were a great success. Shamianas were put up and all the villagers were allowed in. The Maharaja came and spoke to them in very

simple Punjabi and the people were completely won over by his
personality and by the fact that he could talk to them in this personal
way. It was real personal contact with someone who was almost like
a God to them. But the big landowners didn't like it and the Sardars
were eventually successful, I'm afraid, in persuading the Maharaja
to give up these darbars.

A decade earlier Maharaja Hari Singh had found himself in a similar
situation in Kashmir, where the predominantly Muslim community
was in thrall to a powerful Hindu Dogra minority. Mixed populations
of Hindus and Muslims were a feature of many states and this was
nearly always reflected in a representative administration. Indeed,
harmonious relations between the different religions were a very
characteristic feature of the Indian states – in striking contrast to
British India, where the much vaunted *pax Britannica* was often
marred by outbreaks of inter-communal violence. Kashmir, however, had followed a different course and when John Wakefield's
uncle, Edward Wakefield, went there as Dewan in the early 1930s
he found the leader of the Muslim community organising demon-
strations against the government:

> My uncle Ted supported Sheikh Abdullah and went to the ruler and
> said, 'Look, what harm is there if you have two or three Muslim
> ministers on your council?' So the Maharaja said, 'Well, Ted, if you
> think it's the right thing I'll accept it.' Uncle then went back to Sheikh
> Abdullah and said, 'I've got His Highness to agree, so call off your
> agitation.' It was called off and nothing happened for six months,
> during which uncle found it very difficult to get hold of Hari Singh.
> When eventually he did get hold of him and asked him about the
> ministers the Maharaja said, 'I'm sorry. I can't go against the advice
> of all my pundits and all my relatives and advisers. As Dogras they
> are all against it. They say we are selling the land of our forefathers
> to the Muslims.' So uncle told Hari Singh that he had lost face,
> having given this commitment to Sheikh Abdullah, and that it was
> impossible for him to stay on. He packed up and left next day for
> Abbottabad and never came back to Kashmir.

A state in which the ruler was strong and the nobility weak was
equally open to abuse, which was why Conrad Corfield of the Indian
Political Service was not an admirer of Sir Ganga Singh of Bikaner.
Unlike most of his English contemporaries who had the highest
admiration for the man, Corfield regarded Ganga Singh as 'a real
tyrant who obliterated from power and influence of any kind all the
leading nobles of the state until he was the single ruler. He could

do it because he could always say, "Well, they were intriguing against me, so in the interests of law and order I put them in their place."' Corfield regarded a strong nobility as essential to the stability of a state, an attitude based on his own experience of events in Rewa State, where he was sent in 1933 to act as the Maharaja's 'Adviser': 'I soon found that serious trouble was brewing. The farmers were overtaxed, many of the farm labourers were practically slaves and the nobles, who were the chief landowners, had no security. Each had different reasons for discontent, but all were combining against the maharaja and the pot was obviously ready to boil over.' After arranging for the ringleaders of a planned uprising to be arrested, Corfield attempted to regain the loyalty of the nobles by restoring their rights and the loyalty of the farmers by instituting reforms. However, he found it hard to convince the Maharaja that such reforms were needed: 'We gradually arrived at some compromise – until I pressed the ruler too hard over the nobles' rights. The rules necessary to bring the settlement into effect needed the Maharaja's signature but it wasn't forthcoming, so I wrote to my boss in Delhi and asked if I could pay him a visit. When the reply came I asked the Maharaja for a week's leave. He came round the same evening to my house and we shared a whisky on the verandah as usual. Then as he left he asked me who I was going to stay with. "The Political Secretary in Delhi," I said. "Oh, I see," he said. "I hope you have a nice time." That evening the rules arrived at my house duly signed.'

Under normal circumstances a ruler could expect his kinsmen and his nobles to provide the backbone of the state, not only by giving him their support but also by putting their sons into the administration and the state forces. Every state of consequence had its own militia, whether it was Lunawada State's three platoons of Rajput infantry or Patiala's brigade of 1200 infantrymen, 450 cavalrymen and 200 gunners. These small armies were essentially ceremonial, providing protection for the ruler and carrying out formal duties, but forty-nine of the larger states also supplied additional troops to the British Crown in accordance with their treaty obligations. Paid for and maintained by their ruler, who was also their commander-in-chief, and trained by British Military Advisers, these Indian States Forces were barred from service within their own states. However, they served on the North West Frontier and in both World Wars with great distinction. Richer states like Gwalior, Hyderabad and Kashmir contributed units of division strength, while a small state like Suket maintained 'a company of infantry known as the Lakshman Infantry and a company of Sappers and Miners who saw action in Burma and came back with the largest number of Burma Stars of any state force.'

Besides his nobility, a ruler could also draw upon the many commoners in the state whose families traditionally served the state in various hereditary capacities – from the Muslim shikaris who staffed the *shikarkhanas* in so many states to the Brahmins who even in Muslim states often occupied the posts of learning. In every Hindu state it was these Brahmin priests who provided the teachers, doctors and clerical staff. In Lunawada State, Ambalal Radhakrishna Dave's family had held the posts of court physicians and high priests for almost four centuries: 'My father was invited to come from Central India by the Lunawada Highnesses soon after their dynasty was established, and we served them by watching over the health of the royal family. We had to be very cautious of their health and they rewarded us by giving us a jagir and all the honours that went with it.' As *Dharmadhyaksha* or head of the religious department. A. R. Dave had to supervise the running of the temples, bring in other priests for various important religious functions and manage the fire-sacrifices that the ruler performed. As court physician, he practised the ancient skills of Ayurvedic medicine based on 'leaves, herbs and roots' supplemented occasionally by precious metals:

> From father to son we were taught this art which our forefathers had learned after fifteen or twenty years of study with a guru in the Himalayas or in Benares. We used our own clay vessels and made our own furnaces for melting gold, silver and diamonds which were dissolved in the juices of certain vegetables and distilled. We also used conch shells which were very hard and cannot be dissolved easily, and for that we used juice from a plant called *akda* boiled in a pot over a furnace. One pill called *Hiranya garbha*, made purely from gold, was a miracle drug, but it was very difficult to get that gold melted and reduced to ashes, although our forefathers knew all these things. Even at a death-bed, if it was given with ginger in a spoon it was a very good stimulant and a dying man would at once begin to talk, so it was generally used in cases where people wanted a dying man to say something. In the olden days when people used to hide their treasure and nobody knew where it was, then this drug would work like a miracle. However, what we were best at was feeling pulses. If we went to examine a lady patient from the ruler's harem then what could we do, because they would not come out of purdah? A string would be tied round her pulse and my forefathers would take her pulse from the other end of the string just by feeling it. No one will believe that now. It is all gossip, they say.

In many Hindu kingdoms the Brahmins also occupied the most important executive posts. In Bhavnagar two Nagar Brahmin families supplied all the Dewans from 1845 to 1947, playing a key role in developing Bhavnagar into the richest and one of the most progressive states in Kathiawar. When R. S. Bhatt, whose family was also in Bhavnagar state service as teachers and medical officers, joined the administration in 1940 he worked under the Dewan Sir Prabha Shankar Pattani, who during the long minority of its last ruler had supervised his education and ruled the state as its Administrator:

> That was why the ruler always approached him most respectfully, as if he was approaching his own father and always addressed him as *Bapuji* (honoured father). He would always take his advice and say, 'Bapuji, what shall we do in this?' Then Sir Prabha Shankar would give him sage and objective advice, never exercising power in an arbitrary way. And if the ruler wanted to take any strong action that smacked of revenge or disfavour the Dewan would say, 'That is not in our tradition to do so.' But Sir Prabha Shankar also respected the ruler because he sincerely believed that the ruler had some kind of divine spark in him as the head of the state.

As states modernised their administrations, dewans and councils of ministers became increasingly responsible for decision-making. There were always rulers who for one reason or another were content to leave the running of the state in the hands of a capable dewan – and plenty of dewans who took the opportunity to govern discreetly and effectively in the ruler's name. One such state was Rampur where twenty-four-year-old Nawab Syed Raza Ali Khan 'inherited' his father's strong-minded chief minister when he became Nawab in 1930. Colonel Syed Bashir Hussain Zaidi remained Dewan right up to the time of the merger of the states in 1948.

'There's a nice story of how Rampur was industrialised in my late father's time,' declares Zulfiquar Ali Khan:

> Colonel Zaidi used to tell my father, 'Your Highness, why don't you industrialise Rampur?' And my father would say, 'If you industrialise Rampur you won't get any people to join the state forces, you'll get no more cooks or servants. They'll all go into industry.' Then in 1933 Lord Linlithgow came on a state visit and after dinner my father, the Viceroy and the chief minister were sitting down when Colonel Zaidi turned to the Viceroy and said, 'Your Excellency, you'll be very pleased to know that His Highness is thinking of industrialising Rampur.' Whereupon Lord Linlithgow got up and shook my father's hand and said, 'Your Highness, you're so en-

lightened.' When the Viceroy went, Colonel Zaidi thought he would get the sack but instead my father said, 'Zaidi, when shall we start?' Within three months the Raza Bulund Sugar Factory was started and within a decade Rampur had become one of the biggest industrial centres in the United Provinces.

The annals of every state could supply examples of a strong minister controlling the reins of government either with or without the ruler's consent – and not always to the state's benefit. Jaisalmer was one state where ancient intrigues and power struggles continued to weaken the ruling house right up to modern times. One solution was to bring in an outsider, which was why M. M. Sapat's family went from Kutch to Jaisalmer at the beginning of this century: first his uncle – who was ousted by enemies at court – and then his father in 1911: 'Because of all the palace intrigues some code was arranged and a telegram came to my father telling him that he was to come on such-and-such a date. The dewan who had replaced my uncle was then given leave and a message was sent to him saying, "Don't come back."'

The capital of Jaisalmer was a hundred miles from the railhead and 'a world by itself in those days, where you went back two to three hundred years in time. We had to go on camel-back from the railhead. The ladies went in shigrams, two-wheeled landau things pulled by bullocks, but we thought it beneath us to ride in a shigram so we rode with someone on camel-back. As my father was there for a quarter of a century, I must have done thousands of miles on camel-back, going out of the state twice a year for schooling because there was no high school in Jaisalmer.' Because it was 'traditional that the sons of those serving in the states were also employed by the state', M.M. Sapat followed his father into the Jaisalmer administration but came to the attention of the Maharaja of Bikaner in Mount Abu:

My father was sitting having a drink in the lounge of his hotel when His Highness came and saw him and said, 'Dewansaheb, when did you come?' Then he looked at me and said, 'Is this your young hopeful? What is he doing?' My father explained that he was training me and His Highness said, 'A father can never train his son. You send him to Bikaner. I'd like to give him training.' So that's how I went to Bikaner, where I was given proper training in a course that lasted eighteen months – so many months as a receipt and despatch clerk, so many months as a record clerk, noting clerk and so on – but His Highness always used to enquire how I was getting on.

The practice of sending promising juniors for training to Bhavnagar, Mysore or other states known to have first-rate administrations, became common in the twenties and thirties – 'a fine training for any administration service man, because you learned to do things quickly without getting confused and you learned to take immediate decisions'. Another innovation that became increasingly widespread as administration grew more professional was the importation of well-trained and experienced administrators from outside the state as dewans, most notably Brahmins from Madras and South India – a practice that led King-Emperor George VI to ask Conrad Corfield 'why it was that the Indian rulers were continually exchanging divans. A sudden vision of furniture removal was quickly replaced in my mind by the realisation that he was referring to chief ministers and I explained the difficulty the princes had in finding local talent to fill the highest posts.'

It was just such a difficulty that, after two decades of service in Bikaner, brought M.M. Sapat back to his home state of Kutch where a crisis was threatening the future of the elderly Maharao Khengarji II, grandfather of the present Maharao:

His Highness the Maharao was the maternal uncle of His Highness of Bikaner and he had incurred the displeasure of the British authorities without really doing anything wrong. He would not agree to join the Customs Union, because we could then get things in Kutch directly from outside without having to pay British duty. This meant that we could get things very much cheaper – petrol at six annas a gallon, a bagful of sugar for eight or ten rupees – and so the standard of living was very much higher than it was in British India. The other thing was that he used to take his time in replying to correspondence, which the Resident thought was discourteous. But it had got to the stage where the Viceroy was considering divesting him of his powers. Now His Highness of Bikaner took that very seriously since his *Mamasaheb* (maternal uncle) was a very great personality and a doyen among the princes and he wrote a very strong letter to the Viceroy saying that this would be a dishonour to the princely order. So a British Dewan was appointed and His Highness of Kutch asked if, since a Britisher was coming, Bikaner could give him a trustworthy man as private secretary.

Sapat was ordered to leave for Kutch within twenty-four hours: 'But His Highness of Bikaner used to believe in *mahurats* (auspicious days) so he called the Master of Ceremonies and said, "Find a mahurat for Sapat to go to Kutch. When should he go?" When I got home I told my wife with a very sad face that we were leaving for Kutch, but I rang the Master of Ceremonies whom I knew and said, "For God's sake, find a time a few days ahead from now." He replied. "After four days there is a good mahurat." So after four days I was shunted to Kutch, where I became *Huzur* Assistant to the Maharao and Secretary to the Executive Council.'

In addition to the many Indians from other states or from British India who took service with a prince, in nearly all the larger states there was a sprinkling of Europeans who worked in a variety of capacities from dewans to nannies and chauffeurs. Dick Bowles' father came to work for Bhupinder Singh before the First World War more or less by accident:

> He was building this road or railway in the Punjab and one evening he meandered away from his camp over a rise and across a *nullah* (dry river-bed) or two and was taken up by two chaps who said he was trespassing in Patiala State. They took him to the Maharaja's camp, because he was out on a shoot himself. My father was waltzed up in front of the Maharaja and from that moment they made friends. Bhupinder Singh asked my father to join him as State Engineer and that's how it stuck for 25 to 30 years.

After an early childhood of 'total luxury' in Patiala, Dick Bowles was sent to England for his education, returning at sixteen with a large consignment of rare game birds from France that had been reared for the Maharaja's game reserves. Back in Patiala he 'drifted into palace living until one day His Highness said, "Dick, I think I'd better make you one of my ADCs."' In keeping with the 'normal leisurely existence of princely India', his duties were not onerous: 'After breakfast we would look to see who was on the guest list and what visitors were coming. We had to check the guards stationed round the palace at various strategic points and entertain the guests to lunch. I never got involved in the circle of political intrigue. I was quite happy to dart about and entertain guests and take them out riding.' There were always numerous European visitors to be looked after – 'people passing through who were selling things or making things and wanting to make money out of the ruler somehow or other'. Among them was 'a very nice chap with ginger hair from Rankins the tailors of Lahore, who would drive up with his car and driver and samples of the latest cloths. His Highness would order a dozen of this and a dozen of that and a hundred shirts of this, that and the other, and if one or two chaps happened to be standing around at the time he'd say, "You'd better have a couple of suits," or "You'd better have three or four."'

There was also quite a number of other Europeans drawing state salaries:

There was always a British officer seconded to the state forces to make sure they were trained and equipped properly. One was Oz Lovett, a 2nd Gurkha who ran the state forces for a couple of years. There was Dr Fox, His Highness's personal physician. There were the guardians of his children. There was Laurence Tarrant, the son of the Australian cricketer, who looked after the Patiala princes at Aitchison's College in Lahore. Then Frank Tarrant used to emerge and there were always one or two cricketers whom he used to bring out from England to coach during the winter. There was an Australian who used to play for Worcester who was a great chum of mine. Harold Larwood came out once and put the fear of God into Christ knows how many people with his fast bowling. So we had a very formidable cricket side in Patiala. There was a house opposite the polo ground where the younger babies of the Maharaja lived and the nannies there were usually Anglo-Indians. There was Sister Steele, a vast, buxom and formidable lady who lived in the guest house. There was Captain Muir, a World War I fighter pilot who ran His Highness's private aircraft. He had a British engineer, Jameson, and a radio operator, Furness, and these three chaps used to sit around waiting for a take-off that very seldom came, but they had a wonderful life riding, playing tennis, drinking and making merry. Then there was a chap who ran what was called the motor house, with a vast fleet of exquisite and expensive cars, a highly-competent Rolls-Royce-trained engineer called Tweenie who was a teetotaller and drank tea the whole time. The kitchens were in the charge of a most marvellous Spaniard called Frankie Campos, who was responsible for the palace kitchens and arranged all the food whenever we went out on shoots. He was a very amusing, hot-tempered man who stood no nonsense from anybody but would throw tantrums and burst into tears. There was also a most sinister German called Paoli, one of those Germans with rimless spectacles and cropped hair. He had a lovely little house overlooking the Rajindra Gymkhana Club. He was the state photographer and took photographs of the families inside the palace – but you couldn't get very close to him.

Another foreigner who came to work in Patiala – not in Bhupinder Singh's time but a decade later under his successor, Yadavendra Singh – was the teacher Hede Dayal. Her first problem was getting her employer's attention:

I was put into the state guest house, days passed and there I sat. I don't think that it had registered with Her Highness that I had arrived. Then a couple who befriended me took me to the Club. We were sitting there when in charged an ADC who looked round and disappeared and then came back with His Highness. He then sat down and people whom he wanted to talk to were called to his table – and what struck me was how unnatural everybody became on seeing His Highness. I thought what a ghastly situation for this man, never meeting anyone who was being natural or who could be a friend. But he must have asked who this lady was, because he was not the sort who let things hang – unlike his father. 'Why do you bother?' people would say to me. 'When Bhupinder called people for an interview they raised whole families in the guest house before they were summoned.'

Having established herself with the Maharani, Mrs Dayal was then introduced to the four young children whom she was to teach:

The great figure in their lives was Sister Welsh, an Anglo-Indian nurse who had brought them up. She was a very strong personality and had a strict routine for the children, but she also encouraged this 'superiority' business quite a lot. She said, 'One must call the heir-apparent Yuvaraj-Saheb' and when we called him 'Yuvi' she didn't like that. Then Sister Welsh was always comparing the two girls to Princess Elizabeth and Princess Margaret, so Hem, the eldest girl, was quite the princess and would create such a shindig if something was not the way she wanted it. She and Yuvi would fight like hell and he would say, 'When I'm Maharaja the first thing I'll do is to put you in jail.' But I never had any trouble teaching them, because I had a lot of experience and I was very firm, although I remember once after some upheaval they didn't want any lessons and Hem just sat down and said, 'Well, all you have got is my body.' To which I said, 'Your body will do for the time being. You just sit.' But I went there thinking I'd be there for a year – and then I got caught up with the many people who were stuck there.

Only on very rare occasions was a British Political Officer or a member of the ICS sent on loan to work for an Indian prince, usually as an Administrator in a state where the ruler was still a minor. But there were some instances where a ruler agreed – or had his arm twisted by the Political Department – to accept a British official, either as Dewan or as an 'Adviser', and in such cases he worked – officially, at least – as a state employee drawing local rates of pay and not as a gazetted officer of the British Raj. When Cyril Hancock was ordered to go to Bharatpur State as Dewan, he was summoned by the Resident for Rajputana, Sir George Ogilvie, and advised that 'primarily I would be a servant of the Bharatpur State and that if at any time the interests of the Bharatpur State and the Government of India conflicted I was to make it my business to protect the interests of Bharatpur State'.

Bharatpur was then under minority administration. The parents of the new ruler, the present Maharaja Brijendra Singh, were both dead, having reduced the state to a condition of bankruptcy. The boy Maharaja and his three brothers were away in England, being educated under the guardianship of a retired ICS officer, leaving two sisters in their teens in purdah in Bharatpur. In the absence of the Maharaja, Hancock soon found himself with 'a hot potato to deal with' in the person of the elder princess, who refused to marry the man whom her parents had chosen for her while she was still an infant:

> Accordingly I arranged a meeting with the Bibiji Saheba in the palace where I breezed in and said good morning as if we were old friends. I don't think she had met another European before, although she had seen them through the dark glasses of her motor cars, and she kept her sari over her face. I said, 'We have been considering in council what to do about your dislike of the young man you are supposed to be marrying. We are not going to attempt in any way to force you to marry him, but we must ask you to realise that one of the duties of the council is to uphold the good name of the Bharatpur State. So I hope you will tell me that you agree to marry a young man of your own choice.' She was a sensible girl and agreed, so then we sent off messengers to the United Provinces to look for big zamindars with suitable sons and with a good family history. About once a fortnight I took photographs of the candidates and their family history to the Bibiji Saheba and each time I said, 'This is the next one.' The Bibiji Saheba realised that we were trying to do our best for her and eventually we found someone whom she said she would marry.

For the next six years Hancock more or less ran the state, with the assistance of four carefully chosen Members of Council backed by a small secretariat. There was a period of reconstruction with 'strict economy as the order of the day in every department', but with the help of a succession of good monsoons the state's finances rapidly improved to the point where they were able to rebuild roads and public buildings, restore the vast irrigation system upon which the prosperity of the state depended and even revive the famous Ghana duck shoot. 'It was not a brute form of treading over the rights of others and crushing them,' recalls Brijendra Singh, a local Jat who worked under Hancock during this period. 'Major Hancock and the other Europeans who came to Bharatpur were very sympathetic. They tried to solve the difficulties and they applied their imagination. I can remember how Major Hancock would go out on a horse every morning. He would trot and gallop about ten miles and inspect practically every plant by the roadside to see whether it had grown or withered away, and if it had he would have it replaced. The result was that all the roads in Bharatpur had the most beautiful plantations on both sides.'

13
RAJAS AND THE RAJ

(i) The first duty of a Political Officer is to cultivate direct, friendly, personal relations with the Ruling Princes and Chiefs with whom he works.

(vi) He should leave well alone; the best work of a Political Officer is very often what has been left undone.

Notes from the *Manual of Instructions to Officers of the Foreign and Political Department*, 1924

Princely India and British India were two different worlds indirectly bound together by treaties and *sanads* between gadi and crown. The difference between them was that paramountcy allowed the one to intrude upon the other. The British took the view that they were the superior partners in an unequal relationship that left the princes suffering from 'a sense of inferiority that was innate in the whole principle of paramountcy'. The Indian princes, however, saw it rather differently: 'They knew that in order to exist as they were they needed the British. And yet every ruler, major or minor, who was proud of his lineage and his past and the fact that he still ruled a kingdom, did not like his business of state being pried into by outsiders. He could identify closely with the house of Saxe-Coburg and Gotha which ruled England, but he looked down on the minor British functionaries that he was loaded with.' This ambivalent attitude towards the British was widely shared: 'There was no individual hatred or bitterness and there was a lot of affection – but nobody likes to be second to someone else, so there was animosity towards the institution of British sovereign rule over India.' Many rulers took the same view as the Maharaja of Dewas Junior, who regarded the British as a 'necessary evil for India in the times in which we were living. They had done a lot of good for the country, brought in a lot of know-how and education, done away with a lot of practices like *sati*, and more reforms were coming into existence.' But at the same time 'daddy firmly believed in Indian independence, that the British had no right to interfere in what he believed or what we practised. So his relationships with the British were very friendly on the whole but he had one or two tough tussles with them.'

A ruler's direct dealings with the British Raj were limited and many were content to keep it that way, but official visits by senior representatives of the British Crown could not be ignored. There were Viceroys and Governors who looked upon the states as 'playgrounds where they could get a nice free holiday with some good shooting' and there were rulers who used these visits for window-dressing. Ever anxious to create a good impression, they not only displayed hospitality on the most lavish scale but also drew up programmes of civil receptions, banquets, garden parties, official opening ceremonies, parades and march-pasts, tours of local antiquities, polo matches and shikar parties that left little time for the visitor to observe the true conditions that existed in the state – 'indeed, in one state so many foundation stones were laid by visiting Viceroys and Governors without any subsequent foundations being built that the ruler was advised by one cynical political officer to collect them up and use them to pave his palace compound.' Never one to do things by halves, the father of the present ruler of Bharatpur saw every official visit as an opportunity to refurbish or rebuild his guest houses, buy new cars and re-equip his state forces with costly new uniforms. The entertaining alone on one two-day state visit was estimated to have cost him two lakhs of rupees (£15,000).

Even the most fleeting of visits by a passing Resident or Agent to the Governor-General could cause total disruption to the smooth running of the state and provoke a flurry of road-building and cleaning up. In the 1930s the ruler of one of the small Simla hill states had to ask the Political Department to limit the Resident's proposed week's fishing holiday to three days, since the state's finances had not yet recovered from an earlier visit made two years before which had cost the state 1200 rupees (£ 100). Shashi Wallia remembers the preparations leading up to the ball given by her father to honour the local AGG in 1931:

Hectic preparations had been going on for months beforehand. The palace had been white-washed and painted, there were new curtains and the carpets were refurbished. My villa and my brother's villa had been given up to the AGG and his Political Agent so that they could rest in the afternoon. Then around eight o'clock they all started to arrive in their various carriages and, of course, daddy was there in his spotless white angarkha and churidars edged with the gold and red of the state colours and wearing his red pugri but no jewellery or orders other than his KCIE star and sash. My mother was not present because she was in purdah, but there were some rather emancipated high-born Muslim ladies from Bhopal who had been abroad. The guests were made up of the AGG and his various

secretaries and their wives and a number of visitors from as far afield
as Agra and Delhi who had come for the shooting. There was dancing
to an orchestra that was hidden in a side room behind a bank of
flowers, and from time to time one of these ladies would come up to
my father and say, 'Would Your Highness like to join us in the
dance?' But he would say, 'I'd rather watch.' Champagne and various
wines flowed but he personally never drank. There was a complete
English buffet with various game laid out and another table of *Mughlai*
(Mughal) dishes for the Muslims. The only thing he drew the line
at was serving beef.

Some rulers went to great lengths to satisfy the tastes and predilec-
tions of their more important guests. The forceful Lady Willingdon,
whose husband was Viceroy from 1931 to 1936, was known to have
a great attachment to the colour mauve, so mauve flowers were
always presented to her and used to decorate her suites and a
number of princes even wore purple achkans and turbans to please
her. One such attempt backfired during a visit by the Willingdons
to Baroda, when the Maharaja had the state saloon decorated in
various shades of mauve and lilac: 'The only snag was that they
could not find any lavender toilet paper, so the railway authorities
dyed white toilet paper purple. Later Lady Willingdon complained
about it to His Highness and said, "Everything is marvellous in your
saloon, but there is something wrong with your toilet paper because
I am purple all over."' A rather similar mishap had befallen Queen
Mary two decades earlier during her visit to Gwalior, when a
newly-installed marble bath of enormous dimensions sank into the
bathroom floor just as she was about to step into it. It was whispered
that during this same royal tour another Central Indian state had
been unable to get a newly-delivered flush cistern to work. Instead
two lowly sweepers were posted in the ceiling, one with a bucket of
water, the other to observe proceedings in the room below through
a small aperture. When the royal personage was seen to pull the
chain, the signal was given and the water was poured down through
the cistern.

Queen Mary's enthusiasm for collecting beautiful objects placed
her princely hosts in an awkward dilemma. 'We used to hide all the
nice things when Queen Mary came. She would say "Oh, Your
Highness, isn't this lovely! May I take it home and ask someone to
find another like it?" – but it never came back.' Lady Willingdon used
the same technique: 'Maharaja Sadul Singh was always showing us
the pair to something that had been taken or half a toilet set that
was left after the Willingdons had been to Bikaner.'

While doing his best to please a royal guest or an important visitor, every ruler remained very conscious of his own dignity as a sovereign – none more so than the Nizam of Hyderabad. 'He had a chip on his shoulder and rightly so I think,' asserts V. K. Reddy, whose family was closely linked to the Nizam:

> When you are controlling a country the size of France with a population of fifteen million and you are the richest man in the world – then who the hell is the Viceroy? The Nizam didn't need anything from the British and as a 'faithful ally' of the British government he believed he should deal direct with the king. There was a British Resident in Hyderabad who represented the British, but he was so rude to the Residents that they very rarely saw him except on occasions like the Nizam's birthday or the king's, so there were always very strained relations dating right back to his father's time.

Another royal house with an even greater reputation for hostility towards the British was that of the Holkars of Indore, who after a period of 'decline and decrepitude' following their destruction as a military power by the British, began to display a truculence that set them apart from the other princes. 'None of our family has been very fond of the British – except me,' declares Richard Shivaji Rao Holkar. 'My great-grandfather Shivaji Rao was not fond of them at all. He was a keen wrestler who loved to call people off the streets to come into the old city palace to wrestle with him and in 1903 he beat up the British Resident. They said, "This will never do, so out you go", and he had to abdicate in favour of my grandfather Tukoji Rao III. He proved to be rather a good ruler – until he fell foul of the British over the Bawla case.' Although not directly implicated in this affair, in which a member of his police department shot and killed a Bombay businessman who had formed a relationship with the Maharaja's former mistress, Tukoji Rao was also forced to step down. 'He was given a choice of an enquiry or relinquishing the throne. They could have forced him to abdicate in any case, so my father came to the gadi as a minor with a British Administrator. He was educated in England and he hated it with a passion. He was a very democratic and personal ruler and the British were the opposite, while his responsibilities tied him to a position in which he could do nothing.'

Other rulers may have been more cautious than the Holkars, but all were conscious that their treaty relations were with the British Crown and not with the British Raj. When the young Mayurdhwaj Singhji of Dhrangadhara – 'I was quite rebellious, I frankly admit' – was offered a KCIE soon after his accession, he wrote back saying that 'he would be honoured to accept the KCIE if the King-Emperor would accept the Shaktimat Order of Dhrangadhara'. In somewhat similar vein, Jay Singh of Alwar – who regarded himself as a reincarnation of the god Rama and on public occasions wore a hat which he claimed was similar to that worn by this ancestor – once addressed a group of British Members of Parliament in Sanskrit, but was later heard speaking perfect English. When challenged, he replied that when the British came to India they addressed meetings in English, 'So when I come to England, I speak Sanscrit.' Other princes were just as conscious of their dignity. Sardar Malik recalls a story told him by a British Deputy Commissioner about Maharaja Bhupinder Singh of Patiala:

> Barry was in charge of a sub-division which lay between two parts of Patiala State. On one occasion the Maharaja had to pass through this British territory and so Barry met him at the border on horseback, the idea being that he would stay with him while he rode through his sub-division. As they started to ride together Barry rode alongside the Maharaja. Then the Maharaja signalled to him to get behind. 'I knew he had no business to do that because I was representing the King and had every right to ride alongside of him,' Barry told me. 'However, his personality was such that I didn't like to upset him, so I rode behind.'

Royal ladies, too, had their pride. Nirmala Bhonsle remembers an occasion when she accompanied her grandmother, Maharani Chimnabai of Baroda, to pay a call on Lady Willingdon in Delhi in 1934:

> There were my mother and grandmother sitting in the back seat of my grandfather's Rolls-Royce, I on the jump seat. The car stopped at the entrance to Viceregal Lodge and the ADC came and opened the door, but my grandmother said, 'Don't get down. Keep sitting.' We didn't understand, but we sat quietly while she said to the ADC, 'Where is Lady Willingdon?' She kept asking, 'Where is Lady Willingdon?' until he went into the house and out Lady Willingdon came. Then she said, 'Now you can get down.'

Nevertheless, not all British officials were prepared to concede their authority on what they also regarded as due recognition of their own status as Crown representatives. When Conrad Corfield, one of the more forceful politicals of the 1930s and 1940s, had a confrontation with Bhupinder Singh's successor it was the latter who was forced to give way:

I remember going to see Maharaja Yadavendra Singh and when I arrived I was shown into the drawing room – but no ruler. I waited for a quarter of an hour and then I thought, 'Well, this isn't good enough. He's trying it on.' So I said to the ADC, 'I've heard from His Highness that the garden is much improved recently. I'll just go and see it.' The ADC said, 'Oh no, sir. He'll be here any minute.' But I said, 'No, I'd like to go'. So I went and walked away from the house as far as I could on what was a very hot morning, and I'd gone at least half a mile before His Highness came running up, pouring with perspiration and saying he was very sorry. The next time I arrived, there he was standing at the bottom of the steps ready to greet me.

As well as defending their status, rulers like Lalit Sen's father, the Raja of Suket, were very wary of what they regarded as infringements of their sovereign rights:

My father was a very upright, very proud person and very correct in his relationships with the British, but he was very touchy about the slightest interference in the affairs of his state. I remember his telling me about a Colonel Somebody, the Resident in Lahore, and how irked he was by the mere fact that this Resident wanted to meet some of his officials without his permission. He said, 'If this is how our treaty relationships are going to go then I'll leave', – and he left the state and didn't come back until the Viceroy had asked the Resident to go.

No form of interference upset the rulers more than the Paramount Power's insistence on having the last word when it came to recognising a ruler's successor. From the British point of view there were good grounds for refusing to recognise a ruler's right to make his own choice: 'The reason why the Viceroy took it upon himself to exercise control was that many successions were disputed, particularly where a ruler had died without issue or had taken unto himself more than one wife. So all successions had to be accepted by the Paramount Power and in ninety-nine cases out of a hundred where the succession was straightforward, the confirmation was automatic and no interference was exercised.' Official recognition of a new ruler required that a letter of authority from the Viceroy known as a kharita be presented by his representative in person at a formal Kharita Darbar: 'The whole thing was codified. Everybody knew where they stood. All that was laid down in the book and it was followed down to the last "T". The political agent who had this kharita would hand it over to the ruler and say, "Now there you are, Your Highness", or words to that effect.'

This formal recognition may have been resented but rarely was it resisted, although nineteen-year-old Maharaja Mayurdhwaj Singhji made every effort to do so when he succeeded his father in 1942:

> They wanted a ceremonial but I didn't particularly enjoy having a foreigner tell me whether I had succeeded or not, so I had the British informed that as we were in mourning there would be no ceremonial as such, but that I would receive the Resident in the drawing room. They came dressed in their Political Department uniforms with the spiked hats and everything, but I was dressed very simply and so were all the courtiers present.

The presentation of the Viceroy's kharita itself took place when the Maharaja of Dhrangadhara came of age a year later but here, too, he was able to lessen the sting by combining the presentation with his own Dassera darbar. 'My father took the view that he was already the king and that the British were merely coming to acknowledge the fact,' explains his son, Bapa Dhrangadhara. 'During the darbar my father and the Resident sat on two chairs which the Resident expected to be side by side, but my father said, "I'm terribly sorry but I'm the anointed king and he cannot be on a par with me. He may have the first seat on my right above all my nobles but one step below." Everyone said, "My God, they'll depose you tomorrow." But the Resident sat one step below and was quite happy.' The Resident could have insisted on his rights but 'he was a very sweet man, Colonel Gaisford, he agreed with this and that's how it happened.'

The task of maintaining relations between the crown representative in India and the princes rested with a small group of officers who belonged to what was known for many years as the Foreign and Political Department of the Government of India, but latterly became the Indian Political Service. 'It was an exceptionally small department, although its responsibilities were great,' states one of its members, John Cotton. 'At the time of Independence there were no more than 130 officers in the whole service, which included officers working in the Persian Gulf and on the North-West Frontier.' Made up of officers drawn from the Indian Army and the Indian Civil Service, the IPS was essentially the Government of India's diplomatic service, whose members took their orders directly from the Viceroy's Political Department. There were various grades in the service headed by the Residents, formerly known as Agents to the Governor-General:

There were the First-Class Residents responsible for single states such as Hyderabad, Mysore, Gwalior, Baroda and Kashmir and the Second-Class Residents who generally looked after groups of several states. In some of the larger groups the Resident could not himself supervise the day-to-day work and in such cases he had subordinate to him what were known as Political Agents. There were three in the Residency for Central India, two in the Kathiawar States, two in the Eastern States and one in the Punjab States who looked after relations with a number of very small states known as the Simla Hill States. The Resident would also have junior political officers in the capacity of Secretaries and Under Secretaries and even Assistant Political Agents. In the case of Rajputana, where the Resident was equal in status to the Resident in Hyderabad, the states of Udaipur, Jaipur and Jodhpur were considered so important that they also had their own Residencies where the Political Agents had the honorary title of Resident.

The Residencies in which the Residents and their staff lived were often palatial structures, provided in many cases by the rulers themselves. None was more imposing – as indeed it was intended to be – than the Residency built at Hyderabad in 1803, a vast Palladian villa with a classical pillared façade surmounting a broad flight of steps that 'compared favourably with the grander Governor's house in the Indian Provinces'. Over the years it was enlarged and beautified by successive occupants until it became one of the outstanding official residences of India. Like a ruler's palace, it had its own great Durbar Hall for the reception of the Nizam and its grounds were enclosed within a defensive wall complete with ramparts. Within this large compound there were barracks for a company of Indian Army troops, who provided the Resident with a ceremonial escort, and a number of large bungalows for the Residency staff as well as offices. A hot weather residence was also provided by the Nizam not far away at the British military cantonment of Secunderabad, where the Resident passed the summer months.

Another more Indian but very 'gracious' Residency was at Jaipur, where Conrad Corfield served for a period in 1938 – 'originally a Queen-Mother's garden retreat enclosed by a rectangle of 15-foot-high walls festooned with pink and white pelargonium', where 'generations of British Residents had created a garden so English that when I first drove through the gateway I gasped with amazement'. The main building itself was an old Mughal pavilion surmounted by three domes with lesser cupolas at the corners, 'under which one could sit to catch the evening breeze'. The garden and pavilion were said to be haunted by a *fakir* who 'took his life when the sacred tree under which he used to sit was cut down to complete the walls. Echoing steps were heard and bells rang when there was no one there to ring them.'

The Residency at Rajkot was a more down-to-earth establishment, built on a few square miles of British territory in the middle of the Kathiawar princely states. This was where Cyril Hancock, following the footsteps of his father and grandfather before him into the Bombay Political Service, first learned his trade under a succession of Residents. He also came to realise very speedily the truth behind the old adage much quoted in Indian political circles that 'the whisper of the Residency is the thunder of the Durbar':

> One lunch-time shortly after I reached Rajkot in 1920 this very attractive young Indian woman presented herself at my bungalow saying, 'Sahib, I wish to take service with you.' She must have been sent to me by one or other of the disputing states who thought that if they could get a young woman like this employed by me I could be blackmailed sufficiently to decide or propose in their favour. I therefore invited my servants to get rid of her as quickly as possible. I then began to realise that every moment of my day was known, my every kind of pursuit and my every like and dislike.

Every state in the Agency had its own *vakil* or agent accredited to the Rajkot Residency: 'These vakils were nothing more than information-gathering sources of their rulers and this was accepted. We knew about it and they knew that we knew. We also knew that all rulers worth their salt wouldn't be overscrupulous in suborning a junior staff member of the Residency secretariat in order to get the lowdown on what was going on – not only on matters affecting his own state, but possibly affecting other states, because they were all jealous of each other.'

One of the most romantically placed British Residencies was a converted seventeenth-century palace in Udaipur, where Vere Ogilvie came to join her father as a seventeen-year-old in 1926:

> I could hardly have had a more glamorous beginning to life in India, because apart from a few cars there couldn't have been any change in the way of life there for the last several hundred years – but what I really wanted to do was to get onto the back of a horse. Through the good offices of the vakil my desire for a horse was immediately made known to the ruler, and from the palace stables there came several beautiful mounts for me to choose from. So my early days were spent mostly riding with the vakil and my father along the side of one of these lakes on what was known as the bund.

At that time there were very few Europeans living in the state: 'For most of the year we were the only white people in Udaipur, although for part of the time there was an Indian Medical Service doctor and his wife and also a splendid pair of Scottish missionaries who were a source of amusement to my father and mother, I'm afraid, because they had only made one convert in thirty years in Udaipur. It was rather like sending a Hindu mission to the Vatican.' Another feature of Residency life in Udaipur was the thrice-weekly tennis parties:

This was a very useful way of entertaining, because although they were not able to take meals with us because of their caste a lot of the nobles were keen tennis-players. They would arrive very often on their horses with their courtiers behind them and dressed in full Rajput pleated skirts with a sword on one side. The swords would be laid down and a tennis racquet taken up, the long pleated skirts would be tucked into the waistband of their trousers and they would go onto the tennis court and play a very good game.

Rajput women were conspicuously absent on all such occasions and Vere Ogilvie soon learned that 'it was not the done thing to say to a man, "How is your wife?" His wife was a private matter and he was not prepared to talk about her.' But in time she and her mother did get to visit the wives of courtiers and lesser nobles, who turned out to be 'delightfully humorous women, all with a chuckling sense of humour and immensely curious about myself and the sort of clothes I wore – but of course at seventeen I was not aware that they were virtually prisoners and the sadness of it all.'

Her father's duties as a Resident allowed him to tour the state and to pay visits on the lesser estates whose chiefs were vassals of the Maharana:

The first estate we went to was a place called Koraba. We entered on horseback with the Rao of Korabad riding a bay charger with a brilliant red velvet cloth beside my father and behind us came a whole group of mounted attendants and officials. 'God Save the King' was played very badly and guns were fired and we pitched our three tents in an open space near the village. After lunch the Rao paid a formal call on my father dressed in a pink satin outfit, and then in the evening we went through the narrow main street of the village to the palace riding on a brilliantly decorated elephant, and as the houses on either side were lower than the elephant we had a good view of the roofs. The palace took the usual form of a half-ruined fortress and was picturesque without being imposing. We went up some tortuous stairs to a large brightly painted room which was quite bare except for being carpeted by a dust sheet, although the walls were lined with hideous mid-Victorian coloured prints and engravings interspersed with portraits of the Maharana, Queen Alexandra and others. Then from the windows we watched an acrobatic performance put on in our honour. We had been told that our dinner was to consist of a banquet up at the palace, so we had put on suitable evening dress, but the extraordinary thing was that the banquet took place in a small ante-room and with the exception of one course consisted of our own food cooked and served by our own servants. We also dined alone. This was their way of entertaining without offending either us or their own caste regulations and it all went off very well.

The fact that Vere Ogilvie was able to observe the workings of a 'feudal but purely benevolent autocracy' at close quarters was due very largely to the excellent rapport that her father was able to build not only with the Maharana but also with other rulers. Such skills lay at the heart of the Political Officer's job even though his official duty, as Cyril Hancock saw it, was to 'interpret the wishes of the Government of India'. To help him the Political Agent had the manual issued to all political officers with its famous dictum about leaving well alone, as well as the restricted five volumes of Tupper's *Political Practice*, which contained summaries of 'all the more complicated and confidential decisions in the past affecting disputes between the princes and the paramount power'. Tod's *Annals of Rajasthan* also had an honoured place on the Political Agent's bookshelf. Maharawal Lakshman Singhji of Dungarpur remembers George Ogilvie saying to him that, 'for political officers Tod's *Annals* is what the *Gita* is to you. It's the political officer's bible. No political officer can come up to me and say he hasn't read Tod's *Annals of Rajasthan*. If he does, I tell him, "You fool, go and read it and then come back to me."'

It was not part of the Political Agent's job to actively interfere in the internal affairs of a state. Indeed, in the great majority of states there was 'no need for a political agent ever to be objectionable. When the state was well ruled, where the ruler always lived there and was in touch with the people, then the Resident just kept in touch and made himself friendly and did what he could to help.'

Even where there was a good case for intervention, a Resident often felt constrained from taking action by the cherished principle that 'Indian princes should be all-powerful within their dominions' – a concept that many political officers regarded as giving a ruler too much license to do as he wished:

The role of political officer was never properly understood. Even among the other British in India, the prevalent idea was that the political officer spent his time interfering in the internal affairs of whatever Indian state he happened to be accredited to. But the degree of interference was minimal. There were, of course, occasions when interference was called for – cases of gross misrule, mismanagement or injustice on the part of the ruler, in which case the powers of paramountcy would be invoked by the Viceroy through his political officers. The most extreme form of interference would be the deposition of a ruler. There were several such cases that acquired notoriety, but they were so rare that when they did occur, as in the case of the deposition of the Maharaja of Alwar in the thirties, people conceived the idea that such depositions were much more frequent than they actually were.

But deposition was not the only way in which the Paramount Power could influence the affairs of a princely state: 'Where misrule was less serious the crown representative might insist that the offending ruler should accept the services of the British officer who specialised in finance, say, or revenue or something of that sort.' It was just such a case of mismanagement of his state by the Maharaja of Rewa, who 'looked upon the state as his own – *L'Etat c'est Moi* – and would not separate his privy purse from his state expenditure', that brought Conrad Corfield to Rewa in 1934 as his 'Adviser', where he worked 'behind the purdah' to influence the ruler: 'You had to work entirely behind the scenes, so you had to have the ability to influence rather than the ability to direct. I can remember having an argument with the Maharaja who wished a certain line of action to be taken. I eventually persuaded him that it would be safer to follow my plan, because if it went well then he would get the credit for it and if it went wrong he could always say it was my fault.'

However, the Political Agent could not afford to antagonise the ruler:

If you got up against a ruler by interfering in the wrong way or at the wrong time, then the next time the Viceroy visited these parts and the ruler paid his respects he would say, 'Well, of course, we are very happy, but actually I'm not getting on very well with my Resident.' Of course, if they were objected to by the ruler they were probably transferred somewhere else. There were cases where political agents found out something that really needed remedying but didn't get the support – and there were a number, I'm afraid, who would otherwise have taken necessary action but thought, 'This is only going to interfere with my career. I'd much better be kind to the ruler.'

Much depended on the existence of goodwill on both sides. Political officers who displayed an 'unbending attitude which verged on pomposity and arrogance' – as some did – rarely went down well. Conrad Corfield knew one such officer, who was a predecessor of his as Resident in the Punjab States:

> When he decided to pay a state visit to Patiala, he made approaches beforehand to the Maharaja to make quite sure that the right salutes would be fired. When he arrived at the station he got out of his saloon to inspect the guard of honour and the gun salutes started. But the Maharaja, who liked a joke, had only allowed them to use a quarter of the gunpowder, so that they all went off with a sort of derisive poop – which was worse than not having anything at all. He tried to get the Maharaja criticised by His Excellency the Viceroy, but everybody thought it was so funny that they decided that they wouldn't say anything to the Maharaja.

For the most part the political officer was accepted as 'a human being doing a difficult job' and his relationship with the ruler was usually one of 'extreme friendliness, cordiality and good humour'. Many rulers, like the Maharawal of Dungarpur, looked upon the Political Department not as an intruder but as 'a friend, guide and bulwark' whose officers had 'the utmost respect for the princes and saw to it that they were given due respect. There may have been black sheep among them but on the whole they were sincere, honest and devoted to their job, and whatever advice they tendered to the princes was, I think, more often than not to their best interests.' Even when the Political Department acted in a 'high-handed' way and deposed a ruler, it was only done 'after giving the prince a long rope, warning him and then, when they thought there was no corrective, removing him very gently so that they never compromised his dignity'. This was how Tukoji Rao Holkar of Indore was removed:

> The Maharaja Holkar was a very enlightened man, a class-fellow of my father, and I respected him as my father and knew him very well. He had to go but a darbar was arranged, his son was made to sit on the gadi, the deposed Maharaja walked up to the son and put the red *Raj Tilak* mark on his forehead, took five steps back, and then turned about and walked out.

A decade after serving the Maharaja of Rewa as his Adviser, Conrad Corfield in his capacity as Political Adviser to the Viceroy brought about his deposition:

He was a popular ruler, a very nice man and a great expert of Sanscrit, but he could not be persuaded that there had to be a basic division between the privy purse and public funds. I gave him a number of years in which to carry this out but it never happened, so I waited until his son had been trained in administration and was available to take his place. I then put up the proposal through the Viceroy to the Secretary of State for India that he should be deposed. When the approval came, it took the form of saying that the Viceroy should do as he thought fit. Lord Wavell handed this to me with a smile, as much as to say, 'Now you must do as you think fit.' I knew that internally and externally there would be no real criticism, because the heir was not really fond of his father and would be a much better ruler. So my dear Maharaja, of whom I was very fond, had to leave and eventually died a sad death.

14
PIETY AND SIN

Men become deeply devoted to that king who discharges the duty of protection properly, who is endued with liberality, who is steady in the observance of righteousness, who is vigilant, and who is free from lust and hate.

From the *Mahabharata*

'The average prince was a god-fearing man,' declares one such prince from Kathiawar. 'But among them there were despots and very autocratic rulers. The Jam-Saheb Ranjit Singh, the famous cricketer, was a very dominant autocratic ruler. The Nawab of Junagadh had perverse habits and a sadistic nature – although he never ruled, really; it was the Dewan. There were also drunkards and womanisers and those who favoured their own greed or their hobbies – but here in Kathiawar I know of no ruler who was hated by his people. At heart they were not against the people – and the people loved their ruler despite his defects.'

There was much wisdom in the ancient Vedic code of Manu, the primordial lawgiver, which laid down that one-sixth of the *punyam* (piety) and one-sixth of the *papam* (sins) of the people accrued to the ruler. It recognised that a king was part saint and part sinner, reflecting both the virtues and the vices of his subjects. In British times, the average prince was no different, but whereas in the past he had always shared the conservatism of his people his education now made him more conscious of the need for change. Some rulers responded to this challenge, others played for time. Faced with subjects who were far happier with a ruler who fed 4000 Brahmins on his birthday or released his prisoners than one who brought in reforms allowing widows to remarry or forbidding the marriage of young girls to older men, they found it easier to stick to Manu's doctrine, balancing a little sin with a little piety.

Sinning on a grand scale was essentially the prerogative of the rulers of the larger states, where they had the funds and the power to do so. The ruler of a small state with semi-jurisdictional powers – and the majority of the 625 states fell into this category – had little option but to steer a middle course. He had only a limited population to tax and not much private land of his own, so that what revenue he collected went to maintain himself and his family retinue. At this level, the opportunities for reforming his state or for building roads or schools were as limited as the opportunities for excess. The worst he could do was bully his peasants and chase their daughters – and even here redress could be found in a British-Indian court. In the less wealthy salute states, too, revenues had to be spread very thinly indeed to allow the ruling family to exist in the style that tradition and public sentiment expected, while still maintaining a palace staff, a police force and judicial, medical, educational and public works departments. In one of the poorer 9-gun states, the highest paid functionary combined the offices of Lord Chief Justice and Inspector-General for Dancing-Girls, for which he received a total salary of 100 rupees a month.

Only in a salute state with full powers of government could a prince have his head to use his powers for better or worse: to become at one extreme a Sayaji Rao of Baroda, and at the other a Jay Singh of Alwar – a man 'sinister beyond belief' according to one Political Officer who knew him, and the only prince in modern times who actually drove a section of his tenant-farmers to take up arms against their sovereign. The Indian convention was that what a ruler did under his own roof was his own business and that his right to privacy was as inviolate as his zanana. Jay Singh Alwar's chief sin was to carry his private life over into his public one, treating his state as another ruler might treat the women of his zanana. His overwhelming charm won him friends in high places – notably Edwin Montague, Secretary of State for India – and it was this, coupled with the Paramount Power's reluctance to oust one of the most prominent of the princes in the 1920s, that allowed Jay Singh Alwar to remain on the gadi long after he had exhausted the patience of his people and those Political Officers who knew him for what he was. It was whispered about that what finally turned the powers that be against him was an incident involving a young Englishman and a heavy silver table centrepiece: the latter contained a concealed pair of manacles which sprang shut when pressed. Invited to lean over the table and place his hands on the centrepiece, the Englishman found himself suddenly and vulnerably trapped.

The Maharaja of Alwar was deposed in 1933 and sent into exile in France where he died in 1937 – only to make a triumphant return to his state as an embalmed corpse. 'It was the custom in Alwar for the body of a dead ruler to be carried to the funeral pyre seated in state,' explains Corfield:

At the station his stiffened body was fitted with great difficulty into his car dressed in full regalia – and except for the fact that his eyes were closed it was difficult to believe that this ceremonial figure was a corpse. Just before the procession started, one of the princes standing nearby took compassion on the sightless face and adorned it with dark glasses. The effect was so lifelike that the people lining the route began to wail and fall on their faces. The rumour even spread that he was to be burnt alive as this was the only way of bringing his evil influence to an end. A few years later a friend of mine was visiting Alwar and he was having his hair cut in the bazaar, and he said to the hair-cutter, 'What's it like nowadays in Alwar?' 'Oh,' said he, 'it's quieter, you know, but it's very dull.'

As a bad ruler Jay Singh Alwar was not an isolated case, but he was an extreme one. In 1928 the Chamber of Princes passed resolutions calling upon those among its members who had not already done so to draw up law codes to be administered by a judiciary independent of the executive power, and to separate the ruler's privy purse from the public exchequer. Ten per cent of a state's annual revenues was promoted as the ideal amount. Most rulers made serious attempts to conform to these standards, although many more dragged their feet when it came to implementing calls from the Paramount Power to bring in constitutional reforms and set up representative assemblies. Some of these reforms were largely cosmetic, designed to satisfy external rather than internal demands and the oft trumpeted ten per cent privy purse was more honoured by words than deeds. Even the great Ganga Singh, who made much of his self-regulation as an example to other princes, was reckoned by his Congress Party critics to be spending nearer twenty per cent on 'Palace' expenditure than the ten per cent that his published annual budgets stated. It all depended on whether or not such items as the expenditure of 19,000 rupees on the Maharaja's visit to Palanpur to attend the marriage of the heir-apparent in 1936, or the building of a pukka road out to Gajner lake, could be regarded as legitimate state expenditure. Dr Karni Singh certainly has no doubts as to Ganga Singh's code of ethics:

My grandfather fixed his privy purse at 10 per cent as far back as 1912 or 1913 and as time went on the separation between the two departments of 'Palace' and 'State' became very marked indeed. Cars were marked 'Bikaner No. 10P' – that was 'Privy Purse' – and 'Bikaner No. 11S' – that was 'State'. Their maintenance was separate, their petrol was separate and if the family used a car they paid for it. My father was just as particular, to such an extent that when I learnt to fly an aeroplane they charged me 85 rupees an hour, when it only cost ten rupees in petrol.

Another grey area that was open to interpretation centred on the word *dastur*, meaning time-honoured custom, which could be constructed either as inducement – which was the popular attitude – or as corruption – which was the British view, shared by the more Anglicised princes. Attempts to win over British officials by one means or another were commonplace and in consequence all Political Officers were forbidden to accept gifts from a ruler exceeding the value of 250 rupees. Conrad Corfield knew a colleague who at his first Christmas as the Resident of a Central Indian state 'where a Maharani was in charge', received a gift of a large tray of fruit which he learned had come from the State Dewan:

> He started picking at his tribute and at the bottom of the tray found 101 gold mohurs. He was staggered and wrote a furious letter to the Maharani, telling her that he was shocked. She wrote back and said, 'I'm terribly sorry, but 101 gold mohurs is what has been presented to the Resident every year at Christmas and if the amount is not enough will you please tell me what it is?' So they started to make enquiries, and found out that what happened was that five gold mohurs were always kept by the servants of the Residency and the rest sent back to the Dewan's Office, where it was distributed – while on the list it was written, 'Towards Christmas present for the Resident – 101 gold mohurs.'

To lessen the risk of being accused of corruption, all gifts received by Political Officers had to be surrendered to the Government of India Toshakhana in Delhi, to be valued. If an officer wished to keep a gift he had to pay for it. 'My wife and I were in our house once in Rajkot when the Thakur-Saheb of Limbdi came to see us,' recalls Cyril Hancock. 'He felt about his waist-band and opened my baby boy's hand, put in it a gold sovereign and closed his fist. So then I had to write to the Government of India to say that I had been given a golden sovereign by the Thakur-Saheb and would they tell me how much I had to send to the Toshakhana.' However, sometimes these gifts were not quite what they seemed and Corfield remembers the wedding of one of his subordinate officers where the bride received a necklace studded with diamonds and rubies from a ruler: 'The prospective bridegroom came to me and said, "Obviously, I've got to hand it back." I said, "Wait a minute. Send it to be valued first." So it went to the Toshakhana and they valued it at 195 rupees, and I had great pleasure in handing it back to him and telling him that his wife could keep it, because the jewellery that the Maharaja had paid for might have been rubies and diamonds, but the people who had sent it for him knew that it couldn't be accepted, so they had substituted glass.'

In a badly run state corruption was most evident when ill-paid officials supplemented their incomes in any way they could. Such was the case in Patiala before Maharaja Yadavendra Singh appointed H. S. Malik as his Dewan in 1944:

> Our relations were very cordial and very frank and friendly. One day the Maharaja said to me, just in casual conversation, 'One thing you will find, that people in Patiala dress well and eat well.' So I said, 'Yes, I noticed that, and I wonder how they do it, because the salaries they get as government servants are very poor.' The Maharaja realised what I was hinting at and he said, 'Do you mean that they are corrupt?' I said, 'Of course they are. You are paying your chaprassis (office messengers) seven rupees a month. Your magistrates are paid 200 rupees a month, your Sessions Judge gets 500 rupees a month. How do you expect them to live on those salaries?' So he said, 'What can be done about it?' I said, 'Very simple, we must revise the entire pay structure of the services.' And that was one of the first reforms that came. Within a few weeks we were able to put through an entirely revised scale of the salaries of state servants, which in some cases were put up by 300 per cent. Everybody got a rise except the Prime Minister!

Not all rulers, however, were prepared to listen to good advice – which was one of the factors that contributed to the downfall of the Maharaja of Rewa: 'I tried to persuade him that the police ought to be paid 30 rupees a month instead of 15 rupees,' Corfield explains. 'He said, "Oh, I don't understand you English at all. If I paid them 30 rupees a month as you say, then their prices would go up and all the people would have to pay them double to get their services." He believed it was quite good enough to allow the *dasturi* to continue, by which if you went to a policeman you had to hand to him whatever-it-was before you were dealt with.' In Hyderabad there was no need for dastur, according to V. K. Reddy; at least, not among its senior officials:

> People used to say that there was a lot of corruption and that the judges took money. I do not agree, not because my father was the Chief Justice, but because there was a very stern attitude towards bribery and corruption in Hyderabad, very stern indeed. Petty officials used to take money, but in the upper echelons I don't think there was any corruption, and for a very simple reason – which was that

most officers or judges or whatever they were, already had plenty of money. They were all landlords with their private incomes. My father, for example, used to get four thousand rupees a month as a judge. But his personal income was over a lakh of rupees a month, so this four thousand rupees meant nothing to him. it was the prestige of being the Chief Justice or a judge that mattered.

During its last four decades of existence Hyderabad possessed a ruler in Nizam Osman Ali Pasha who was as much of an enigma to his subjects as to outsiders. He was arguably the richest man in the world, with more than 400 *Arabs* of coinage in his coffers (about £30 million), jewellery estimated to be worth at least as much again, rooms full of gold bullion and lands that brought in 35 crores of rupees annually. Yet he was 'always slouching around in a very dirty pair of old shoes and dirty pyjamas and wearing a *rumitopi* (fez) which always had an inch of grease around the bottom. He chain-smoked local Golconda cigarettes and he really didn't care about his appearance.' But to describe him simply as a miser was to do him an injustice, argues V. K. Reddy: 'Osman Ali Pasha was a poet, a philosopher and an eccentric. At the same time he was a shrewd judge of men and a very capable administrator. He spoke abruptly, but that was his manner, for by nature he was a very kind man and a tolerant one. He lived simply and ate very little himself, but the food that was given to the rest of the palace was fantastic.' On Christmas Eve, the Nizam and all the womenfolk from his zanana would be driven to a local Catholic mission: 'The whole shooting match had to go to midnight mass. The Nizam sat in the front pew and when he left he always gave a big donation to the Sisters who were there. He also attended the Hindu festivals like Holi and Dassera. He would go to the Hindu temples but remain outside in his car – and of course, he went to the mosque every Friday.' The Nizam rarely remitted even the smallest sums offered as nazar – yet possessed inherited treasures on a scale that almost defied belief:

One fine morning the Nizam said to my grandfather, 'Rama, I think it's high time we sorted out the pearls. I want them all graded.' So they went to the treasury and there they pulled out buckets and buckets and buckets of pearls of all shapes and sizes. First they washed them all in boric acid and then they poured them through these grading machines like you use for grading gravel, so that they were sorted out according to size. Then they were laid out to dry on huge sheets on the roof, covering the entire roof of the palace.

But pearls made up only part of the Nizam's treasures. Some of his jewels he had acquired himself, such as the ten square emeralds 'each the size of a flat egg' bought from a Persian jeweller for eighty lakhs of rupees at the time of the 1911 Delhi Durbar. Some were inherited from his father, Mahbub Ali Pasha – including the famous 162–carat Jacob diamond, which the Nizam had had mounted on a gold base and used as a paperweight. One of the stranger tales that V. K. Reddy heard from his grandfather concerned an instruction from the Nizam to reopen the English Palace within the grounds of King Kothi Palace, which had remained closed since the death in 1911 of Mahbub Ali Pasha: 'When my grandfather opened up the cupboards in the bedrooms he found expensive jewellery scattered all along the floors. Mahbub Ali Pasha had carried jewels everywhere in his pockets and given them out here and there as favours. When he died everything had been locked and sealed, the clothes had rotted and the jewels had fallen on the floor.'

After Hyderabad, the finest collections of precious jewels were reputed to lie hidden in the family toshakhana of the ruling house of Jaipur, the best pieces dating from the time of its close association with the Mughal Court. Every royal family was secretive about these private assets, representing as they did that dynasty's insurance against hard times, but none had better cause than Jaipur to be so and none guarded its secrets more effectively. The family treasures were said to be hidden under a fort perched high above their ancestral home of Amber, the ancient capital of the Kachhwaha Rajputs, itself clinging to the side of a mountain on the edge of the Jaipur plain. The Kachhwaha clan had wrested this land from the original inhabitants, the aboriginal Minas, and it was the chiefs of the Minas who were entrusted with guarding the treasure – a task their descendants carried out so faithfully that even the ruler himself was only allowed access three times during his tenure of the gadi. That, at least, was the story, for the rulers themselves guarded their secrets just as securely as the Minas kept their treasure.

Kashmir and Gwalior were said to be next in the league table for jewels and treasures, followed by Baroda and Jodhpur. Sahibzada Ata Muhamed Khan remembers going to see Maharaja Hari Singh of Kashmir with his uncle and watching the Maharaja measuring emeralds for his *sarpech*, the jewellery that was worn draped over a turban: 'Most of the leading jewellers from Calcutta and Bombay were there, but His Highness was very particular about colour and couldn't find what he wanted. My uncle said to him, "*Hukum*, let's see what you've got in your toshakhana." "What's there to see?" replied His Highness. "There is nothing left." But he called his toshakhana custodian, a young man named Dewan Iqbal Nath, and asked him to bring something. We sat there and a little velvet package which hadn't been cleaned for years was brought in. Inside was a yellow velvet tray which was put before us. On it were about 200 fantastic emerald drops. I've never seen anything like it in my life.'

Baroda, too, had some outstanding jewellery, much of it built up by Sayaji Rao's spendthrift predecessors Khande Rao and his brother Mulhar Rao, who had such items as salute cannons and elephant chains cast in silver and gold. Included among their treasures were four sumptuous tapestries of threaded pearls studded with gems, and a single necklace made of enormous diamonds with the 128–carat Star of the South as the centrepiece. A lesser Baroda diamond was the 70–carat Akbar Shah, believed to be one of the eyes of the fabulous peacock throne of the Mughals, looted by Nadir Shah of Persia at the sack of Delhi in 1739. Less glittering but just as impressive was the seven-stringed Baroda pearl necklace, with pearls 'almost the size of marbles'.

Patiala, too, had a spectacular pearl necklace but one made up of ropes of black pearls. Then there was a necklace of emeralds 'each the size of a teaspoon' and a breastplate studded with the auspicious number of a thousand and one diamonds. Yadavendra Singh of Patiala was by all accounts a thrifty man but his father was one of the last of the big spenders. This was made possible by the rich, well-irrigated soil of the Punjab, which gave Bhupinder Singh an annual revenue from his subjects of 15 lakhs of rupees (£1¼ million), of which at least half went into his privy purse. Maintaining the 11–acre pink sandstone Moti Bagh Palace with its 'bathrooms like ballrooms', plus half a dozen other royal residences, together with occupants, staff and dependants numbering four or five thousand swallowed up half a dozen lakhs – but still left the Maharaja with enough funds to indulge himself handsomely. 'The tendency to buy things up *en masse* was part of the Patiala tradition,' maintains Sardar Malik, who first met the Maharaja in London while serving with the Royal Flying Corps during the First World War: 'The entire fifth floor of the Ritz was occupied by the Maharaja and his suite and the corridors outside were stacked with new suitcases. I asked his ADC what had happened and he said, "Well, His Highness went to Finnegans today and he bought all this to give as presents when he gets back to Patiala."'

The Darbar Hall in Patiala was festooned with crystal furniture, with more crystal furniture and glass stored away in packing cases which even in the 1940s were still unopened. This all dated back to the time of Bhupinder Singh's great-grandfather and had been bought more or less by accident when the Maharaja entered a well-known Calcutta store owned by a European named Lazarus; 'The Maharaja had with him another Sikh, simply dressed like himself, and they had wandered around the shop examining things and asking Lazarus the price of various items. Lazarus thought they were ignorant peasants wasting his time and he spoke sharply to them. This angered the Maharaja, who asked him how much he wanted for the entire contents of the shop; Lazarus, even more irate at what he considered an idiotic enquiry, quoted some relatively low figure – whereupon the Maharaja turned to his aide and instructed him to pay the man in cash on the spot.'

There was still considerable evidence of bulk purchasing when Hede Dayal came to Patiala in 1945: 'Once when I was in the music room I found stacks of scores and when I asked Max Geiger, the Viennese conductor of the Patiala orchestra, why this was so, he said, "Well, the old man went to Vienna and I gave him a list of the music I wanted. But they lost the list so he just went to the shop and told them to pack up the whole shop and send it to Patiala."' 'The Patiala toshakhana itself was filled with knick-knacks bought up during various European shopping sprees – tin trunks with layer upon layer of pearls with diamonds, pearls with rubies, pearls with emeralds, jewels for *nuths* (nose-rings), jewels for the feet, jewels for the belly-button and for God-knows-what. There was so much of it that I found myself incapable of taking in their beauty. It was like costume or stage jewellery.'

However, it was not for this particular indulgence that Bhupinder Singh would be best remembered. Every Indian state had its share of *mirch masala*, the 'chillies and peppers that added spice to the daily ration', and in Patiala that spice came from the 'goings-on' in Bhupinder Singh's zanana. What they were, no man knew for sure – but much was guessed at. 'Quite rightly, His Highness had two lives,' remarks Dick Bowles. 'He had his private life with his personal household and he had his public life. His private life *was* private, but whatever it was I'm sure it was on a grand scale.'

Bhupinder Singh's great rival among the Sikhs was Jagatjit Singh of Kapurthala, whose life-style was closer to that of the French monarchs whom he so greatly admired than to that of any oriental prince of old. 'He enjoyed the pleasures and high society of the West,' declares his grandson. 'But he also enjoyed the company of interesting and attractive young ladies and he brought many back from Europe to stay in Kapurthala as his guests and personal friends, some of them the most beautiful women I have ever seen.' That these liaisons damaged his reputation in the eyes of the British authorities, there can be no doubt, yet it was equally true that the Maharaja always behaved with the utmost discretion in public. He treated all his guests with great charm and courtesy and retained the friendship of his lady friends even after they had ceased to enjoy the comforts of Jagatjit Palace or Chateau Kapurthala.

A much safer but equally traditional princely indulgence was gastronomy, which in a number of states was raised to the level of an art form. Every region in India had its traditional dishes and specialities and this was reflected in the cooking and the kitchens of the royal palace. In the larger establishments every cook had a speciality and might spend his entire working life preparing and refining one particular rice dish, based on a recipe taught him in his youth. Once learned, these recipes remained a closely guarded secret which was rarely divulged to outsiders. Only when a daughter of the royal house was about to leave the palace would these secrets be passed on – and then only to those who would be accompanying her. Such recipes related not only to food but also to the many forms of semi-alcoholic drinks such as sherbet, which the Mughals had introduced as a substitute for alcohol. In the North there was *thundai*, a cooling drink based on *bhang* or Indian hemp; in Rajasthan, various kinds of liqueurs known as *ashas*, supposedly made up of as many as seventy-five different ingredients as diverse as human blood or crushed pearls and drunk 'mainly for potency'. Ashas were essentially elixirs intended for royalty alone, as were some of the more exotic dishes served up at great feasts, such as the dish whose recipe began: 'Take a whole camel, put a goat inside it and inside the goat a peacock, inside which put a chicken. Inside the chicken put a sand-grouse, inside the sand-grouse put a quail and finally, a sparrow. Then put the camel in a hole in the ground and steam it.' Even more improbable was a recipe acquired by the present Maharaja of Sailana, who used to travel from state to state with his father collecting traditional recipes: 'There are *puris* (deep-fried wheat cakes) which would puff up and in certain of the smaller Rajasthan states, they would stick a live bird in the puri, quickly deep-fry it and bring it to the table – where the bird would fly out. It was not for eating, just an extravaganza.'

The preparation of *paan* was another delicacy surrounded by secrecy, 'because paans could have all sorts of potent and expensive ingredients such as gold and pearls'. Paan was also a much favoured method of poisoning, and for this reason it was always prepared by only the most trusted servants: 'We were always taught that wherever we used to go we had to take the paan offered to us, open it up and look inside and only then eat it.' The kitchen itself was another obvious source of danger and in earlier days, 'certain animals were kept in the kitchen and their behaviour watched when the food was being cooked. It was said that a peacock cried in a certain way if poison was present in the room.' The *thalwalla* charged with bearing in the thali of the ruler at mealtimes was another trusted retainer, and the thalis themselves sometimes had lids which could be locked and secured. The young heir-apparent was an obvious target for poisoning by an ambitious second wife with children of her own, which was exactly what happened to Princess Padma Lokur's father when he was a teenager:

> His step-mother came from a very poor family and her mother was very ambitious. She told her daughter that if the eldest son died, then her own son would get the gadi. My grandmother was very young at the time and listened to my great-grandmother and poisoned my father by putting poison in what we call a *karanji* (crescent-shaped fried sweetmeat). He ate it, but luckily vomited, but even so he had to lie in bed for six months. While he was lying there he started eating a little food and the maid who brought him his food was bribed by my grandmother so that every day she used to put a little poison in the food. This puzzled the doctors until they got in a very trusted woman who had been his wet nurse; she looked after him and he was cured. My grandfather found out about the poisoning and my grandmother was given a sound beating and thrown out of the palace but after six months she was pardoned. She repented what she had done and used to say to my mother, 'I made a grave mistake in trying to poison your husband and until you get a son I shall not be happy.'

Far more damaging than poison, however, was alcohol, which threatened to become virtually an occupational hazard in some quarters. One of the best known casualties was the ruler of the smallest salute state in Western India, 'a very intelligent, well-read, handsome man who could not cope with having ideas that were bigger than his state'. Nawab Iqbal Mohamed Khan was among those who tried to persuade him to give up drinking: 'I explained to him that if he was not able to contribute to his own state and to the princely order, it would be a loss to both as he was such an intelligent man. He promised he would give up drinking and he did for a few days – but he could not give it up permanently.'

Nevertheless, heavy drinking was far less widespread among rulers themselves than it was among their immediate relatives, particularly their brothers and younger sons – precisely those whom greater professional expertise in state administration made increasingly redundant. Sayaji Rao's Baroda was only one of a number of progressive states weakened in this way. Some tended to blame the British because 'keeping company with the British induced you to drink'.

Increasing British influence certainly brought about a change in eating habits, which meant the addition of European kitchens and European or European-trained chefs to palaces; as much for the satisfaction of Westernised palates among ruling families as for visiting Europeans. Jagatjit Singh's Kapurthala naturally had its French cuisine and its French-trained chefs. However, the best cooking was said to be derived from the Mughals, and this Mughlai cooking found its highest expression in the kitchens of the Muslim states. 'My grandmother's cooking was famous,' asserts Nirmala Raje Bhonsle of Baroda. 'All her cooks were packed off to far-away places to learn these things – to France for French cuisine or for Mughlai cooking to Avadh (Oude). A lot of cooks went to Lucknow, where the old Nawabs used to keep these men in the kitchens for a while and teach them. One day a batch of them came back and my grandmother asked them, "What have you learnt?" "Many things," they said, "but it was so dirty there. *Maharaj*, they don't cut the coconut, they just bite it off with their teeth and drop it into the cooking pots."'

The finest cuisine in India was said to come from the kitchens of Rampur State. 'It was my grandfather, Nawab Hamid Ali Khan, who developed this art to the highest perfection,' Zulfiquar Ali Khan maintains:

In those days he had about 90 to 100 cooks and one cook only cooked one thing. They were all Rampur trained, but the unfortunate thing is that they never taught their sons. They taught them 80 per cent but never 100 per cent of what they knew, because they were afraid that if they did so they would be sacked and their sons would be cooks in their place. My grandfather developed Mughlai cooking to a point that not even Akbar or Jehangir could have enjoyed, because he improved on what they ate. He himself only ate one meal in twenty-four hours, at half-past seven in the evening. He ate at least two and a half seers (approximately five pounds) and then he only drank iced water and smoked Turkish cigarettes until the next meal. He spent 2½ lakhs a year on Indian food and another 1½ lakhs on English food just for his personal kitchens alone. My father in his turn had about 60 to 70 cooks during his rule, of which 25 to 30 were left when he died. Now I have only three or four, which I retain only with great difficulty because they're offered better jobs in hotels.

One of the many rulers who sat at Hamid Ali Khan's table was Shashi Wallia's father, the ruler of Dewas Junior:

> Daddy and the Nawab-Saheb were seated at their own circular tables with a huge thali on each the same size as the table, on which there were two hundred dishes in silver bowls. My father just folded up and said, 'Your Highness, I'll never get through the first two dishes.' But the Nawab-Saheb said, 'This will all be distributed among the palace servants so nothing will be wasted, but you must have one spoon from each dish.' Then he pointed out thirty different preparations of chicken, twenty-five types of *gosht* (meat) and another forty of shikar meat of various kinds. Then there were fifty dishes of *dals* (lentils) prepared in different ways, ten different types of pulao, and so it went on. It took my father two and a half hours to taste every one of them, and afterwards he called his personal physician and said, 'For God's sake get me some Eno's quickly, because this banquet has killed me.'

If gourmandising was the Nawab of Rampur's chief indulgence, it could be set against other forms of patronage that he undertook which exemplified the major role played by the Indian States in preserving and encouraging some of the main strands in Indian art and culture. Not only did Rampur maintain one of the finest libraries of Arabic, Persian and Urdu manuscripts in the world, but its rulers were almost without exception active patrons of literature, music and painting. The last Nawab, Syed Raza Ali Khan, was himself a gifted musician who brought the best classical musicians in India to play at his court and encouraged them to stay and teach their skills to others:

> We had a complete Department of Music called the *Arab-e-Nishak*. A lot of money was spent on instruments and keeping the musicians happy. Ustad Mushtaq Hussain Khan and Ustad Vilayat Khan were among the great musicians who learned from my grandfather and father. Even the greatest of the Indian musicians, Ustad Allauddin Khan, belonged to Maihar, a small state in Central India, but learned from my grandfather. So too did the best *tabla* (drum) player, a fellow named Ahmed Jan Tirakhwa, who belonged to Rampur.

This form of patronage was sufficiently widespread to be considered commonplace in many Indian States, whose rulers both encouraged and preserved Indian classical music, dancing and painting to a quite remarkable degree. Many of the most famous musicians and dancers in India today either enjoyed this patronage themselves in their earlier years or were taught by masters who had done so. 'This was patronage in a real sense when a musician feels he is wanted and that his music is being loved,' maintains Pushpendra Sinh:

> In Lunawada we had our own court musicians, but often others would come for special occasions. The great Ustad Fayyaz Khan, who was my father's great friend, would often come from Baroda, sometimes uninvited because he wanted pleasant company – and when a good musician is in good company, he opens up and expounds what he really knows and wants to do. So it was not only money but appreciation. My father himself is not only a great lover of music but a great exponent of the harmonium, which he learned from Gulam Rasul Khan Saheb, who was India's number one harmonium player.

Nearly every major salute state – and many a minor one, too – had its *Gharana* or music school where a particular style of music evolved, and every city palace its *naubatkhana*, the 'drum house' where the palace musicians had their quarters. 'It was generally above the gate,' recalls M. M. Sapat, 'so that it overlooked the interior of the palace while the music that was played there could also be heard by the public. At Jaisalmer the *naubat* was played four times a day, with *ragas* on the *shehnai* (reed instrument) accompanied by the *nagara* (drums) and the *sarangi* (stringed instrument). His Highness Jawahir Singhji would stand and listen and say, "*Wah, wah!*" to encourage them. He himself was a great patron of music and would play the harmonium and sing.'

The same patronage extended rather less dramatically to the crafts in many different forms because, as Raja Shrimant Shivram Sawant Bhonsle explains, 'You had to have certain master-craftsmen who were painters or silver-smiths, carpenters or artisans of various types. They were retained as part of the ruler's retinue and lived off the revenue of lands that they were given. In Sawantwadi, for example, we had what were called *Jindgars* or saddlemakers who excelled in embroidery, because in those days saddles were made of cloth that was highly embroidered. But apart from making saddles, they also used to make other things involving embroidery, such as fans or the gadis on which you sat. It was not only the ruler who got the benefit, because the aristocracy also had to have these things, so the craftsmen thrived.'

Royal patronage also extended to numerous expressions of piety: from the many mosques, *gurudwaras*, shrines and temples built and maintained by the rulers to the wide range of religious activities in which they played a leading part. Every religion represented in the state had its peculiar observances and festivals scattered through the year, in which every single ruler in India participated to some degree, quite irrespective of his religion. Here he acted as a true father and mother of his people, representing them at the most important occasions in a way which helped to bind all his subjects together as one people. These festivals loomed very large in the lives of royalty and commoners alike, who celebrated them with an enthusiasm and fervour that is hard to imagine today. For Muslims of the Shia sect, their chief devotion went into the *Mohurram*, a 'very serious and grandiose affair which we had to observe for forty days', recalls Princess Shahvar Sultan of Cambay. Its high moments were the acts of public self-flagellation in the streets which were accompanied by a religious ecstasy bordering on hysteria, with young men whipping themselves with chains and hooks or dancing on swords to show their devotion, and the carrying in procession of flower-bedecked towers called *taziahs*. In Cambay a heavy wooden structure called a *zari* was carried by the faithful through the town:

> This zari was as big as a room and was covered in silver and gold plating donated by the ruler. It was assembled for the tenth day of Mohurram outside the Darbar and at nine o'clock sharp they say it used to rise off the ground by itself. Hordes of people, including Hindus, used to come for this *ashura* ceremony, all waiting for that one moment. Just four people stood there, at the stroke of nine they would put a finger under the zari and lift this very heavy thing, which was then taken through the streets to a place called the Kerballa, where it was dismantled.

The patterns of the many Hindu festivals were far more complicated, varying greatly according to place, caste, sectarian grouping and even sex. The Ganpati festival honouring Ganesh was very much a Maratha festival, marked with five days of processions, fairs and sing-songs and ending in the immersion of images in a river or the sea; whereas Lakshmi puja was essentially a merchants' festival, celebrated by shopkeepers and by women in the Diwali feast of lights in late autumn. For the Kshatriya warrior caste, the highlight of the year was the last day of the Dassera or 'ten day' festival of early autumn, celebrating the victory of good over evil and marking the day on which Rama set out to conquer Ravana – a day also chosen in the past by the Marathas to start their autumn campaigns. In almost every state in India this was the leading festival of the year, a time when the men made animal sacrifices and performed penances, culminating in the *shastra puja* on the tenth day when 'your arms, swords, bows and arrows were laid down in front of the temple and puja done to them, led by the ruler'. In every Rajput

palace courtyard, the women of the household would perform their
Ras Garba dances and the men the *Banaoli Dantia*, a stick dance for
two or three dancers in turn to the accompaniment of drums and
beaten thalis. These sticks had replaced the swords of earlier times:
'You treated the stick in exactly the same manner in which you
treated a sword, with respect, touching it to your forehead. You
could either use two sticks, one for offence and one for defence, or
you carried a stick and a *dhal*, which was a shield made out of steel
inlaid with gold or sometimes a tortoise-shell. So it was a dance
with a purpose behind it and not just a celebration. The drumming
itself was very martial and gave you unbridled energy so that you
could keep dancing and leaping for an hour at a time.'

Dassera culminated in a grand parade that invariably began from
the City Palace: an annual display of pageantry enjoyed in every
Hindu state. The most famous Dassera took place in Mysore and
drew British visitors from all over India. 'Hundreds of guests came
every year for the Dassera Darbar,' recalls Rani Vijayadevi, sister of
the late Maharaja:

> On the first day of the festival my aunt and my uncle at the early
> morning puja would both take a vow to do certain pujas for the next
> ten days. During that time they were not allowed to go out of the
> palace, they tied on a red silk cloth that they always wore and my
> uncle did not shave. Every day he had to say special prayers to our
> goddess Chamundeshwari, waking every morning at five. Then every
> evening there was a public darbar, after which my uncle would go to
> the ladies' apartments where they would throw flowers over him and
> offer garlands and do what was called *arti*, to take away the evil eye.

The Darbar on the ninth day was reserved for the British. At a
ceremony that was unique in India the Resident – acting, it was
stressed, in an unofficial capacity – would lead the guests in offering
homage to the Maharaja, a ceremonial which took place in the
privacy of the Private Darbar Hall. Finally, on the afternoon of the
tenth day the ruler would go out in solemn procession from the
palace to the parade ground:

> At the head of the procession were the camels and the elephants,
> holding navy-blue and yellow flags. Then came the elephants with
> big drums followed by the Mysore Palace Infantry in red and green
> uniforms, the palace guards, the Mysore State Forces in red and
> white, and then a mounted escort of the Mysore Lancers (8th King
> George V's Own Light Cavalry) who would always come down
> from Bangalore for this event. They had a very famous uniform of

navy-blue and white with a leopard's skin on their horses, all black Walers imported from Australia. Finally there came the elephant carrying my uncle and my father, with my brother sitting at the back, in a golden howdah. They all wore the old Mysore brocade coat worn with a sash and loose brocade pants. Their turbans were of Benares silk made up for them by a Parsi family in Mysore who made all the turbans for my family.

At the parade ground there was a hollow tree held sacred by all Kshatriyas as the tree in which the Pandava heroes of ancient legend had hidden their weapons while in exile: 'A little house was built with this tree in the centre and there my uncle would get off his elephant, perform puja and change and then come back on horseback to take the parade. By then it was about seven thirty and getting dark, so it was lit with thousands of little bulbs. After the march-past there would be refreshments and then at about half-past nine the procession would return, lit by old gas-lamps and burning torches and with the palace lit up and looking very pretty.'

An equally popular festival in the Indian States was the spring saturnalia called Holi, a time of license when everybody from the ruler downwards joined in throwing red powder or coloured water at one another. In Bharatpur proceedings lasted for a week, as Brijendra Singh remembers:

People would greet each other by throwing *gulal* powder, moving about in small groups. Everyone wore white, even the police constables on traffic duty, and His present Highness wore two sets of white clothing alternately because in those days the pink dye that was used was washable. For seven days his officers would gather in one place called the Holi Darbar. His Highness would throw *kumkumas*, which were pellets filled with dye that broke on impact and we would throw them back. Then on the last day there was a big bonfire in the evening and next day there would be what was called a colour Holi, when His Highness would come out into the city on an elephant with a big water tanker filled with coloured water behind him. He would have a hosepipe and with this he would hose the water on people while they would throw water and colour on him using hand-pumps.

The annual cycle of festivals traditionally began with the arrival of the rains after two months of heat and drought, and ended in Rajasthan with the Gangaur festival that followed Holi, and was as colourful and dramatic as any festival in India. *Gang* was a synonym for Shiva and *Gauri* was his consort Parvati, who symbolised the ideal woman's devotion to her husband. 'Gangaur was a festival for ladies and typical of Rajasthan,' explains the Maharani of Wankaner:

'As Parvati goes from her father's home to the Himalayas she blesses the women with *saubhagya* (long life for your husband). In Dungarpur there were huge wooden Gangaur statues that were bedecked with clothes and jewellery and then taken from the old palace down to the lake by the new palace. At the lakeside there was singing and dancing and a lot of people came, including the Maharawal.' It was a 'terrific show in its own way', but only a pale reflection of the spectacle of the Udaipur Gangaur in its fairy-tale setting on Pichhola lake. As a little boy, Mahendra Singh witnessed the last two such Gangaur ceremonies held before the death of his grandfather, the last ruling Maharana of Mewar, in 1955:

> The procession was taken out on four consecutive days and each day had its own colour, so that all the men came in the same coloured turbans and kamarbands and the womenfolk in the same coloured *odhnas*. Every day there was a full procession from the palace down to the ghat at the lakeside; bands, infantry, cavalry and the Maharana on elephant-back surrounded by the state insignia. On the water were two enormous gangaur boats which had platforms at the front and rear. On one of them would be the Maharana with his *umraos* (noblemen) sitting in order of court precedence on two sides above the oarsmen, and on the other boat a Mohammedan family, the Satravan Umrao, who had helped the Mewar family in battle against the Mughals and were honoured in this way. These two boats could take about one hundred persons and moored together they were rowed across the lake to another ghat, where they visited the Ban-nath Shiv temple before returning for the end of the ceremony. This was timed so that the procession on land was in bright light; the first boat procession was as the sun was setting and the second after sunset, so that it was possible to have illuminations and fireworks. Like so much else in the Hindu states, its religious significance was on two levels. At the one level there was the pageantry of the boats, the music, the light and all the people dressed up, and at the other there was the symbolism of the crossing of the water, with the thought that Shiva in the form of Eklingji, the chief deity of Mewar, through his consort Parvati would guide the ruler and his people safely through life.

15

MOTHER AND FATHER OF THE PEOPLE

*The King should always bear himself towards his subjects as a
mother towards the child of her womb. Hear, O monarch, the
reason why this becomes desirable. As the mother, disregarding
those objects that are most cherished by her, seeks the good of
her child alone, even so, without doubt, should kings conduct
themselves. The king that is righteous should always behave in
such a manner as to avoid what is dear to him, for the sake of
doing that which would benefit his people.*

Bhishma to Yudhishthira, from
the *Mahabharata*.

So much has been written about the Princes being womanisers and
spendthrifts, but I ask you, where was the time? I worked with my
father as his secretary after I had done my Senior Cambridge Exam
and he started work at five o'clock whether it was winter or the hot
weather. I would write up his notes for him and then take them to
his secretary to be typed; that was my routine. He would sit in his
office till 12:30 in the afternoon, have his lunch and a nap and then
go for a walk; sometimes hundreds of people used to wait for him so
that they could put their grievances to him face to face. Later he
would sit in the club and play tennis or billiards, come back and have
his meal at 8:30 and go to sleep. When did he have time to do
nautch-gana (dance parties), tell me?

This complaint, from the daughter of the late Maharao of Kutch,
was a familiar one. 'So many of the rulers were very, very simple,'
argues the widow of the last ruler of Porbandar. 'Many were strict
vegetarians who never drank or smoked and lived very simple and
very disciplined lives – but those were the rulers one never heard
about.' The son of the last Raol of Mansa State insists that 'in a
small state like ours there was no question of indulging in ostentatious luxury. We lived in a certain luxury of a type, but there was
no question of sitting back and enjoying the goodies. My father,
grandfather and great-grandfather were almost puritanical, in fact.
None kept concubines or were addicted to opium or liquor – and

had there been the slightest rumour of misbehaviour it would have been really looked down upon by everyone in the state.'

Few persons were in a better position to observe a ruler go about his business than his wife or children – and a father seen through his son's eyes was not necessarily a paragon of virtue. 'Looking back, my father appears as rather a tragic figure,' says Dr Karan Singh of Maharaja Hari Singh of Jammu and Kashmir:

> What happened to him reminds me of the confrontation between Charles I and Cromwell – and perhaps my father was lucky to have escaped without losing his head. He was virtually a king within his state, with the British very distant, and the area he ruled was only just less than England, Scotland and Wales put together. In many ways he was a remarkable man, a great organiser and very meticulous in everything he did. He selected his prime ministers with great care and got men of great ability who later on played important roles in Free India. He didn't interfere with day-to-day administration, which he left to the prime minister, so to that extent he was constitutional. But the people in his personal court had somewhat limited vision, which was one of the reasons why he wasn't adequately aware of the changes taking place.
>
> Then he himself was a bit of a loner in a way. I think the 'Mr A' blackmail case which he had the bad luck to get caught up in as a young man had a deep impact on him, so I don't think he liked fraternising much. It seems to me that he didn't really have a feel of what was happening in the sub-continent. He was so immersed in the system, as it were, that he never really thought it would come to an end.

In striking contrast, Maharaja Yeshwant Rao Holkar of Indore saw 'quite clearly and quite early on that it was a bit of a dead end'. To Richard Shivaji Rao Holkar, his father was 'a person who would have liked to have been a wealthy American. His education and his leanings led him to conclude that the institution of rulership was not really something of the twentieth century – and he wanted desperately to be part of the century and to have the opportunity to lead a fairly private life.'

If Hari Singh and Yeshwant Rao had few ideas in common, they did at least share the burden of being rulers of large states. It was Conrad Corfield's experience that neither such big states nor the many more smaller states were easy to govern and that 'the state which had a settled feeling of contentment and belonging was about the same size as a District in British India; in other words, the kind of area where one man, who really was the mother and father of the people, could exercise his influence.' This was a feeling shared by his colleague, John Cotton, who also believed that 'in the context of the time, a well-ruled Indian state was a better form of administration than anything we had in British India, because it was an Indian ruling his own people – and not just a governor, but a man whose dynasty had always ruled, so that *ma-baap*, the mother and father of his people, was what he was.'

Two states that conformed to this ideal size were Rampur and Sawantwadi, both just under 1000 square miles in area: the former an isolated Muslim state surrounded by British territory in the United Provinces; the latter a Maratha state in hilly country close to the Western seaboard between Bombay and Goa.

From 1930 until the merger of the states in 1948, Rampur was ruled by Nawab Sir Syed Raza Ali Khan. During that period, the state underwent its own industrial revolution which brought a trebling in the state income in less than two decades. 'It was a complete revolution,' says his son. 'Canals, electrification, roads, sanitation, schools – this was all his work, turning Rampur into a very progressive and healthy place.' The Nawab placed great reliance on Colonel Zaidi who headed his State Council, but still 'saw to it personally that his Council of Ministers and secretaries did a good day's work – as he did himself. There were never any papers left pending on his table and he would not get up from his desk until the last file was completed, which might be at nine or ten o'clock at night.' Rampur had a mixed population of Muslims and Hindus:

> In the city it was about 77 per cent Muslim and 23 per cent Hindu, while in the rural areas there were more Hindus than Muslims, so it worked out about fifty-fifty. My father took a very enlightened attitude towards this. On his seven-man council he had three Muslim ministers, three Hindu ministers and one ICS officer on deputation. It was the same in the Army and the other services. In my grandfather's day, the State Forces consisted of two infantry battalions and four squadrons of horse which were 100 per cent Muslim. My father started bringing in Hindus until there were about one in every three in the army and a little more in the police and the civil services.

Sawantwadi State was slightly bigger than Rampur, but had only half its population and less than a sixth of its state revenue. Here the ruler was Rajabahadur Khem Sawant V, the present Raja's father, who was born in 1897 and educated very largely in England. 'He came back to India after serving in Mesopotamia during the First World War, and although he had been under a strong English influence from the age of three or four he became very enamoured with Eastern philosophy, so that even today people consider him to have been a saint king with a very strict moral character.' The Raja also became a supporter of the Swadeshi Campaign against imported goods and started wearing *khadi* or home-spun clothes, even for state occasions. In 1927, at the height of the Civil Disobedience Movement against the British, he invited its leader, Mahatma Gandhi, to come over and spend a month convalescing in his state: 'When the British objected, my father's answer was that he could see no reason why he should not entertain a personal friend. After Gandhi left us, he publicly acknowledged my father to be an ideal ruler and Sawantwadi to be a *Ramrajya* (ideal kingdom).'

What had particularly impressed the Mahatma were the many fundamental reforms which the Raja had carried through:

> One of the first things he did was to abolish the *Devadasi* system. This was a system whereby girls belonging to a particular community were dedicated to the temple at an early age and had to perform various services to the village deity. Some were attendants who looked after visitors who stayed at the temple, others were supposed to sing devotional songs or dance at the temple, but this system had led to other things and the devadasi had become almost the village prosti-tute. So Sawantwadi became quite free of this devadasi system. Then there was another class called the *kunbin* class, meaning those who work as maid-servants. Now these kunbins were being exchanged from family to family as gifts. So that was abolished and with it was introduced the Sharada Act, which forbade old men to marry young girls. Such reforms were very strictly enforced, with the idea of creating a welfare state where no physical or moral cruelty took place.

Mahatma Gandhi had been born in Porbandar State, where his father had served for a period as Dewan. 'It was the influence that he experienced during his childhood that made Gandhiji what he was,' suggests Rajmata Anant Kunverba of Porbandar. 'I've lived with it myself and most of our people are like that, with an intrinsic simplicity. For instance, my husband always wore khadi, both for his pyjamas and his suits, all spun in Porbandar. My mother-in-law used to be quite displeased with him, because he would never wear any jewellery around his neck and never used gold except for his puja.'

Maharaja Rana Sir Natwarsinhji Bahadur ascended the gadi of Porbandar State in 1908 at the age of seven:

> My husband got his ruling powers when he was eighteen years of age. Until that time he was supervised, educated and trained by British tutors who were with him constantly. At the age of ten he was

removed from the palace in which he had lived with my mother-in-law
and went to live with his two British tutors, who were great discipli-
narians. It was a very spartan upbringing which lasted him all his life.
I have never met anyone so disciplined. He could never understand
anyone wasting anything, not even a tiny scrap of paper. He used to
cut up all his envelopes and use them for scrap paper.

After leaving Rajkumar College the young ruler of Porbandar
underwent training in all the departments of the state administration, 'so that by the time he really acceded to the gadi he was a
well-trained and disciplined person'. This essentially British education did, however, leave the Maharaja somewhat out of touch with
the ways of his own people:

I remember my husband telling me how foolish he once felt over an
incident that happened soon after he had been installed. In the Barda
hills of Porbandar live a very ancient tribe called the Rabaris and a
meeting had been arranged where they all gathered to meet my
husband. At the end he said, 'Are there any problems?' And one man
got up and said, 'Yes, one problem we do have. We have been given
an order that our camels are not to graze off the trees in the hills.
What are they going to eat?' Now we had certain large areas of land
that were kept purely as grazing grounds and so my husband said,
'Well, they can eat like all the cattle do that go out grazing.' To which
one man replied, 'But, Bapu, camels can't bend down and graze like
cattle off the ground. They only take leaves off trees or off bushes.'
Now my husband, having been brought up in the way he had, did
not know this. Then my husband said, 'If you have been given an
order that your camels are not to graze off the trees, how do you
manage?' They pointed to the forest *chowkidars*, who were the forest
rangers looking after the forests, and said, 'You see these chowkidars.
We pay them the same amount as the state pays them and they allow
our camels to graze in the forests.' My husband was so impressed
that he announced that the order was cancelled, whereupon the
spokesman for the Rabaris turned to these chowkidars and said,
'Your salaries are also stopped.' My husband told me that he realised
then that unjust laws that could not be kept led to corruption, whereas
if laws were made that people could cope with, then there would be
no room for corruption.

As a ruler the Maharana-Saheb had the authority to do very much
as he liked:

He had the power but never misused it. He was too simple and
humble for that, being a Hindu in the real sense of a *vedanta* – 'We
come with nothing and we go with nothing, so that we must not think

of what we have or of possessions, nor concern ourselves with the fruits – only with our actions.' So my husband never put his name to anything and yet the new part of Porbandar was all planned and designed by my husband and built under his supervision. Not a building went up without his approval. He would say to the state engineer, 'You build it up to the level of the plinth, then let the Dewan know and I'll come and see it.' They knew that Bapu would come and see it and so everything was 100 per cent. We've had two cyclones recently when all the old buildings from my husband's time stood like rocks, while the new buildings just collapsed.

Like so many of his contemporaries who had a similar upbringing, Maharaja Natwarsinhji followed a strict routine, rising early each morning and going for a ride or a round of golf before breakfast and then starting work promptly at the same time every day: 'As soon as my husband arrived at the Secretariat the flag would go up, so people would know he had come. Then he himself saw to everything, working together with his Dewan. If he wasn't in the office he would be visiting the villages, because he kept very close contact with all his people and never left the state unless it was absolutely necessary.' The working day ended at five o'clock, when the Maharana-Saheb returned to the palace, changed and went off to the club to play tennis, billiards or bridge before returning home at exactly seven-thirty, which in the summer months was when the little ceremony of the bringing on of light took place:

The Hindu thinks of light as God, so that when the sun goes down and the *mashals* (lamps) are first brought on to replace the light of the sun, we always put our hands together and bow to the light as God. In the old Indian States this started the evening. In Porbandar a live flame was brought in a huge urn carried by a dwarf, an elderly man named Jivo who had a deep voice. First would come the light and then others following playing a *shehnai*, flute and soft drums. It was really very lovely because it was at that time of evening when it wasn't dark and it wasn't light. Then while my husband held his hands together they would blow the flame, as it were, with their hands. That was done outside. Then as he went up the steps one of our very old maids would stand at the top of the staircase holding a large flat cake of rye, which is the staple food of Kathiawar. This she would twirl around my husband's head three or four times and then it would be thrown away. This was a wonderful custom of taking the evil off the head of the *annadata*, the provider of grain. You saw it also in the streets, when the women would clench their fists and crack their knuckles. Our women, so graceful and so beautiful, would take the ends of their saris and touch my husband's head on either

side, again taking the evil off his head and then cracking the evil, as
it were, as they cracked their knuckles.

The bringing on of light also signalled the start of the evening
darbar: 'We never had any dancing in our evening darbar, but we
had music, poetry, recitations, oratory, complaints and, of course,
discussion – discussions on the *Ramayana* and the *Bhagvad-Gita*,
discussions on politics. We had four or five outstanding Gujerati
poets in Porbandar and, of course, there would also be pilgrims
wandering about or minstrels and so you met all sorts of people. It
was like a kind of club, but it was also the theatre and the parliament
and everything else rolled into one.'

Little Porbandar was a state without illiteracy and without slums,
where its culture and the best of its ancient traditions were respected
under a ruler widely regarded as an ideal raja – 'even now they say
that during Bapu's time, we had a Ramraj.' Like every other state
in India, its population of some 147,000 persons (in 1941) was
mixed, made up of a number of different castes, tribes and religions
that co-existed without rivalry or friction. This was by no means
unique to Porbandar, for whereas inter-communal rivalries in many
parts of British India led to frequent clashes between Hindus and
Muslims, in the vast majority of Indian states the problem was
virtually non-existent. 'There was never any ill-feeling between
Muslims and Hindus,' says Iqbal Muhamed Khan of his father's
period of rule in Palanpur from 1918 to 1948. 'With only 15–20
per cent Muslim population, he could not have ruled had it not been
for complete harmony with the other communities. Hindus and
Muslims mixed everywhere and it was taken for granted.'

It was no different in Kutch – except that here the ruling family
was Hindu. 'The population was one-third Muslim to two-thirds
Hindu,' says the present Maharao, Madansinhji Savai Bahadur, who
succeeded his father in 1948. 'In very few places did the two
communities live so very close to one another. When there was a
Mohamedan fair my grandfather would do the salaam at the Mosque,
just as a lot of Mohamedans came to do respect to the Hindu deity.
I, too, would go and make obeisance as Mohamedans do. When all
the riots took place in India during Independence there was no
incident in Kutch.'

One of the great virtues of a monarchy was that it united people
and gave them a common cause, overriding tribal or religious
loyalties. The duty that he owed to his subjects to treat them as one
people was something that no well-brought-up young heir-apparent
could be allowed to forget. 'There are very few things that my father

told me,' declares the Maharawal of Dungarpur,' but I remember him telling me that one day I would be called upon to rule over a quarter of a million people. "You must be fair-minded," he told me. "You must look upon the Hindus and *Mussalmans* (Muslims) as your two eyes. If you differentiate between Hindus and Mussalmans, you will be cock-eyed. So if you want to maintain your two eyes, you must look upon your subjects in terms of absolute impartiality and equality."'

In Lakshman Singh's case, his father's early death robbed him of any further tutelage, but the fathers of other young heirs-apparent generally saw to it that they were adequately trained and prepared for the roles that, even as late as 1945, every Yuvaraj or Walihad continued to take for granted as his birthright. After completing his education at Mayo College, the young Yuvaraj of Kotah was set to learn how the various departments of the state were run: 'I was sent to each head of department who explained how everything was done, and while they carried on the business of running their departments I used to sit there in their offices and watch how it was done. Then I went to sit with my father in his office and watch things and whenever they were discussing some business they would ask me what was my opinion, would it be all right if we did it this way or that way. So I gradually got to know something about it.'

Some rulers took this training a stage further by sending their sons off for a few months to a state like Mysore which was generally recognised as having a model administration. Few princes, however, received as thorough an education in practical administration as the young Raja Shrimant Shivram Sawant Bhonsle, who succeeded to the gadi at the age of ten:

After my father's death in 1937 my mother became Regent and it was she who really brought me up to rule. Normally a ruler was given his powers when he was about twenty or twenty-one, but before that I had two years of army experience and then underwent training in civil administration. I was put under the Commissioner of the Southern Division of Bombay Presidency, based at Belgaum, where I trained for almost eight months. I started by being asked to take over a village while the village clerk went on leave. Then I went to the Tehsildar's office and worked with him and from this I went to the Assistant Collector's office and finally the Commissioner's office. This was followed by training in the judiciary under two very eminent Indian Magistrates, doing the Criminal Procedure Code with one and Criminal Appeals with the other. After that I worked as personal assistant to my mother, taking decisions on my own, ruling the state unofficially until I got my powers.

The young Raja of Sawantwadi was perhaps fortunate in so far as he knew when he would be assuming full ruling powers. For other young princes there was no such certainty, while the stresses of being the heir-apparent to a ruler made it difficult for them to enjoy a natural father-son relationship: 'When you had a powerful head of state he would not brook any interference from an upstart, which his son very often was because he was a generation younger. The son, on the other hand, considered himself fully prepared to take over, because he knew that, with or without training, the moment his father died he would step into his shoes.' An additional difficulty was the natural rivalry between brothers, in which 'the younger sons wanted their fathers to live forever, because while he was still alive they were still equal, whereas once the eldest brother came to the gadi they would automatically fall – unless they were good friends'. Even more damaging was the effect of court intrigue, which could raise all sorts of suspicions in people's minds, because 'the system was right for mischief-making. Pass a word here, pass a word there. Say, "Your Highness, I am deeply hurt to even say this, but I feel it is my duty as a loyal subject to mention to you that your son said the following about you."' The problem became particularly acute when a ruler lived for an unusually long time, as happened in Kapurthala:

> When one lives under the overpowering shadow of a personality like my grandfather, it does generate its own problems. My father, for example, a very erudite person and a person of very gentle habits, never really could quite foresee where he fitted in, but my grandfather handled this remarkably well by giving him a great deal of responsibility in his absence. Even during his presence he would delegate a vast amount of responsibility, making him President of the State Council, which virtually meant that all governance was in his hands except for the executive decisions which had to be taken by the ruler. It's natural that, when one has lived as an heir-apparent for very long, a certain amount of pressure would be generated, but I must say to the credit of my late father that I never found him allowing that to colour his vision.

As it happened, Jagatjit Singh's eldest son never did rule in his own right. When the old patriarch finally died after a long illness in Bombay in 1949, the state, upon whose gadi he had sat since 1876, had already ceased to exist. His son and grandson accompanied the cortège as it entered Kapurthala with a full military guard of honour:

> Following the cortège was a mass of humanity. I have heard of people lamenting the loss of somebody very dear to them, but to see

shopkeepers, petty tradesmen, farmers, village elders, old grizzled grey-beards with tears streaming down their eyes, was something I'll never forget. After my grandfather's body had been cremated in the place called Shalimar Gardens where members of our family are cremated, I remember the State Pandit, Sri Ram, a venerable old gentleman who used to do the pujas and who officiated at the last rites of my grandfather, came to see me. He was very old and walked with great difficulty, but he came to offer his condolences and sat down and wept. He was very dearly loved by my grandfather, who had consulted him in many things, not just as an astrologer but as a venerated elder, very knowledgeable in folklore and custom and ritual in the scriptures. So Pandit Sri Ram broke down and wept and said, '*Maharaj badi hasti thi, Riyasat bana gaye aur sath le gaye* – Here was a very great man and the strange thing is he built the state and he took it with him.'

Even after the merger of the states with the Indian Union in 1948–49, the imminent prospect of accession to the gadi was enough to fill many a Yuvaraj and Walihad with alarm and foreboding. The present Maharana of Mewar was a grown man when his invalid father finally died in July 1955, but that did not lessen the trepidation with which he anticipated becoming the 75th in line of his great dynasty: 'The night before His late Highness died I was sitting in front of him and I looked at him and our eyes met. I felt more depressed than words can say, for I felt that he wanted to know how, if he were to die, I should conduct myself. Whether I would be able to hold the dignity of the gadi together, whether I'd be reasonable, fair, honest and upright in my dealings, whether his choice in adopting me had been the correct one. A whole wave of such thoughts swept through my mind.'

Four decades earlier the Maharana's fellow-clansman in neighbouring Dungarpur had succeeded to the gadi in very different circumstances – and almost without being aware of it. 'There was an epidemic of influenza in 1918,' the Maharawal of Dungarpur recalls. 'In a small place like Dungarpur, ten to fifteen people were dying from it every day because there was no known cure for it in those days. I was very, very ill – in fact, worse than my father, but he caught a chill and then double pneumonia and died – while I happened to survive.'

The passing of a ruler was always a traumatic and momentous event in a state's history. Dick Bowles was present in Patiala in March 1938 when, after a period of increasing ill-health, Maharaja Bhupinder Singh died at the relatively early age of forty-eight:

From 1937 onwards His Highness's health began to deteriorate. He wasn't as active as he had been and didn't appear as often. A great fleet of European doctors, nearly all of them from Switzerland, kept coming out and living at the palace, but he didn't seem to be getting any better. Towards the end he allowed himself to be somewhat taken over by his own religious leaders, because he was, after all, regarded as the leader of the Sikh nation. One of these chaps announced that His Highness was going to die a violent death in an earthquake, so Bhupinder decided to move out of Moti Bagh Palace into an earthquake-proof establishment of lightweight timber which he had built in the gardens of the palace. But, as it happened, he died in the palace. I was just twenty-one at the time, and I recall the appalling atmosphere of that time so vividly. It was an atmosphere of total gloom as word spread through the corridors that he was unlikely to make it. That afternoon the walls round the gardens of the palace at the back were lined with crows and they were all silent. He died in the true Sikh tradition. He was lifted from his bed and placed on straw on the ground, the idea being that you are born with nothing and die with nothing. I was waiting in a library where there was a side entrance into his private quarters, an area where we often stood around and gossipped, and when he died a terrible noise of wailing emerged through this door. It seemed absolutely unnatural and quite horrific and against all the rules I walked into the zanana. I never saw him, but got as far as the ante-room next to the room where he was lying. All the Maharanis and ladies were there wailing and crying and the floor of this room was littered with exquisite Indian and European jewellery, because the custom among the Sikhs is for all the women to remove all their jewellery and throw it on to the ground. I went out and ordered a bloody great whisky and that was the first time I drank. A lot of whisky was drunk that night.

It was customary in India for funerals to take place between the sunrise and the sunset following the death of the deceased: by interment among the Muslims, by cremation among the Sikhs and Hindus. But before the funeral a number of important rituals had to be carried out and, among Hindus and Sikhs, certain social taboos observed. While the deceased's body was being washed, anointed and dressed for the funeral, his successor was privately acknowledged as the new ruler, most commonly by the placing of an auspicious red *tikka* mark on his forehead by a close relative: 'The moment His late Highness passed away I became a ruler instantly,' explains the Maharaja of Dhrangadhara. 'It was just assumed. I was addressed as Bapu straight away and my sister came along and did the *tilak* (mark) on me.'

Alone among his family the new ruler was not considered to have been made impure by the death that had occurred in the house, nor was he required to wear the traditional white colour of mourning. Brijendra Singh of Bharatpur was ten when his father died in exile outside the state in 1929:

> I don't remember anything of the emotional part of it, but I was rushed over to the palace and kept there and made to wear coloured clothes. However, my mother made me shave my hair to show that I had gone into mourning. Then my father's body was attended to, not by ourselves – for we never touch the dead body – but by our *bhai-bands*, Sinsinwar Jats descended from a common ancestor, who had always to be available to lift the dead body, clean it and bathe it and to perform the cremation ceremonies – just as they also put the new ruler in the gadi, for it was they not the servants who carried me in a palanquin to the place where we are crowned.

Nor was the new ruler expected to perform what was generally regarded as one of the most solemn duties a son was required to carry out: that of accompanying his father's body to the royal cremation ground, kindling his funeral pyre and remaining in attendance until the body had been consumed by flames. In nearly all the Rajput and Maratha states, the new ruler accompanied his father's funeral cortège only as far as the palace gates, the idea being that 'the gadi is not supposed to be left vacant'. This seeming lack of filial piety was based on a well-founded need to secure the succession at its most vulnerable moment, as the Maharaja of Dhrangadhara explains:

> A practical reason for it is evidenced in Jhala history, when in about 1400 Raja Rajadharja died and his two elder sons, Ajoji and Sajoji, accompanied their father's bier to the burning-ground. On their return they found the gates of the city shut against them. Ranjoji, the third son and my ancestor, was a boy then but his maternal uncle had distributed largesse to mercenary soldiers who had been recruited in their war against the Gujerat Sultan. The two brothers had to go off and seek their fortune elsewhere, ultimately taking service with the Rana of Mewar. So in Dhrangadhara a ruler is never allowed to accompany a funeral to the *samshan*, which is the cremation ground.

The womenfolk, too, were confined to the palace. Before the bier was taken out, usually with the body lying in repose but sometimes arranged in full ceremonial garb in a seated position, they heaped garlands and rice over it and broke their bangles. Then, as the cortège moved out of the palace grounds, they saw it off to the accompaniment of ullulation and wailing. 'I remember very well walking in this procession,' states Dick Bowles, 'listening to the

Indian music and the sound of the ladies through the lattices of the zanana right along the front of the palace weeping and wailing. It was a terrible sound, terrible.'

Once the body had left the building, it was the responsibility of the women to see that the whole house was washed and purified. All would remain in mourning for twelve days, with those closest to the ruler taking no baths for ten days. For the widow of the ruler the mourning period really only ended with her own death. She would go into retreat, wear only black and eat only vegetarian food. Until the recent past these and other restrictions dictated by custom were practised with almost ruthless severity, as Chichibai of Pratapgarh recalls of the two wives of Yuvaraj Mansingh of Pratapgarh who died in 1931:

> Mansinghji died in the palace five years after he had married my mistress. She was taken from the *quila* (fort) to the palace to have a last look and then the two widows were made to stay in one place for twelve months, just sitting in this hovel of a room in the palace – one widow being about thirty, the other thirty-five – and during this period of mourning they were not allowed to meet anyone. After the twelve months of mourning she was taken to her father's house at Dhrangadhara for the *barsi* (one-year death ceremonies), where she stayed for another year before returning to Pratapgarh. She lived in the quila for the rest of her life and was known as the *quila-ma*, but while the other rani just lived the life of a recluse and hardly left her room in the palace for fifty-odd years, my mistress started a boarding school for Rajput girls. Her father-in-law, Maharaja Raghunath Singhji, told her that it was not the custom for Rajput girls to be educated, but she had an independent spirit and started the school despite the objection of her in-laws, spending money from her own allowance.

The mortifications of widowhood had been practised in Hindu society for many centuries and they were, for the most part, willingly and even enthusiastically embraced as an act of devotion. In royal circles, the highest expression of wifely devotion to a dead husband took the form of *sati*, the act of self-immolation in which a widow – or even a number of widows – joined a late husband on the funeral pyre. Among the Rajput clans in particular, no action by a woman was more highly regarded than this final act of self-sacrifice. Even after the practice had been outlawed by the Paramount Power in the early nineteenth century, isolated instances of sati continued to occur from time to time. Nowhere in Rajasthan were satis more honoured by memorials and by worship than in Jodhpur, so it was entirely fitting that the last recorded instance of a royal sati should have been performed in Jodhpur by a Bhati married to a Sisodia, the grandson of Sir Pratap Singh of Jodhpur and Idar. Her name was Sugankunverba, widow of Brigadier Jabbar Singh Sisodia of the Jodhpur Lancers, and her act of self-immolation took place illegally and in secret in the late 1950s. Maharani Padmavati Gaekwad of Baroda, only daughter of Maharaja Umaid Singh of Jodhpur, was a close friend of hers:

About a month before he died she stopped eating and drinking. She went about her household chores, looked after her husband and nursed him, but without letting on she got together all the things required for the last rites. I used to go to their house to cheer them up and one evening just a little before sun-down as I drove into the compound, I heard this very deep chanting of *Ram-Ram* as if coming from a deep, echoing chasm. He had passed away two minutes earlier and she had already announced that she was going to commit sati when he was cremated at sunrise. While they attended to his body she went to her bathroom, had a bath and put on the brand new clothes that she had stored in her trunk. For sati we don't wear widow's clothes but wedding clothes, with the ivory bangles and everything. The colour she chose was a sort of light pink called *saptalu*, which none of the wives of the Sisodias can now wear because they now do puja to that colour. When she had dressed she sat with her husband's head on her lap all night. Twice his body perspired and twice she wiped it down saying, 'Why are you so impatient, I am coming with you. Be calm. The sun's first rays are still to come.' Morning came and her *devar* arrived, her husband's brother who was going to perform the last rites. When he doubted her intentions she got up and sat over the lamp which they kept burning near the dead body. She fanned the flames with the hem of her sari and sat there for five minutes until he said, 'I'm satisfied.' Now normally when a sati goes to the pyre she is accompanied by a procession, but the word had spread like wildfire through the whole city and people started gathering. So she said, 'We can't walk, bring cars and a truck,' and in this way they avoided the police who were waiting at the entrance to the big burning ghat. She had sent for me, but I didn't get the message and got there late and by that time the flames had got too high for me to see her – but I heard her voice saying '*Ram-Ram*', which never stopped for a second until she died. She is worshipped today not only by Rajputs but by everybody and so many *artis* (songs) and *bhajans* have been composed about her, and her funeral pyre burnt for almost six months non-stop with all the coconuts that people kept putting on it. That was after they had picked out the remains and immersed them in the Ganges at Hardwar.

RULER OF THE STATE

Reduced in power, circumscribed in territory, compelled to yield much of their splendour and many of the dignities of birth, they have not abandoned an iota of the pride and high bearing arising from a knowledge of their illustrious and regal descent.

Lt. Col. James Tod,
Annals and Antiquities of Rajasthan, 1829

'My first reaction was one of total bewilderment because all these people who had been surrounding my father suddenly started surrounding me. It was a new experience that somehow I had never anticipated.' Although it seldom came as a surprise, the elevation to the gadi meant an alteration in circumstances so complete as to be overwhelming at first and difficult to absorb. Private acceptance of the new ruler's authority by his family and by those in close attendance was usually followed on the third day by a public proclamation of the succession. In Bikaner drums were beaten in the town square, the announcement was made and a silver coin was struck bearing the new ruler's name. The period of official mourning continued for twelve days and on the thirteenth the ruler was officially and publicly installed in what was the Indian equivalent of the European coronation ceremony – although crowning itself played no part in the ritual. In Bikaner this installation was preceded by the ruler's recognition by his leading nobles:

> Before the ruler could sit on the gadi he had to be asked to do so by the four chief nobles of Bikaner – the Raja of Mahajan, the Raja of Bidasar, the Rao of Bhukarka and the Rao of Rawatsar. These four nobles were the pillars of the state and this was the recognition of the ruler by the Rajput clan. Next, recognition had to come from the Godara Jats, who were the original inhabitants of Bikaner before the Rao Bika conquered them. The Godara Jats recognised the ruler by one of their number cutting his finger and putting his blood-mark on his head.

The installation, however, only came after the long and complex rituals of the *Rajyabhishek* ceremony had been completed. One ruler who underwent this ancient ceremony of anointing was the Raja of Sawantwadi:

> In Sawantwadi the ritual of the Rajyabhishek purported to be that followed by Rama, and the various Vedic mantras used were said to be the same as those recited at that time. The whole ceremony took about eight days, beginning with various prayers directed to appease the nine signs of the zodiac. This was followed by the other ceremonies directed at various aspects of life so as to 'clear the air', as it were, and at the end of each ceremony fire was worshipped. This went on for about a week before the actual day of the Rajyabhishek, for which an auspicious day and time was found by the court astrologer.

On the morning of his anointing the ruler was given a ritual bath known as the *Mangal Snana* or holy bath, as the Maharaja of Dhrangadhara describes:

> The ruler's body is smeared with earth brought from all kinds of places – from the top of a hill, from the bottom of a hill, from outside a prostitute's house – I don't know why, but from all kinds of places. Then you are washed clean with an enormous basin with 108 holes in it, into which waters from various rivers in the state have been poured. Now this was in February in my case and during a coronation no door or window can be closed, so it was blowing very hard and I was absolutely drenched, yet curiously enough right through this pouring of the waters I was feeling steaming hot at times and freezing cold at times. After that you changed and came before the sacred fire for the anointing.

While the ritual bath took place in private in the ruler's palace, the anointing ceremony was performed in public in the temple, as the Raja of Sawantwadi continues:

> First you prayed to your family deity and asked for blessing. After that you worshipped your weapons, your horses and your cows, then you carried a bow and arrow four or five times around the fire and sat down on a low stool. The family priest then poured water through a golden vessel containing a thousand holes and the hereditary chief minister did the same thing. Immediately after that you were anointed with the *panchamrit* (five nectars), consisting of honey, sugar, curds, milk, ghee and finally water again. Now this was the same ceremony of anointing observed when we worshipped our deities, so that once the Rajyabhishek had taken place, then the ruler was symbolically elevated at that time to the level of Vishnu. He is then installed on the gadi and actually worshipped by the *Raj-guru* (royal priest) as any deity is worshipped.

With his anointing completed, the ruler was then led to the gadi to be given his tikka mark, which in Pratapgarh was done in blood – not by a Bhil, as was the case in a number of other Rajput states, but by the Raj-jyotish after cutting his thumb on his sword: 'There's an old saying that the amount of blood that flowed down the nose predicted how long that particular ruler was going to rule.' In Dhrangadhara, however, the mark was made with the more usual *kum-kum* paste, while the ruler was seated on a tiger skin: 'In our case the tilak was made by the Raj-purohit, who makes a long mark right from your nose right up to your scalp in red. That's when the trumpets are sounded, the guns are shot off and the drums begin to be beaten for the rest of the day, because that is the moment when you are confirmed as ruler.' It was at this moment that Mayurdhawaj Singh admits to feeling 'terribly humble that all these splendid people were accepting you and anointing you as something above them and someone distinct and separate from them – because this was really a ceremony of death in which you died in a state of man and were reborn as a king. Thereafter you are cut off from your family and previous connections. No ritual impurity thereafter attaches to you. You emerge as *Varpaguru*, the head of all castes.'

With the ritual complete, the Hindu raja became a true king in the eyes of all his people – although not in the eyes of the Paramount Power.

The Maharawal of Dungarpur was invested with full ruling powers in February 1928, the Maharaja of Dhrangadhara in October 1943, the Maharaja of Benares in July 1947. For the Maharawal, the cares and responsibilities of office seemed 'overwhelming' at times, 'but I always prayed and said to myself that God in his good grace would show me the right path'. Part of the responsibility called for a certain detachment on his part: 'Your friends have got to be forsaken. You can't be free with people, which in itself was a sort of solitary confinement and suppression of your feelings to an unreasonable degree, but one had to do it as part of the game. Some princes made the mistake of having favourites, women and men. I never did. I was lucky.'

In his style of government, the Maharawal believed in being very closely involved in the running of the state:

At least fifty per cent of the rulers – especially rulers of the larger type of states – didn't take much interest in the affairs of the state and left everything to their Dewans – often very capable, eminent men. Whether it was the Dewan or the Political Agent or both together ruling the state, as far as these rulers were concerned they just signed the papers and their work was done. But as far as I was concerned, I believed in personal rule and in spending five or six hours every day going through files and cases. So much depended on the personal equation, which is why I believe monarchy to be one of the best forms of government. On alternate days, I saw anyone and everyone who came. I had two secretaries who screened petitions and these were forwarded for disposal to the department concerned. If a man persistently came to me with the same request, then I went into it personally and took such action as I saw fit under the rules of the department. It stopped red tape, ensured efficiency and prompt disposal of cases.

Like his father before him, the Maharawal believed in getting out and about as much as possible, spending 'at least 150 days in the year' going round the villages in the morning and returning to his office before noon:

There are very few princes in Rajputana who can talk the Bhili language as well as I can. I've lived with them, spent many nights in their huts, drunk their goats' milk and their toddy and eaten their chickens and eggs. I've entertained them at the palace, played and danced with them. And if you maintained that personal touch, then the people looked to you for advice and redressal of their grievances, they gave you their devotion and loyalty. Today there is no such personal touch. A Chief Minister starts his excursion with twenty-five cars, two or three Superintendents of Police and a horde of officers and Members of the Legislative Assembly. He makes a speech of five minutes' duration and then his entourage starts moving out and in this way he covers fifteen villages by noon.

The Maharawal ruled with a Cabinet of five ministers headed by the Dewan, a post that for many years was filled by the ruler's younger brother, Veerbhadra Singh, an Oxford MA. In later years there was also a State Legislative Council, but throughout his reign power remained concentrated in the Maharawal's hands:

I was head of the Executive and head of the Legislature. I had a Judge of the High Court, Rao Bahadur Chunilal Harilal Setalvad, who was a retired Chief Presidency Magistrate of Bombay and one of the best men in the entire judicial service of Rajputana. He used to come once in ten weeks, stay for ten days, take a fee of 5000 rupees and go. He advised me on the disposal of court cases and I signed all his decisions. Only once did I interfere. There was famine relief going on, a large dam was being constructed and there were complaints from about 120 labourers that their wages were not being paid. I made enquiries on the spot and felt there was a *prima facie* case and told the Inspector of Police in charge of that circle that this man should be prosecuted. But the Magistrate let him off and that was the end of it. As the head of the state I shouldn't have done that, but I was a young man and felt that this man should be punished, which was wrong. However, as far as the courts were concerned there were practically no pending cases – and that was a characteristic feature of the Indian States. I used to see to it that statements of case law from all the courts were produced and if the number of pending cases more than three years old exceeded ten or twelve, then the Magistrate or Civil Judge was called upon to dispose of them straight away – and if he didn't, his pay would be stopped. Justice delayed is justice denied and even a crude decision is a decision. Now nothing happens for years on end, with thousands of under-trial prisoners languishing in jails for ten years and more.

The Maharaja of Dhrangadhara was born fifteen years after the Maharawal and this age difference was reflected in their different attitudes towards their roles. 'I thought of myself more as an administrator than a ruler who must always be in touch with his people,' declares Mayurdhwaj Singh:

> Some rulers ruled and some merely reigned. I wanted to be a good and popular ruler, moving in the direction of the ultimate ideal of *Ram-Rajya*, Rama's kingdom in which there was no injustice, where taxes were few and where he heard the public voice. I was very young and I had various ideas about rural reconstruction but I had a very elderly Dewan, Sir Harilal Gosalia, who regarded it as improper for any Minister other than himself to come to the palace and who believed that his officers should only meet me during the State Council meeting that I attended once a week. So I felt cut off and a time came when I had to say, 'Sir Harilal, I would like to justify my existence and do something. In what way can I contribute?'

As the Maharaja became more closely involved in the business of government, he found that whereas a ruler who reigned could always let his ministers take the blame for unpopular reforms, 'when you are actually governing you cannot help but tread on people's toes'. A number of progressive Labour Laws were enacted and such reforms as a Hindu Woman's Right to Property Act and a Widows' Remarriage Act, but there were other issues where he found himself having to 'soft pedal'. He also had to learn by experience that 'the personal touch, which I had not regarded as important, was very important. I took the view that the hours I spent preparing things and making things right were more important than merely listening to petitions and complaints and grievances and saying, "Yes, yes. We will do something about it," and not doing anything about it. I thought all that was a waste of time and so access to me was reduced to a minimum. But I think this was a great mistake. If there is a famine and you're there saying "terrible, terrible", that is something that people will appreciate more than if you're being busy behind the scenes ensuring that food comes.'

During his six years on the gadi, Maharaja Mayurdhawaj Singh's main preoccupation was paying off a major debt which had built up in the state during his father's time: 'During my short reign I cleared that quite enormous debt and we were all prepared to go forward when the eclipse happened. If I could have foreseen the integration of the states I would certainly not have paid the entire debt. I could have used that money for all the wonderful schemes that I had in my head.'

Maharaja Vibhuti Narain Singh of Benares was just four years younger than the ruler of Dhrangadhara. For him, the period of ruling with full powers was to be measured in weeks rather than years. 'While I was still at Mayo College, Conrad Corfield (then Political Adviser to the Viceroy) called me to Delhi. I said, "Let me complete my education," but he said, "There's no time. If you waste a day you may not be a Maharaja." Then a Political Agent came and read out the letter from the Viceroy that gave me the powers of a Maharaja on 11 July 1947. The people in Benares were very good to me. The Cabinet of Ministers, presided over by Khan Bahadur Syed Ali Zamin during my minority, asked me to preside over Cabinet Meetings and so I was able to play the leading part.'

The young Maharaja's first major public act was to announce the formation of a 'Responsible Government', with an administration made up of members drawn from an elected *Praja Mandal* or popular assembly: 'The leaders came and met me and said they were not satisfied and wanted more powers. I said, "All right, I'll form a committee to make the necessary constitutional changes."' By the time this new constitution had been drafted, the states had merged and Benares State had ceased to exist. A new India had come into being in which the Princes and their states were to be allowed to play no part.

The three decades following the end of the First World War had seen dramatic developments on the Indian political scene and far-reaching changes in the fortunes of the Indian Princes. With the inauguration of a Chamber of Princes in 1921, they had been provided with a forum that could have been used to their political advantage. But to Conrad Corfield it appeared as if the annual meetings of the Chamber of Princes that followed were primarily concerned with attempts to 'get away from the control of the Paramount Power. They said, "If you leave us alone, we'll run it very well, we don't like to be interfered with," and the whole of their intention was turned to that, instead of trying to work with the other two governing bodies of the Council.' Of the 118 salute States entitled to membership of the Chamber in their own right, the rulers of ten states, including Hyderabad, Mysore, Baroda, Indore and Travancore, opted to stay out. And whilst 127 non-salute States were given the privilege of electing twelve members by a system of group voting, the remaining three hundred or more fiefdoms dotting the sub-continent were left out in the cold with no representation at all.

Year after year one Viceroy after another appealed to the Princes to usher in constitutional and administrative reforms, but the advice was not pressed home and fell on polite but largely deaf ears. 'From the time of the Minto-Morley Reforms in 1909,' says Divyabhanu-sinh Chavda, 'the writing was very clearly on the wall: that with autocratic rule the Indian Princes would not be able to last out very long in isolation. On the one hand everything pointed to change, on the other the weight of tradition tied down people of my father's generation and they could not change with the times.'

A year prior to the formation of the Chamber, the Indian National Congress had appealed to the Princes to grant full responsible government in the states and in 1927 the All India States Peoples' Conference was formed under the aegis of the INC, to provide leadership to popular movements in the states. Attempts to politicise the ordinary inhabitants of the Indian States met with very little success, but there were few Princes who did not respond to the emotional appeal of Mahatma Gandhi's call for Indian self-government and to the benign personality of the man himself. 'One did feel a kind of sympathy with the Nationalist Movement,' says the present Nawab of Palanpur, whose father was one of a number of rulers who got to know the Mahatma well:

Gandhiji always informed us whenever he passed through Palanpur. In those days the rulers could stop a train at any particular station in their territory if they informed the station-master beforehand, so the train would be stopped and my father and I travelled three or four times with him in his third-class carriage, talking to him and giving him his goat's milk and dry fruits and whatever he wanted. As a matter of fact, one of the local rubbishy newspapers wrote an article saying that the Nawab of Palanpur even fools Mahatma Gandhi by giving him goat's milk and dry fruit and that Gandhiji is very friendly with him even though he doesn't do anything for the people of Palanpur!

Yet for most Princes the idea of power-sharing, either in the form of a self-governing Indian Federation (as proposed in 1935) dominated by democratic forces, or in terms of a surrender of internal sovereign rights, remained an unacceptable anathema. One notable exception was the saintly Raja of Aundh, who became the first ruler to introduce genuine constitutional reforms of a far-reaching nature, helped by his second son, Apa Pant, and a remarkable Polish Jew named Morris Frydman who had become a sadhu and whom Apa Pant had met while under training in Mysore State:

> I used to meet him often and we discussed all kinds of things and when I returned to Aundh, I wrote and asked if Mr Frydman could come for six months. One day, a month or two later, he just walked into my room in Aundh and announced, 'I've come.' I said, 'I can't even pay you thirty rupees, Aundh is a poor state,' and he said, 'Apa, I have not come for the money'. Now Frydman had great influence with my father and on his seventy-fifth birthday, he said, 'Raja Saheb, why don't you go and make a declaration to Mahatma Gandhi that you are giving all power to the people because it will help in the freedom struggle.' Now to my father, ruling the state meant very little and freedom for India was a great thing. So Morris Frydman made a draft declaration and I went with my father by the *Deccan Queen* to Bombay and on to Wardha where the constitution was written by Gandhiji. So on 21 January 1939, this constitution was declared giving full responsible government to the people of Aundh. This period, from 1938 to 1947, was the most wonderful time for us, working on what came to be known as the 'Aundh Experiment', because it was a great success. In the beginning the people were a little hesitant because they couldn't understand why their Raja was doing this. They were suspicious and I walked from village to village trying to explain. But after two years it clicked and they were so enthusiastic afterwards that in 1945 they didn't want to merge.

With the outbreak of the Second World War in 1939, schemes for Federation were shelved as Britain became preoccupied with the war effort. As they or their fathers had done in the First World War, the Princes rallied to the banner of their King-Emperor, contributing unstintingly of their resources and personal services. The State Forces of Jaipur, Jodhpur, Kashmir, Gwalior and Patiala were only some of those to see action on many fronts, while a number of rulers distinguished themselves in action, including the Maharajas of

Jaipur, Cooch Behar, Nawanagar, Kolhapur and Bundi, the last being awarded the Military Cross for gallantry.

The Indian National Congress, however, took a very different stand, intensifying its agitation for Independence at about the same time as the Muslim League made its call for the creation of a separate state of Pakistan. Unrest and lawlessness began to spill over into some of the Indian States. In Dungarpur this occasioned the one instance of firing during the present Maharawal's long rule:

> The rates of grain and essential commodities in Dungarpur were probably the cheapest in India and there was a lot of maize being smuggled to Gujerat to manufacture starch for washing clothes. I said I would not allow this, so I sent a platoon to the border to catch the smugglers, who gathered together and started to throw stones. My police force fired two or three shots into the hill-side and one bullet struck a rock and ricocheted and killed a girl of eleven years. To immortalise the incident, a statue of the girl was erected after Independence and a park was named after her. I confessed before Congress leaders that it was a blot on my administration. I said that I was extremely sorry, but it was in the interest of thousands of people that I had to stop the smuggling of grain outside my state.

It was the Nawab of Palanpur's conviction – shared by many others – that the Indian States were peaceful 'right until the merger. But a few years before, a kind of uneasiness and restlessness came to the people, not because they were against the ruler, but because they had learned to agitate from the people in British India. No agitators came to Palanpur. A few people would write articles in various papers criticising the states, but otherwise it was just like a virus of restlessness.'

When the Second World War ended, it seemed at first as if nothing had changed. 'Nobody thought that princely rule would end at that time,' declares the Maharawal of Dungarpur. 'Even in 1945 I never thought it would end, but when Churchill lost that vital election, I thought then that something was going to happen.' With the arrival of the Cabinet Mission in India in March 1946, with instructions to draw up plans for the transfer of power from Britain to the sub-continent, it became apparent that England meant business. A number of rulers met members of the Cabinet Mission to put forward proposals which would allow the Princely States to remain in existence after Independence. They were advised that British Paramountcy would lapse with the transfer of power and that they would do well to organise themselves into large administrative units so as to fit into the framework of the new Indian Constitution.

Riven by dissensions and rivalries, the princes failed to meet the challenge.

In February 1947 the new British Prime Minister, Clement Attlee, announced that the transfer of power would take place not later than June 1948. He also announced the appointment of a new Viceroy, Lord Mountbatten of Burma, specifically charged with executing the task. This was devastating news to both the rulers and the officers of the Indian Political Service. 'The mood was one of astonishment,' declares John Cotton:

> The general feeling had been that when the war came to an end, all the schemes for democratic advancement in India which had been placed in abeyance would be revived and we could persuade the Princes to put their houses in order. We had thought there would be an interval during which we could achieve this long-term scheme. There was a mood of helplessness among my colleagues in the Political Department, who had the future welfare of the Indian States at heart, because it couldn't be done in that time. All the promises, all the agreements made over the years since India had become a part of the British Empire, were set at nought at a stroke of the pen.

Cotton was one of those who attended the Conference of Residents and Political Officers called by Lord Mountbatten soon after his arrival in India:

> I watched with dismay, sitting against the wall. The Viceroy presided, supported by the advisers he had brought out from England, and I listened while these experienced Political Officers were told – whatever their objections and whatever protests they had heard from individual Princes – that time was short, that there would be no opportunity to solve the manifest problems of the Princes who were relying on the treaty relations of the Crown towards them, and that all these matters would be dispensed with in the hope that the successor government would do their best to care for the Princes. It was a very sober occasion. I think a lot of Residents gathered round the table were aghast at what they were hearing. A number of them, and notably Sir Conrad Corfield, attempted to tell the Viceroy that certain matters could not be overlooked and that the Princes deserved better treatment, but all the Viceroy could say to that was, 'Look, I have been sent out here to preside at the conferment of Independence on India. It has been decided that the sooner this is done the better, and if there are any problems, then they must be settled after Independence, because there isn't time to deal with all these matters. So you can leave here and tell the Rulers that the die is cast.'

Early in June the Viceroy suddenly announced that the date for the transfer of power to the two independent nations of Pakistan and India was to be brought forward to 15 August 1947. He advised the Princes to negotiate with one or other of the two successor governments, taking the view that small states which could group together or larger states which were 'viable' units would have a future. 'He told us that "viable" states had nothing to fear,' maintains the Maharawal of Dungarpur – one of the few alive today out of those who played an active part in these traumatic events:

> This doctrine of viability ultimately slaughtered the Princes at the altar of Accession. Some of the Princes who fell in line with the theory of viability took the Viceroy's word as gospel truth, coming as it did from a person so closely related to the British Royal House. These Princes did not even wait to examine the strength of the doctrine in relation to the provinces of India. So on the one hand there was this theory of viability which proved to be a myth, leading the Princes up the garden path and creating disunity among their ranks, and on the other hand there stood the doctrine of unity repeated by the then Chancellor of the Chamber of Princes, the Nawab of Bhopal, that 'United we stand and divided we fall'. There were a few far-sighted rulers like him who firmly believed that the states derived their strength from their weakest link – that they had to combine in order to live. Unfortunately he lost most of his support in the Chamber, and the Princes, regardless of judging the man's ability as Chancellor, just relegated him to the background and rather than be dishonoured, the Nawab read the writing on the wall and he resigned.

With less than a month to go before the handover of power, a new States Department was set up under the veteran Hindu politician Sardar Patel, who urged the Viceroy to use his influence with the Princes to get them to sign individual "Instruments of Accession". These Instruments expressly reserved and retained sovereignty and continuity of state government but would bind them either to Pakistan or to the new India, who would in effect become the new paramount powers. Mountbatten promised Sardar Patel that he would deliver 'a full basket of apples'. Addressing the Chamber of Princes for the first and last time on 25 July, the Viceroy urged the rulers to accede to either of the two dominions, keeping in mind geographical contiguity, and assured them that there would be neither any financial liability on their part nor any encroachment on their sovereignty. Prominent among the absentees was the Nawab of Bhopal, who felt that the Princes had been invited 'like the oysters to attend the tea party with the walrus and the carpenter'. One of the 'oysters' present on this occasion was the Maharawal of Dungarpur, who recalls Mountbatten's virtuoso performance:

> The session lasted only for about two hours instead of the normal two or three days. The Viceroy came dressed in his white Admiral's uniform, unlike his predecessors who invariably came to the Chamber dressed in civilian clothes with long grey morning coat, and a special seat was given to the then Home Minister, Sardar Patel, whereas in all former sessions only the Viceroy occupied the seat on the dais. I think a departure from this practice was made on this occasion to bring pressure on the Princes. Mountbatten looked magnificent and spoke in the most lucid terms. When the Dewan of Kutch sought elucidation on what he should do since the Maharao was away in England for medical treatment, Mountbatten promptly picked up a paperweight lying on his table and said, 'I can see clearly through this crystal that the best course for your Ruler to adopt is to accede to India.' One or two Princes tried to get up and say something, but chits were sent round stating that the Viceroy was rather occupied and busy and he did not want to prolong the Session.

One by one, the Princes started filling Mountbatten's 'basket of apples'; some willingly, determined to carve out a niche for themselves in the mainstream of national life; some confused and apprehensive, carried along by the inexorable tide of circumstances. Others signed only with the greatest reluctance, knowing of no other viable options to exercise. The first to sign the Instrument of Accession on 7 August was Maharaja Sadul Singh of Bikaner, who according to his son, Dr Karni Singh, 'had put his faith in Mountbatten and in the leaders of free India'. For many like the Maharaja of Dhrangadhara, it was this 'free India' that really mattered: 'I wanted India to be free. Everything else was secondary to that prime consideration because it involved so much of one's self-respect to be governed by others. At that time nothing else mattered, but of course one didn't visualise then that events would necessarily happen the way they did.'

There were also those amongst the Princes, like the young Maharaja of Bharatpur, who were called upon to take an irrevocable decision without ever having been allowed to exercise full responsibility.

> I was sitting next to Mountbatten at a dinner party and he said, 'You have still not acceded.' There was dead silence at the dinner table, so I told him, 'Your Excellency, I'd like ten minutes with you after dinner instead of talking at the table.' After dinner I said, 'You're

accusing me, but may I also remind you that the British gave me restricted powers, not allowing me to sign or do anything without the Viceroy's permission; now do I have your permission to sign the Instrument of Accession?' and within twenty-four hours I got my powers!

At the other end of the spectrum were those Princes who were waiting to see the direction of the general drift before committing themselves to an unpalatable decision, or who were holding out for independence on grounds of viability, like the rulers of Travancore and Hyderabad who declared that they would set up as sovereign states on the lapse of British paramountcy. Conrad Corfield recalls the Nizam's reaction when he called on him to convey the news that the British would no longer exercise any control over his state when paramountcy lapsed: 'His Exalted Highness bounced up in his seat and with a gleeful grin said, "Do you mean I can do then as I like?" I suggested that perhaps his ministers and people would have something to say about that, and reminded him that when we left he could no longer rely on our support to maintain his rule, but he remained quite unconcerned, so I left him to enjoy his confidence in the future.'

As 15 August approached, rulers who had long procrastinated began to arrive in New Delhi in ever-increasing numbers to sign on the dotted line. Amongst the most dramatically obtained signatures was that of the Maharaja of Jodhpur, who pulled out a revolver and told Sardar Patel's secretary that he would 'shoot him down like a dog if he betrayed the starving people of Jodhpur'. The Nawab of Bhopal signed on the condition that his Accession would not be made public for ten days, whilst the Maharaja of Travancore only acceded after a physical attack had been made on his Dewan. The anti-climax in accessions was provided by Yeshwant Rao Holkar of Indore, who after having caused great anxiety with his procrastination, finally sent in his signed Instrument of Accession by ordinary post.

The Maharaja of Benares, who had been given his powers prematurely at the insistence of Conrad Corfield, describes the unreality and pathos of the situation in words that reflect the thinking of a majority of his fellow Princes at the time:

The Independence and Merger periods were something for which we were not fully prepared and we couldn't believe it, but when it came, we had to face it with a challenge and make the best of a bad bargain. I feel now that the British didn't have the foggiest idea what to do with the Princes or how to use them. On the one hand they said we'll do something for you, and on the other they said you should be with the people, so the Princes didn't know which way to go. If they went with the people they were afraid they might be deposed, and if they went against the people, they wondered what would happen when the British went. In the whole business there was no clear thinking, it was all done in haste and hurry.

As the last hours of 14 August 1947 ticked away, it became clear that Sardar Patel's 'basket of apples' was almost full. Only the rulers of Hyderabad, Jammu and Kashmir and Junagadh had held out. At the stroke of midnight, India threw off the shackles of foreign rule and met its 'tryst with destiny'. In Dhrangadhara, the three-year-old Yuvaraj – acting in his father's stead – raised the Indian tricolour: 'The courtiers had instilled in me a kind of belief that this was only a temporary phase. "Don't worry, it's only some evil men who have taken our kingdoms away, but you're going to get it back one day!"' However, there was to be no fairy-tale ending for the Indian Princes.

EPILOGUE: BROKEN PROMISES

Let us do justice to them; let us place ourselves in their position and then assess the value of their sacrifice. The rulers have now discharged their part of the obligations by transferring all ruling power and by agreeing to the integration of their States. The main part of our obligation under these agreements is to ensure that the guarantees given by us in respect of privy purses are fully implemented.

Sardar Valiabhai Patel speaking in the
Indian Parliament on 12 October, 1949

No account of the lives of the Indian Princes would be complete without some explanation of the events during the years following the transfer of power in August 1947 which finally brought about the extinction of the Princes as a ruling species.

The euphoria generated by Independence was soon overshadowed by the holocaust of Partition, its wanton Hindu-Muslim bloodshed and its two-way human exodus of unparalleled magnitude. Those princely states closest to the borders of Pakistan could not insulate themselves from the horrors of those tragic times. '1947 was, I think, one of the worst years in my recollection,' says Sukhjit Singh of Kapurthala:

The whole world seemed to have gone completely crazy. The entire genesis of the problem in Kapurthala was from the refugees who came in, who having lost everything had nothing further to lose. They had no feelings for the state, therefore they had no compunction or hesitation about spreading that madness. Once the trouble spread it was really difficult to control, but luckily, because of the tremendous amity between the religions that had existed traditionally, we were spared the worst of the holocaust. We had one or two bad incidents, but these were nothing compared to what happened elsewhere in the Punjab where families were wiped out by villages.

Hede Dayal remembers how in Patiala 'the trees were full of vultures and canals full of bodies' as the killing continued: 'As the refugees came in, the Maharaja set up a big kitchen and I know that for some time he fed sixty thousand people every day. His Highness also sheltered about twenty-five thousand Muslims in Bahadurgarh Fort near Patiala and the Maharani used to send me to go and find out who was there and what people needed. I went there and what a fort it was! Whole villages with guards to protect them till they could be sent out in convoys.'

The little Muslim state of Pataudi, south-west of Delhi, was also badly affected. 'A lot of refugees went through both ways,' recalls the present Nawab, who was only a small boy at the time:

I remember sitting on top of a house with my father and you could see a whole village burning. He'd get into his jeep and he would personally go and see what was happening. When it got worse my father's brother, who was in the Army, evacuated us and we went to Bhopal to stay with my grandfather, but my father stayed back till the whole thing was over. It was a very sad affair for him because Pataudi was so peaceful prior to this. We had about ten so-called policemen who were armed, but who didn't have any ammunition because we hadn't ever needed it! We had a jail in which we used to tie a goat because a jail couldn't remain empty and we had to justify having a jailer. So what could we do? All around us there was killing.

Of the three states which had opted to go it alone at the time of Independence, Junagadh dropped into Sardar Patel's 'basket of apples' when, following the Nawab's sudden flight to Pakistan in the company of some of his favourite dogs, the people of the state opted under a referendum to join India. The second apple was secured when the Maharaja of Kashmir was constrained to accede following a 'tribal invasion' of his state from Pakistan six weeks after the Transfer of Power. His eighteen-year-old son, Karan Singh, was appointed Regent in his stead – with his father's old enemy, Sheikh Abdullah, as Prime Minister. The third apple was Hyderabad, which continued to dangle out of the reach of the Indian government for another two years until a short, sharp 'police action' in September 1949 brought the Nizam to his senses. In the meantime, the Indian States Ministry had begun to implement a policy which culminated in the complete unification of India – but left in its wake a string of broken promises.

The first to lose their internal sovereignty were some forty-one Eastern states, which were bulldozed into merging with the province of Orissa, so providing a model for other mergers. Under the deal struck between the government and these minor Princes, the rulers surrendered all their governing powers, their state's cash balances and all state properties in return for an annual privy purse amounting to approximately ten per cent of the state's annual revenue as it stood in 1946. Every ex-ruler was allowed to retain his palaces and other private properties and his personal privileges.

Two months later it was the turn of the Kathiawar rulers, whose privy purses were individually settled by negotiation. Maharaj Dharmakumarsinhji remembers how when his brother, the Maharaja of Bhavnagar, was asked how much he wanted for his privy purse he replied, 'You cannot compensate me for parting with my land and my people and my rights, but whatever you think fit, you may give me. I am not going to say a word.' Maharaja Natwarsinhji of Porbandar 'gladly gave over almost everything to the government', recalls his widow, the Rajmata. 'My husband said, "It doesn't belong to me, it belongs to the state and to my people."' In Dhrangadhara, the Maharaja summoned a meeting to announce his decision to merge to his people:

> There was stunned silence when I told them that what we had done was for their interest, and that it would be a more economic kind of government and a more cooperative situation would prevail. Nobody had any comment to make and only one person, an elderly village head, said to me in Gujerati, 'That is all very well Sir, I know what you have done, but who will now wipe our tears?' I was so taken aback by that one and only remark that I was not able to proceed any further with the meeting and I left, but I did feel that it had been a tribute not necessarily to me alone, but to my whole line – that they had wiped tears in their time.

The first two mergers paved the way for the swift integration of all the princely states in the succeeding months, each being justified on logical grounds. In the case of the Deccan states, the rulers met in Bombay in February 1948 and formally requested a merger with the province of Bombay. The Raja of Sawantwadi failed to attend, having written to Sardar Patel to say that he would rather merge with Kolhapur State: 'I didn't attend the meeting and Sawantwadi was literally taken by force. They sent a contingent of my own Maratha Regiment which didn't do anything, along with police from Belgaum and Ratnagiri and under the garb of a movement from the *Praja Parishad* (People's Movement) they just took it over.'

In April, a number of states in Rajputana led by Udaipur merged to join the Rajasthan Union – an act which provoked Nathudan, the leading bard of Mewar, to lampoon the crippled Maharana Bhupal Sinhji's surrender with the stinging couplet:

'Oh Eklingji, why was he incapacitated in his legs?
It should have been in his hands,
so that he would have been unable to sign.'

In May 1948 it was the turn of the Central India states, the Maharaja of Gwalior alone surrendering 55 crores of rupees (£41¼ million), enough to pay for the privy purses of all the Princes for years to come. Next came the Gujerat states, with Maharaja Pratapsinh of Baroda proving a major princely fly in the ointment by refusing to merge with the other local states, even though two years earlier he had been one of the first to accede to India. According to his son, Fatehsinghrao Gaekwad, 'He was misguided and badly advised and not allowed to read the writing on the wall.' Matters came to a head when it was found that large sums of money had been removed from the state treasury and priceless jewellery had been taken abroad, primarily to satisfy the extravagance of the Maharaja's second wife, Sita Devi. The Bombay government finally took over the administration of Baroda in May 1949 and the Maharaja was persuaded to return most of the state funds and jewels – including the famous seven-row Baroda diamond necklace.

The last state to merge with the Indian Union was Mysore in November 1949. In return for the surrender of their states, as well as cash and investments amounting to something like 95 crores (£74½ million), the ex-rulers received privy purses that cost the Government of India 580 lakhs (£4 million) in the first year and less with each succeeding year. It was, in the words of Sardar Patel, 'a small price to pay for the bloodless revolution which led to the great ideal of geographical, political and economic unification of India, an ideal which – for centuries – remained a distant dream'. In order to reassure the Princes that the covenants signed by them were sacrosanct, Sardar Patel agreed to back them with constitutional guarantees to ensure that any future government would honour them. When the Indian Constitution came into being in January 1950, these guarantees were incorporated in four articles: Article 291, which guaranteed the payment of tax-free privy purses; Article 362, which covered privileges; Article 363, which guaranteed that any agreement with the rulers would not be justiciable and Article 366 (22) which defined the term 'Ruler'.

The actual loss of sovereign power hit some rulers harder than others, but most were able to take it in their stride. 'For a few days it was awful,' admits the Maharawal of Dungarpur:

I felt like leaving and going away. I was so bitter, I was downhearted because I was devoted to my state. I had worked very hard for twenty years and all this labour was going to waste. But I do feel it was a sacrifice which in certain respects was well worth it, regardless of my feelings. Looking to the circumstances in which partition was brought about and to how the Princes faced the problem of Indian Independence, I think it was inevitable. As to what happened, one must take it philosophically and that's the best way to look at it.

On the day his state was integrated, the Maharaja of Porbandar left to settle in Ootacamund, because 'he felt that the people who took over from him would feel more comfortable if he happened to be away'. The Maharaja of Morvi could not bear the thought of signing his state away and abdicated in favour of his son. The Maharajas of Bikaner and Kapurthala died within months of signing away their states, their deaths hastened by the personal traumas incurred. 'My father felt very let down,' declares Dr Karni Singh of Maharaja Sadul Singh of Bikaner:

He had been very much carried away by the euphoria of Independence and had placed his faith and trust in the word of our great leaders that they would not be interested in annexing the states. Then a sudden shift started which became a whirlwind almost when, without any apparent reason, the Government of India started shifting its stance and going in for integration of states and finishing them off. I have a file on which 'Why this sudden change?' is written in my father's own handwriting. A big meeting was held in Bikaner at which the people said they didn't want to merge and then the whole thing was rail-roaded through. My father felt let down, because he couldn't imagine that the great people who had brought about Independence could go back on their word in such a short time, and he died soon after. It was the fact that assurances had been given and that they went back on their word.

Among the younger Princes and those who had the resourcefulness and willingness to adapt to changed circumstances, there were many who were soon able to carve out successful careers for themselves in various fields of commerce and industry. Many Princes also distinguished themselves in the Armed Forces and in the Foreign and Administrative Services. Quite a few could not adjust and found solace in alcohol and dreams of past glories.

For those who had never enjoyed the powers of a ruler, the merger of the states came as less of a blow. 'Power is such a self-consuming passion that its loss does leave a wrench in the heart,' declares Lalit Sen of Suket. 'If you have known power for

generations and generations as my family had for 1180 years in
unbroken line then you take it for granted – and only when it went
did the people who had enjoyed it feel what was going away. My
father did feel the loss but he was a deeply religious man and he
didn't take it to heart as so many others did. And as far as I was
concerned, maybe I was too young, maybe I hadn't tasted any of
that power. Then the education that my father had given me enabled
me to see India as one nation, so I was drawn quite naturally into
the national mainstream like a duck to water. I was barely twenty-four
when I first contested the elections.'

Having been encouraged earlier by Sardar Patel to take to politics
as a career best suited to their training, a number of Princes
contested the first General Elections of free India in 1952. Some,
like the Maharaja Rana of Porbandar, were asked by their former
subjects to stand for election, but refused to enter the fray. 'My
husband would not allow our late Yuvaraj to enter politics, because
he felt that a ruler should not do that,' says the Rajmata of Porbandar.
'However, quite a number did go into politics, either because they
were encouraged to or because they felt it would benefit them
perhaps, and the day the first Prince went into politics, my husband
said, "That is the end of our privileges and that is the end of our
privy purses." And what he said came true.'

Unmindful of future repercussions, increasing numbers of Princes
and other members of their order took to the hustings, proving with
each successive election that their popularity with their former
subjects had not waned. Had they chosen to stand for elections on
the ruling Congress party ticket, their fate might have been different.
Some, however, felt that they would be more effective either as
independent candidates or in alliance with right-wing opposition
parties. The Rajmata of Jaipur fought the 1962 elections on the
Swatantra party ticket, but voiced her apprehension to a group of
villagers prior to the day of voting:

> When they came I said to them, 'If you don't want me to represent
> you, I can still withdraw my candidature because there's two days
> left. Because, you see, I don't know your problems and I have to tell
> you quite frankly that I can't do anything for you because I am
> standing in the Opposition. All I can do is voice your grievances in
> the Parliament and Parliament doesn't deal with local affairs, so you
> make up your own minds.' So they kept quiet for a little bit and then
> they said, 'No, you stand and we'll vote for you.' So I said is it because
> I'm your Maharaja's wife? They said it was partly that, yes. And then
> they said, 'The other thing is that you're doing it for us, you can't be
> doing it for yourself otherwise you wouldn't be in the Opposition.

You'd be like the other Princes who have joined the Congress party.'
Then I knew that I had their confidence and their love and that they
trusted me.

The Maharani subsequently registered a record-breaking victory at
the polls. Five years later in the 1967 elections, twenty-four Princes
were elected to the *Lok Sabha* – the Lower House of Parliament –
twelve on the Congress ticket, seven on the Swatantra ticket and
four as Independents. In the state assemblies too, princely candidates
swept the polls. 'The Princes were asking for it,' says Rajendrasinh
of Idar:

> No political group is going to allow the survival of people who are
> out to pull it down. The Princes stood for elections and swept the
> Congress almost out of power in Orissa, Madhya Pradesh, Gujerat
> and Rajasthan – and that was done by a very small number of Princes.
> Wherever we stood we just wiped them out. Now the feeling grew
> among Congressmen that this was a very dangerous group of people,
> so something had to be done to curb this particular group. It was as
> simple as that.

Pressures now built up within the Congress party to set about
clipping the wings of the rulers and when the All India Congress
Committee met in June 1967, a resolution was passed calling for
the abolition of all princely privileges and privy purses. The Princes'
response was to attempt to rally together, but princely unity – that
ever-receding mirage – continued to be just as elusive as it had
always been and at their meetings internecine strife was once again
at the forefront, as a dismayed Nawab of Pataudi observed:

> I found many of them having the fights that they used to have two
> hundred years ago, one not talking to another because somebody's
> great-grandfather had done something to so and so's great-
> grandfather. It was mind-boggling in many ways to me, but it showed
> me that if they could not get together in 1970, there was no way they
> could have got together in 1947. There was even one prince who
> stood up and said, 'I'm afraid this is the last meeting I'm going to
> attend because my privy purse is 192 rupees and I cannot afford the
> train fare.'

During the three-year period of negotiations between the government and the Princes, a serious rift manifested itself in the ranks of
the Congress party which caused the party leadership to seek the
support of leftist groups, who in their turn demanded a speedy
abolition of the princely order. Just when they seemed to be on the

brink of a solution, the negotiations broke down. To the Maharaja of Dhrangadhara it appeared that 'for some reason or other, the Government of India got the impression that the Princes and the princely negotiators were trying to lead the government up the garden path and that they did not mean business'. This proved to be the last missed opportunity in the Indian Princes' chequered history, in all probability caused by misunderstanding on both sides. In December 1970, a two-day debate began in Parliament for the consideration of the Constitution 26th Amendment Bill, which sought to abolish the princely order by the omission of Articles 291 and 362 from the Indian Constitution. Some of the Princes who were members of the Congress party resigned, some abstained from voting and a few voted in favour of the bill. In the Lower House, the Amendment Bill was passed by a margin of eight votes over the necessary two-thirds majority, while in the Upper House it was defeated by just one vote because 'some fellow had diarrhoea and he didn't come'. Almost immediately, a Cabinet decision was taken to de-recognise the rulers through a Presidential Order. A plane was chartered and sent to Hyderabad to get the President's signature on the ordinance, which was obtained at around midnight on 22 December.

There was a brief reprieve when the matter went before the Supreme Court and the Presidential Order was declared *ultra vires*, but before the Princes could enjoy their victory Parliament was dissolved and fresh elections announced. The Congress party fought the election on the slogan of the eradication of poverty and was returned with a thumping majority. In December, in the midst of a war with Pakistan, the Constitutional Amendment Bill was re-introduced and swiftly passed by both Houses of Parliament.

Brigadier Sukhjit Singh of Kapurthala, who together with the Maharaja of Jaipur was to be awarded the gallantry award of the *Maha Vir Chakra*, heard the news of the abolition flashed on the radio as he was about to lead his brigade into action on the war front:

I had very mixed feelings, because here was the country I was trying to serve having no compunctions about reneging on solemn constitutional guarantees. I had always accepted the basic fact that change must occur, but I did not for one moment believe or accept the fact that the removal of four crores of the Union budget would materially affect the poverty line in India, because ten times that amount was being lost in bad management, embezzlement, bad procurement and various other losses to the exchequer. But this four crores a year that was paid out to the Princes helped maintain vast establishments, kept people who had no other form of sustenance going, people who had given their lives in the execution of what we call the honouring of their salt.

Lalit Sen of Suket was among the few Princes in Parliament who voted in favour of abolition, feeling that 'the whole thing was anachronistic, out of date and antedeluvian. The government, on the other hand, underestimated the human misery which would be caused and over-estimated the credit they would get out of a move like this, because it was such an infinitesimal part of the budget.'

Maharaja Karni Singh of Bikaner had always felt that 'living on the privy purses was like living on borrowed time'. To him it now seemed as if 'the sword of Damocles that was hanging over our heads had finally been lifted. I feel it really made men out of the Princes. It consequently brought the best out of us, to be able to stand on our own two legs and face the world by the Grace of God and the blessings of our ancestors.' When the Maharaja returned to Bikaner after being de-recognised, there was a crowd of fifty thousand people waiting for him at the railway station who greeted him with garlands in their hands shouting, 'Maharaja *Ki Jai Ho* – Victory to our Maharaja, long may he live!' To his former subjects, at least, he was still the *Annadata* they had always known and honoured.

Some years after the Indian States and their rulers had ceased to have any legal existence, Bapa Dhrangadhara and his younger brother, accompanied by a friend, made a journey on horseback from Dhrangadhara to Jodhpur:

It was a lovely trip of 450 miles, roughly following the route taken by one of my ancestors when he went to get married. But at one village we stopped for a glass of water and suddenly this old man came out and went up to Rajrana Saheb directly and said, 'Who are these men? Something tells me that they are royal.' 'You're right,' said Rajrana Saheb, 'they are princes of Dhrangadhara.' 'Then you must stop. I am a Charan and it is my *haq* (right) to stop you. You will eat at my house.' We explained that we had a long way to go before we camped that night, but we agreed to have a glass of *chhas* (butter-milk) or a little *dahi* (curd) if he had some. This five-minute halt became ten minutes, then an hour, for this Charan was a descendant of Ada Dossa, the man who had carried Maharana Pratap's sandals on his head and had walked into the Mogul Emperor Akbar's headquarters to announce his master's death. But before he bowed to the Emperor he had put the slippers down saying that 'Even my master's slippers will not bow to you.' Then he had sung the praises of his Lord to the Emperor. Everyone thought that he had had it, but the Emperor was so pleased with his loyalty that he granted Ada Dossa a jagir of so many villages. Now here was his descendant left with just a part of one remaining village. As we were leaving, I gave him fifty-one rupees. He said, 'I refuse.' I smiled at him and said, 'What haq have you to stop me? I have the haq to give to all Charans.' So he smiled and folded his hands and then we rode on.

GLOSSARY

Achkan: Long coat with high collar

Adaab: Muslim salutation, bowing with right hand raised to mouth, brow and breast

Adhiraj: Supreme ruler, overlord, hence Maharajadhiraj; from Sanscrit Adi – chief, first

Angarkha: Long, double-breasted coat

Anna: Unit of currency worth a sixteenth part of a rupee, formerly in use in India

Annadata: Giver of food, honorific applied to rulers in certain states

Arti: Oil lamp or flame moved round circularly as an act of homage or devotion

Attar, Ittr: Fragrant essential oil of jasmine, roses and other flowers

Ayah: Maid-servant, nanny

Baba, Bapa, Bapu: Father: honorific applied to rulers in certain states

Badshah: A king, sovereign

Bahadur: Brave, champion, hero; title used by both Hindus and Muslims, often bestowed by government

Bai: Mistress, lady, title added to names of women; dancing girl

Barat: Marriage procession

Barot: Keeper of historical records and genealogical trees; hence *Raj-Barot*

Begum: Common title for Muslim ladies of high rank; feminine of Nawab

Betel: See *Paan*

Bhai, Bhaiya: Brother; *bhaibund*: brotherhood, relation of man of same caste or community

Bhajan: Hindu hymn

Bhala: Spear, javelin, lance; *Bhaldar*: lancer

Bhang: Dried leaves of hemp plant, an intoxicant and narcotic (see *charas, ganja*)

Bhat: Man of a tribe of mixed descent, whose members are professed genealogists and poets; a bard

Bhil: Race inhabiting the hills and forests of the Vindhya, Malwa and North-western Deccan, believed to have been the aborigines of Rajputana

Brahmin: Member of the priestly caste

Bundobust: Any system or mode of regulation; discipline

Burkha, burqa: Coverall with eye-holes worn by Muslim women in public

Chaprassi: Peon, orderly

Charan: Poet, bard credited with certain powers

Chaurang: (Marathi) low stool; lit. of four colours

Chhadidar: Staff-bearer

Chhatri: An umbrella; domed building such as cenotaph; *Chhatrapati*: one of sufficient dignity to have an umbrella carried over him; commonly used to describe Shivaji and his descendants

Chik: Screen made of split bamboo sticks

Chobdar: Mace-bearer and court herald who announces the arrival of guests on state occasions. From *chob*: an ornamented club covered with gold or silver plate

Chowkidar: Watchman, sentry, guard

Chowrie, chauri: Yak-tail fly whisk used as part of royal regalia

Chudidar: Lit. of the form of rings; leg-hugging tapering pyjamas which gather into folds around the ankle, when worn

Crore: Ten millions or 100 lakhs, a crore of rupees was worth about £750,000 during the inter-war period

Dacoit: Bandit, robber

Dal: Lentils

Dandi: Sedan chair for carrying people uphill

Darbar, Durbar: The court of a princely state; in some Rajput states used to denote ruler

Dasi: Maid-servant

Deccan: Southern plateau of India between the Eastern and Western Ghats

Dewan: Prime Minister to an Indian Chief, Hindu and Muslim

Dhoom-dham: Tumult; pomp and grandeur

Dhol: Drum

Gadi: Cushion or throne of royalty

Gaekwad, Gaekwar: Surname or title of the Maharaja of Baroda. It was once a caste name and means 'cowherd', i.e. protector of the sacred animal. Later it became a dynastic appellation of the rulers of Baroda

Ganesh: Elephant-faced god of success, son of Shiva

Garh: Fort, as in Pratapgarh

Ghagra: Long, gathered skirt

Ghee: Clarified butter

Ghunghat: Veil which conceals the face

Gurdwara: A Sikh place of worship

Guru: Teacher, spiritual guide

Haldi: Turmeric

Havan: Sacred ritual fire

Holkar: Surname or title of the Maharaja of Indore

Howdah: Seat on elephant without a canopy

Hukka, hookah: Indian hubble-bubble for smoking tobacco or marijuana filtered through water

Huzra, Huzuri: Courtier, attendant

Huzur: The presence; term of respectful address; also used for aides such as Huzur Secretary – ruler's private secretary

Id: Muslim festival to commemorate Abraham's offer to sacrifice his son Ismail; Muslim festival of the Passover; festival at the breaking of the fast after Ramzan

Idgah: Enclosed place outside a town where Muslim prayers are held at festivals

Izzat: Honour, respect, prestige

Jagir: Hereditary assignment of land given by government or ruler; *jagirdar*: holder of jagir

Jam: Chief. e.g. Jamsaheb of Nawanagar: title used by certain rulers in Kathiawar, Kutch and Sind

Jamadar: Guard, head of soldiers

Jheel, jhil: Natural lake or swamp

Kala Pani: Black Water; the ocean

Kalgi: Ornament on turban, aigrette

Kamarband, Cummerbund: Waistcloth or belt

Kamdar, Karbhari: A manager; also Dewan in smaller states in Gujerat and Maharashtra

Kanyadaan: Bestowing of a daughter in marriage

Katha: Religious discourse

Katori: Small cup or bowl

Kavi: Poet

Kesar: Saffron

Khannazads: Women attendants in the zanana (Hyderabad)

Kharita: Official letters between an Indian prince and the Viceroy, contained in a sealed silk bag

Khazana: Treasure, treasury

Khazanchi: treasurer

Kotwal: Head of police in a town; in Hyderabad, official in charge of internal security

Kshatriya: Hindu military caste

Kumar, Kunwar: Heir of a Raja; every son of Chiefs of Gujerat and Kathiawar

Kum-kum: Red powder, saffron, used in *pujas* and for making *tikka* mark on forehead by Hindus

Kutcheri: Office

Lakh: A hundred thousand. A lakh of rupees was worth about £7,500 during the inter-war period

Lungi: Cloth wrapped around the waist like a sarong

Maa-Baap: Mother and father

Machan: Raised platform

Mahabharata: Epic of the great war between the Kauravas and Pandavas

Maharaja, Maharana, Maharao, Maharawal, Maharawat: The highest of hereditary rulers among the Hindus (see *Raja*); *Maharani*: Queen; *Maharajkumar*: son of a *Maharaja*

Mahurat, Muhurta: Propitious moment fixed by astrologers for an important happening such as a marriage, *puja*, etc.

Mandap: Porch or pillared hall especially of a temple; marriage pavilion

Mardana: Men's quarters in a house, also the men occupying it

Mashaal: An oil torch

Matka: Earthen pot

Maund: About 42lb

Morchal: Fan of peacock's feathers, part of royal insignia

Mujra: Formal salutation; also professional singing of *tawaifs*

Mullah: Muslim priest

Nagara, nakara, naubat: drums; *Nagarkhana, naubatkhana*: place where drums are beaten

Namaskar, namaste: Hindu salutation made with palms pressed together

Nawab: Title of a Muslim ruler; governor of a town under Mughal rule; *Nawabzada*: son of a *Nawab*

Nazar, Nazrana: Offerings of presents or coins on ceremonial occasions to a ruler as tokens of respect or allegiance

Nikaah: Muslim marriage contract

Nilgai: Blue bull, a large antelope

Paan: The betel vine; the leaf is chewed with slaked lime, catechu and dried areca nut or *supari* as a savoury

Paan-supari, ittr-paan: Offerings made to guests at the end of ceremonial functions and *Durbars*

Pagri, pugree, pug: Turban

Paigah: Nobility of Hyderabad state; those required to maintain *paigah* or mounted troops

Panchayat: A committee for

Pankah: Fan

Pat, patla: Low stool or platform

Pattakars, pattawalas: Attendants

Pir: Muslim saint or religious teacher

Poshak: Outfit of clothes (Maratha states)

Praja: People

Puja: Hindu worship; *pujari*: priest who performs *puja*

Purdah: A veil or curtain; practice of keeping women in seclusion

Purohit: A Hindu chaplain; *Raj-purohit*: Court chaplain

Quila, Killa: Fort

Raj: Government, sovereignty, reign, often applied to British rule in India

Raj-chinnha: Royal insignia

Raja: Hindu ruler of exalted rank but inferior to *Maharaja*. Variations: *Raj, Rana, Rao, Rai, Rawal, Rawat, Raikat*; *Rajkumar*: son of *Raja*; *Rajkumari*: daughter of *Raja*; *Rajmata*: mother of *Raja* or *Maharaja*

Rajput: Lit. king's son, a Hindu of the Kshatriya (warrior) caste in Central and Western India from one of 36 so-called 'royal' clans originating from a sacred fire on Mount Abu; thus *Rajputana*: the country of kings' sons, and *Rajasthan*: the land of kings

Ramayana: Hindu epic whose hero Ramachandra or Rama is one of the incarnations of Vishnu

Ramraj, Ramrajya: Ideal rule, as exemplified by the Kingship of Rama

Rupee: Standard unit of currency, worth about 1s.6d. during the inter-war period

Safa: Turban worn by princes

Salaam: Form of salutation – the blessing and peace of God be with you

Sambar: A deer

Samshan, smashan: Cremation ground

Sanad: A charter or grant; deed of grants; diploma; signature

Saptapadi: Lit. seven steps; performed during Hindu wedding ceremonial

Sardar, Sirdar: Nobleman, a leader; honorific used among Sikhs; *Sardarni*: wife of *Sardar*

Sarpech: Ornament worn in the turban

Sasural: Home of the in-laws

Sati, suttee: Suicide by Hindu widow on funeral pyre of husband

Shamiana: Open-sided tent

Shehnai: Wind-instrument like a clarinet

Sherwani: Long coat

Shikar: Hunting; *shikari*: professional hunter or tracker

Sikh: A sect of the Punjab, the disciples of Guru Nanak

Singh, Sinh, Sinhji: Lion; used as a surname by Rajputs, Sikhs and other communities

Tablas: Small drums

Tahsil: Revenue sub-division of a district; *tahsildar* local revenue collector

Talukdar: A landholder with peculiar tenures in different parts of India; an officer in Hyderabad State corresponding to magistrate and collector

Talwar: Scimitar

Tawaif: Courtesan dancer

Thakur: Petty chief; title of respect applied to Brahmins

Thal, thali: Circular feeding dish made of silver, copper, brass

Tikka: Ceremonial anointing on the forehead with *kum-kum* or sandalwood paste; *tilak*: mark made on forehead; *raj-tilak*: tilak made to king at the time of coronation

Tikka-Saheb, *Tikka-Raja*: Heir-apparent in several Northern states; *tikka-rani*: wife of tikka-raja

Toda: Anklet

Tonga: Horse-drawn carriage

Toshakhana: Treasury; a special department in the Foreign and Political Department for gifts received by Political Officers

Vakil: An agent; attorney; ambassador

Wali: Muslim ruler as in Wali of Kalat; *walihad*: heir-apparent in Muslim state

Yuvaraja: Heir-apparent in Hindu state; *Yuvarani*: wife of heir-apparent

Zamin: land; *zamindar, zemindar*: a landholder; *zamindari*: an estate, the system of tenure in which land revenue is imposed on an individual occupying the position of a landlord

Zanana, zenana: Female, feminine; women's apartments, harem, forbidden to all men over the age of twelve except close relatives

KEY DATES

c. 1500 BC	First Aryan migrations into North India
c. 950 BC	*Mahabharata* written down, longest epic poem in existence, describing fortunes of royal Pandava brothers and their struggle to regain their throne after being driven into exile
c. 750 BC	*Ramayana* written down, story of Kshatriya warrior-king Rama, banished for fourteen years before being raised to the *gadi* and establishing a *Ramarajya* or utopian kingdom
321–185 BC	Mauryan Empire in North India, first imperial government in India
c. 300 BC– c. 500 AD	Chera, Chola and Pandya kingdoms in South India
319–415	Gupta Empire in North India
c. 413–453	Court poet Kalidasa flourished
c. 450	First Hun invasion of North India
470	Traditional date of the founding of Kanaui kingdom by Rathor Rajputs
c. 550	Beginning of second wave of invasions by Huns and other tribes, ancestors of many of the Rajput rulers of Rajputana, Kathiawar and Central India
725	Occupation of Gujerat by Arabs, Chauhan Rajputs driven from Ajmer
c. 728	Bapu Rawal, chief of the Sisodia Rajputs, captures Chittor fort and founds kingdom of Mewar
c. 928	Dhola Rae founds kingdom of Amber
1001–1026	Mahmud of Ghazni raids North India
1156	Jaisalmer founded by Jaisal, chief of the Bhati Rajputs
1192	Muhammad of Ghor defeats Prithvi Raj of Delhi, takes Ajmer
1211	Marwar founded by Rathor Rajputs, driven from Kanauj
1297	Gujerat falls to Alu-ud-din Khilji, Pathan king of Delhi
1303	First siege and fall of Chittor
1323	Muhammad-ibn-Tughlaq conquers Deccan
1336	Vijayanagar kingdom founded in South India
1459	City of Jodhpur founded by Rao Jodha, king of Marwar
1485–1535	Muslim Kings of Gujerat, Cambay their capital
1488	Bikaner founded by Rao Bika from Marwar
1526	Mongol invader Babur defeats Sultan Ibrahim Lodi of Delhi at Panipat

1527	Emperor Babur defeats Rajput Confederacy at Khannua and establishes Mughal Empire
1535	Second siege of Chittor by Sultan of Gujerat
1556–1605	Reign of Emperor Akbar 'the Great'
1565	Deccan Muslims defeat Hindu Vijayanagar Confederacy at Talikota. Bolacharama Wadiyar, Viceroy of Vijaynagar, founds Mysore kingdom
1567	Last siege and sack of Chittor by Akbar, Udaipur founded by Rana Udai Singh as his new capital
1599	British East India Company founded
1641	Foundation of Fort St George, Madras
1656	Maratha chieftain Shivaji murders Afzal Khan of Bijapur at Partabgarh fort
1658	Aurangzeb deposes father, Emperor Shah Jehan
1681	Bharatpur State founded by Jat Zamindar Churaman
1687	Aurangzeb conquers Shia Muslim Deccan kingdoms
1707	Death of Aurangzeb signals Mughal decline
1723	Marathas exact tribute from Gujerat
1724	Hyderabad State founded by Asaf Jah Nizam-ul-Mulk
1728	Jaipur State founded by Raja Jai Singh II, ruler of Amber
1732	Malhar Rao Holkar of Indore takes Malwa
1739	Nadir Shah of Persia sacks Delhi
1761	Ahmad Shah Durani of Afghanistan defeats Marathas at Panipat
1764	Sikh Confederacy defeats Ahmad Shah
1775	First Anglo-Maratha war
1784	Madhaji Rao Scindia recaptures Gwalior Fort
1788	Rohilla chief Ghulam Qadir blinds Mughal Emperor Shah Alam
1793	Permanent Settlement of Bengal
1795	Marathas defeat Nizam of Deccan
1799	Fourth Mysore war, Wadiyar dynasty restored; Ranjit Singh establishes Sikh Empire in Punjab
1804	War against Holkar of Indore
1817–18	Pacification of Marathas; first treaties signed between East India Company and Rajput and Maratha rulers
1845	First Anglo-Sikh war
1848	Second Anglo-Sikh war
1856	Annexation of Avadh (Oude)
1857	Indian Mutiny
1858	Government of India transferred from Company to Crown; Queen Victoria's Proclamation undertaking to 'respect the rights, dignity and honour of the Native Princes'
1877	Proclamation of Queen Victoria as Empress of India
1911	George V Durbar in Delhi
1918	Montague-Chelmsford Report

1921	Chamber of Princes inaugurated
1927	Indian National Congress forms All-India States' Peoples Committee
1930	Round Table Conference in London
1935	Government of India Act
1942	Gandhi's 'Quit India' Campaign
March 1946	Cabinet Mission in India
March 1947	Arrival of Viceroy Lord Mountbatten
4 June 1947	Mountbatten announces date of Transfer of Power
5 July 1947	States Department inaugurated, first rulers sign Instruments of Accession
14–15 Aug. 1947	India and Pakistan become independent
December 1947	Eastern States merger with Indian Union, followed by other groups of states
September 1949	Police action in Hyderabad completes merger of all states
December 1971	Princely Order finally abolished

ACKNOWLEDGEMENTS

Our deepest gratitude first of all to all those whose names are listed separately as contributors to this book and who gave unstintingly of their time and hospitality. In particular, we should like to thank H. H. Nawab Iqbal Muhammed Khan of Palanpur, who first suggested that this book ought to be written and who provided help and encouragement throughout, and to Their Highnesses Maharana Bhagwat Singh of Udaipur, Brigadier Sukhjit Singh of Kapurthala, Maharani Gayatri Devi of Jaipur, Maharao Bhim Singh and Maharani Shiv Kumari of Kotah, Maharaja Brijendra Singh of Bharatpur, and Maharaja Virbhadrasinhji of Lunawada for their kind hospitality. We should also like to thank the following for their help: in India, Their Highnesses the Maharaja of Mysore, Maharaja Amrinder Singh of Patiala, Maharaja Gaj Singh of Jodhpur, Maharajkumar and Maharajkumari Ambika Pratapsinh of Banswara, Maharajkumar Pulin Behari Deb Burman of Tripura, also Bhagirath Dwivedi, Satish and Anjula Bedi, Dileep Gupte, Sandhya Uberoi, Foy Nissen, Jimmy Ollia, Habib Issa, M. Mardani, Rajni Lakhia, Govind Talwalker, Dr Aroon Tikekar, Amrita Garewal, Amenah Ahmed, the *Times of India*, Bombay University Library, and the Maharaja's airline, Air India; in England and America, Evelyn Battye, Edwin Binney III, Patrick Ducker, Faith Evans, Giles Eyre, John Fasal, Mollie Kaye, Pat Kattenhorn, Michael Mason, Alice Rockwell, Stuart Carey Welch.

LIST OF CONTRIBUTORS

*Listed by state. § indicates present Maharaja,
Nawab or Begum*

AKALKOT/BARODA Ranji Nirmala Raje Bhonsle: married late Raja
  Vijaysinh Bhonsle of Akalkot; granddaughter of late Maharaja Sayajirao
  Gaekwad of Baroda.

AUNDH Apasaheb Pant, second son of late Raja Bhavanrao Pant Pratinidhi
  of Aundh.

§ BARIA Maharaol Jaydeep Sinh: grandson of late Maharaol Ranjitsinhji
  of Baria; married late daughter of late Maharaja Sawai Man Singh
  of Jaipur.

§ BARODA Maharaja Fatehsinghrao Gaekwad: son of late Maharaja
  Pratapsinh Gaekwad of Baroda; great-grandson of late Maharaja
  Sayajirao Gaekwad.
  Dr N. G. Kalelkar: awarded scholarship by Sayajirao to study in Paris.

§ BENARES Maharaja Vibhuti Narain Singh: son of late Maharaja Aditya
  Narain Singh.

§ BHARATPUR Maharaja Sawai Brijendra Singh; married late sister of late
  Maharaja Jaya Chamarajendra Wadiyar of Mysore.
  Brijendra Singh: Bharatpur State Service.

BHAVNAGAR/GONDAL Rajmata Vijaiba Saheba: married late Maharaja
  Krishna Kumar Sinhji of Bhavnagar; daughter of late Maharaja
  Bhojrajji of Gondal.

BHAVNAGAR Maharaj Dharmakumarsinhji: younger brother of late
  Maharaja Krishnakumar Sinhji of Bhavnagar.
  Ravi Shankar Bhatt: Bhavnagar State Service; father and grandfather
  served in Bhavnagar State.

§ BHOPAL/PATAUDI Begum Sajida Sultan: married late Nawab Muhammad
  Ifitkhar Ali Khan of Pataudi; daughter of late Nawab Hamidulla Khan
  of Bhopal.

BHOR Rajkumari Padma Lokur: grand-daughter of Raja Raghunathrao
  Pant Sachiv of Bhor.

§ BIKANER Maharaja Dr Karni Singh: son of late Maharaja Sadul Singh
  and grandson of late Maharaja Ganga Singh; married daughter of
  Maharawal Lakshman Singh of Dungarpur.
  M. M. Sapat: Bikaner State Service, Kutch State Service; father and
  uncle were Dewans of Jaisalmer.

BILKHA/MANDI/KAPURTHALA Rani Nirvana Devi: married Darbar
  Jaswantsinhji, Chief of Bilkha; daughter of Raja Joginder Sen of
  Mandi; grand-daughter of late Maharaja Jagatjit Singh of Kapurthala.
§ CAMBAY Nawab Mirza Hussain Yawar Khan.
  Nawabzadi Shahvar Sultan: daughter of Nawab Mirza Hussain
  Yawar Khan of Cambay.
COSSIMBAZAR (zamindari) Dr S. C. Nandy of Cossimbazar.
DEWAS (Junior) Maharajkumari Shashiprabha: daughter of late Maharaja
  Malhar Rao Puar of Dewas Junior.
§ DHRANGADHARA Maharaja Mayurdhwaj Singh; married daughter of
  Maharaja of Jodhpur.
  Maharajkumar Shatrujit Deo (Yuvaraj): married late daughter of
  Sahibzada Ata Muhamed Khan of Palanpur.
§ DUNGARPUR Maharawal Lakshman Singhji: married grand-daughter of
  Raja of Bhinga and daughter of late Maharaja Madan Singh of
  Kishengarh.
§ GWALIOR Maharaja Madhavrao Scindia: son of late Maharaja George
  Jivajirao Scindia.
  Rajmata Vijayaraje Scindia: married late Maharaja George Jivajirao
  Scindia.
  Sardar Krishnarao Narsingrao Sitole: premier nobleman of Gwalior
  State.
  Leela Moolgaokar.
HYDERABAD Begum Ali Yavar Jung: married Nawab Ali Yavar Jung,
  nobleman of Hyderabad.
  V. K. Reddy: son of Chief Justice of Hyderabad State.
IDAR Maharajkumar Rajendrasinh (Yuvaraj): son of Maharaja Daljitsinhji
  of Idar and great-great grandson of late Maharaja Sir Pratapsinhji of Idar
  and Jodhpur; married daughter of late Maharaja of Gondal.
INDORE Maharajkumar Richard Shivaji Rao Holkar: son of late Maharaja
  Yeshwantrao Holkar.
  Shalinidevi Holkar: married Richard Sivajirao Holkar.
JAIPUR/COOCH BEHAR/BARODA Rajmata Gayatri Devi: married late
  Maharaja Sawai Man Singh of Jaipur; sister of late Maharaja
  Jagaddipendra Narayan of Cooch Behar; grand-daughter of late
  Maharaja Sayajirao Gaekwad of Baroda.
§ JAMMU & KASHMIR Maharaja Dr Karan Singh: son of late Maharaja
  Hari Singh of Jammu and Kashmir.
JAUNPUR (zamindari) Nandini Dev.
JODHPUR The late Maharani Padmavati (Rajendra Kumari): married
  Maharaja Fatehsingh Gaekwad of Baroda; daughter of late Maharaja
  Umaid Singh of Jodhpur.
§ KAPURTHALA Maharaja Sukhjit Singh: son of late Maharaja Paramjit
  Singh and grandson of late Maharaja Jagatjit Singh.
  Raja Ranbir Singh.
  Jaya Thadani.
KISHENGARH/PALITANA Rajmata Gita Kumari: married late Maharaja

Sumair Singh of Kishengarh; daughter of Maharaja Bahadursinhji of Palitana.

§ KOTAH Maharao Bhim Singh.

KOTAH/BIKANER Maharani Shiv Kumari: married Maharao Bhim Singh of Kotah; daughter of late Maharaja Ganga Singh of Bikaner.

§ KUTCH Maharao Madansinh: son of late Maharao Vijayarajji; married daughter of late Maharaja Madan Singh of Kishengarh.

LUNAWADA Maharajkumar Bhupendrasinh (Yuvaraj): son of Maharaja Virbhadrasinh; his mother is the sister of M. Wankaner.

Maharajkumar Pushpendrasinh: second son of Maharaja of Lunawada; married daughter of Leela Moolgaokar.

Maharajkumar Harish Chandrasinh: younger brother of Maharaja; married sister of Maharaja Mayurdhwaj Singh of Dhrangadhara.

Maharaj Virvikramsinh: cousin of the Maharaja.

A. R. Dave and L. P. Mehta: Lunawada State Service

A. P. Shah: Dewan, Lunawada State.

MANSA Rajkumar Divyabhanusinh: second son of late Raol Sajjansinhji of Mansa; mother is the sister of Maharaja Pratap Sinh of Wankaner.

MYSORE Rani Vijayadevi: married late Thakoresaheb Pradyumma Sinh of Kotda Sangani; sister of late Maharaja Jaya Chamarajendra Wadiyar of Mysore.

§ PALANPUR Nawab Iqbal Muhammed Khan: son of late Nawab Taley Muhammed Khan of Palanpur.

Sahibzada Ata Muhammad Khan: cousin of Nawab Iqbal Muhammed Khan.

Nawabzada Muzaffer Khan (Walihad): son of Nawab Iqbal Muhammed Khan.

§ PATAUDI Nawab Mansur Ali Khan: son of late Nawab Muhammad Ifthikar Ali Khan of Pataudi; grandson of late Nawab Hamidullah Khan of Bhopal.

PATIALA Hede Dayal: Patiala State Service.

Dick Bowles: Patiala State Service; father was also in Patiala State Service.

PHALTAN Rajkumari Sarojini Devi: daughter of late Raja Malojirao Naik Nimbalkar.

PORBANDAR Rajmata Anant Kunverba: married late Maharaja Rana Natwarsinhji of Porbandar.

§ PRATAPGARH Maharawat Ambika Pratapsinh: son of late Maharawat Ramsingh of Pratapgarh; his mother is the sister of Maharaja Mayurdhwaj Singh of Dhrangadhara.

Chichibai: maidservant who accompanied Princess of Dhrangadhara when she married the Yuvaraj of Pratapgarh.

RAMPUR Nawab Zulfiquar Ali Khan: second son of late Nawab Raza Ali Khan.

REWA/KUTCH Maharani Pravin Kunverba: married Maharaja Martand Singh of Rewa; sister of Maharao Madan Sinh of Kutch.

SANGLI Rajmata Padminiraje Patwardhan: daughter-in-law of late Raja Chintamanrao Patwardhan of Sangli.

SANTOSH (zamindari) Protap Roy.

§ SAWANTWADI Raja Shivram Sawant Bhonsle: son of late Raja Khem Sawant Bhonsle of Sawantwadi; married sister of Maharaja Fatehsingh Gaekwad of Baroda; his mother was the grand-daughter of late Maharaja Sayajirao Gaekwad of Baroda.

§ SUKET Raja Lalit Sen: son of late Raja Lakshman Sen of Suket; married daughter of Maharawal Lakshman Singh of Dungarpur.

TIKARI (zamindari) John Wakefield: father Manager Tikari Raj, uncle Indian Political Service.

TRAVANCORE The late Maharani Setu Lakshmibai (Senior Maharani): adopted as niece by Maharaja of Travancore.

Maharajkumari Rukmini Varma: grand-daughter of Maharani Lakshmibai.

§ UDAIPUR The late Maharana Bhagwat Singh: son of Maharana Bhupal Singh of Udaipur; married sister of Maharaja Karni Singh of Bikaner.

Maharana Mahendra Singh: son of Maharana Bhagwat Singh.

Rao Manohar Singhji of Bedla: Nobleman of Mewar.

§ WANKANER Maharaja Pratap Sinh: son of late Maharaja Amarsinhji.

WANKANER/DUNGARPUR Maharani Rama Kumari: married Maharaja Pratap Sinh of Wankaner; sister of Maharawal Lakshman Singh of Dungarpur.

LADY BIRDWOOD (née Vere Ogilvie): father Sir George Ogilvie, Indian Political Service.

late SIR CONRAD CORFIELD: Indian Political Service.

SIR JOHN COTTON: Indian Political Service.

LT COL. SIR CYRIL HANCOCK: Indian Political Service.

SHAVAX LAL: Indian Legal Service: Law Secretary.

SARDAR H. S. AND MRS MALIK: Indian Civil Service; on deputation as Dewan of Patiala 1944–47.

MRS IRIS PORTAL (née Butler): father Governor, Central Provinces.

V. VISHWANATHAN: Indian Civil Service, Home Secretary.

L. P. SINGH: Indian Civil Service, Home Secretary.

Extracts from the interview with Sir Conrad Corfield recorded by Charles Allen in 1975 are quoted by kind permission of the BBC and the Director of the British Indian Oral Archive.

TABLE OF SALUTE PRINCES

The Indian Salute States in local order of precedence, 1931

Name of state	Area in square miles	Title, Race and Religion of Ruler	Gun Salute of Ruler

States in direct political relations with the Government of India

1. Hyderabad	82,698 (excluding Berar)	Nizam; Sunni Muslim	21
2. Mysore	29,528	Maharaja; Kshatriya; Hindu	21
3. Baroda	8,135	Maharaja; Maratha; Hindu	21
4. Jammu and Kashmir	85,885	Maharaja; Dogra Rajput; Hindu	21
5. Gwalior	26,382	Maharaja; Maratha; Hindu	21
6. Bhutan	18,000	Maharaja; Bhotia; Buddhist	15
7. Sikkim	2,818	Maharaja; Tibetan; Buddhist	15

States forming the Rajputana Agency

1. Udaipur (Mewar)	12,915	Maharana; Sisodia Rajput; Hindu	19
2. Jaipur	16,682	Maharaja; Kachhwaha Rajput; Hindu	17
3. Jodhpur (Marwar)	35,066	Maharaja; Rathor Rajput; Hindu	17
4. Bundi	2,220	Maharao Raja; Hara Chauhan Rajput; Hindu	17
5. Bikaner	23,315	Maharaja; Rathor Rajput; Hindu	17
6. Kotah	5,684	Maharaja; Hara Chauhan Rajput; Hindu	17
7. Karauli	1,242	Maharaja; Jadon Rajput; Hindu	17
8. Kishengarh	858	Maharaja; Rathor Rajput; Hindu	15
9. Bharatpur	1,982	Maharaja; Jat; Hindu	17
10. Jaisalmer	16,062	Maharawal; Jadon Bhati Rajput; Hindu	15
11. Alwar	3,213	Maharaja; Naruka Rajput; Hindu	15
12. Tonk	2,586	Nawab; Pathan; Muslim	15

Name of state	Area in square miles	Title, Race and Religion of Ruler	Gun Salute of Ruler
13. Dholpur	1,200	Maharaj Rana; Jat; Hindu	15
14. Sirohi	1,964	Maharao; Deora Chauhan Rajput; Hindu	15
15. Dungarpur	1,447	Maharawal; Sisodia Rajput; Hindu	15
16. Pratapgarh	886	Maharawat; Sisodia Rajput; Hindu	15
17. Banswara	1,606	Maharawal; Sisodia Rajput; Hindu	15
18. Jhalawar	810	Maharaj Rana; Jhala Rajput; Hindu	13
19. Shahpura	405	Raja; Sisodia Rajput; Hindu	9

2 non-salute states

States included in the North-West Frontier Province Agency

1 Chitral	4,000	Mehtar; Muslim	11 personal

4 non-salute states

States included in the Baluchistan Agency

1. Kalat	73,278	Wali, Brahui; Sunni Muslim	19

1 non-salute state

States forming the Western India States Agency

1. Kutch	7,616 (excluding Rann of Kutch)	Maharao; Jadeja Raput; Hindu	17
2. Junagadh	3,337	Nawab; Babi Pathan; Muslim	13
3. Nawanagar	3,791	Jam Saheb; Jadeja Rajput; Hindu	13
4. Bhavnagar	2,860	Maharaja; Gohil Rajput; Hindu	13
5. Porbandar	642	Maharaja Rana Saheb; Jethwa Rajput; Hindu	13
6. Dhrangadhara	1,157	Maharaja Raj Saheb; Jhala Rajput; Hindu	13
7. Palanpur	1,769	Nawab; Lohani Pathan; Muslim	13
8. Radhanpur	1,150	Nawab; Pathan; Muslim	11
9. Morvi	822	Maharaja; Jadeja Rajput; Hindu	11
10. Gondal	1,024	Maharaja; Jadeja Rajput; Hindu	11
11. Wankaner	417	Raj Saheb; Jhala Rajput; Hindu	9
12. Palitana	289	Thakor Saheb; Gohil Rajput; Hindu	9
13. Dhrol	283	Thakor Saheb; Jadeja Rajput; Hindu	9

Name of state	Area in square miles	Title, Race and Religion of Ruler	Gun Salute of Ruler
14. Limbdi	344	Thakor Saheb; Jhala Rajput; Hindu	9
15. Rajkot	282	Thakor Saheb; Jadeja Rajput; Hindu	9
16. Wadhwan	243	Thakor Saheb; Jhala Rajput; Hindu	9

185 non-salute states

States forming the Madras States Agency

1. Tranvancore	7,625	Maharaja; Kshatriya; Hindu	19
2. Cochin	1,418	Maharaja; Kshatriya; Hindu	17
3. Pudukkottai	1,179	Raja; Kallar; Hindu	11
4. Bagnanapalle	255	Nawab; Saiyd; Shiah Muslim	9

1 non-salute state

States forming the Central India Agency

1. Indore	9,519	Maharaja; Maratha; Hindu	19
2. Bhopal	6,902	Nawab; Afghan; Muslim	19
3. Rewa	13,000	Maharaja; Baghel Rajput; Hindu	17
4. Orchha	2,079	Maharaja; Bundela Rajput; Hindu	15
5. Datia	911	Maharaja; Bundela Rajput; Hindu	15
6. Dhar	1,777	Maharaja; Puar Maratha; Hindu	15
7. Dewas (Senior)	449	Maharaja; Puar Maratha; Hindu	15
8. Dewas (Junior)	419	Maharaja; Puar Maratha; Hindu	15
9. Samthar	180	Raja; Bargujar; Hindu	11
10. Jaora	601	Nawab; Pathan; Muslim	13
11. Ratlam	693	Maharaja; Rathor Rajput; Hindu	13
12. Panna	2,596	Maharaja; Bundela Rajput; Hindu	11
13. Charkhari	880	Maharaja; Bundela Rajput; Hindu	11
14. Ajaigarh	802	Maharaja; Bundela Rajput; Hindu	11
15. Bijawar	973	Maharaja; Bundela Rajput; Hindu	11
16. Baoni	121	Nawab; Pathan; Muslim	11
17. Chhatarpur	1,130	Maharaja; Bundela Rajput; Hindu	11
18. Sitamau	201	Raja; Rathor Rajput; Hindu	11
19. Sailana	297	Raja; Rathor Rajput; Hindu	11
20. Rajgarh	962	Raja; Umat Rajput; Hindu	11
21. Narsingarh	734	Raja; Umat Rajput; Hindu	11

Name of state	Area in square miles	Title, Race and Religion of Ruler	Gun Salute of Ruler
22. Baraundha	218	Raja; Rajput; Hindu	9
23. Nagod	501	Raja; Parihar Rajput; Hindu	9
24. Maihar	407	Raja; Kachhwaha Rajput; Hindu	9
25. Jhabua	1,336	Raja; Rathor Rajput; Hindu	11
26. Barwani	1,178	Rana; Sisodia Rajput; Hindu	11
27. Ali Rajpur	836	Raja; Rathor Rajput; Hindu	11
28. Khilchipur	273	Raja; Khichi Rajput; Hindu	9
61 non-salute states			

States in relations with the Government of the United Provinces

1. Rampur	893	Nawab; Saiyed; Shia Muslim	15
2. Benares	875	Maharaja; Bhumihar Brahmin	13
3. Tehri-Garhwal	4,500	Raja; Kshatriya Panwar; Hindu	11

States in relations with the Government of Bihar and Orissa

1. Patna	2,399	Maharaja; Chauhan Rajput; Hindu	9
2. Mayurbhanj	4,243	Maharaja; Kshatriya; Hindu	9
3. Kalahandi	3,745	Raja; Kshatriya; Hindu	9
4. Sonpur	906	Maharaja; Chauhan Rajput; Hindu	9

States in relations with the Government of Bengal

1. Cooch Behar	1,318	Maharaja; Kshatriya; Hindu	13
2. Tripura	4,116	Maharaja; Kshatriya; Hindu	13

States in relations with the Government of Assam

1. Manipur	8,456	Maharaja; Kshatriya; Hindu	11
15 non-salute states			

States in relations with the Government of the Central Provinces

15 non-salute states

States forming the Punjab States Agency

1. Patiala	5,932	Maharaja; Sidhu Jat; Sikh	17
2. Bahawalpur	15,000	Nawab; Daudputra; Muslim	17
3. Jind	1,259	Maharaja; Sidhu Jat; Sikh	13
4. Nabha	928	Maharaja; Sidhu Jat; Sikh	13
5. Kapurthala	630	Maharaja; Ahluwalia; Sikh	13
6. Sirmur	1,198	Maharaja; Rajput; Hindu	11
7. Mandi	1,200	Maharaja; Chandra Bansi Rajput; Hindu	11
8. Bilaspur	448	Raja; Rajput; Hindu	11

Name of state	Area in square miles	Title, Race and Religion of Ruler	Gun Salute of Ruler
9. Maler Kotla	168	Nawab; Sherwani Pathan; Muslim	11
10. Faridkot	643	Raja; Berar Jat; Sikh	11
11. Chamba	3,216	Raja; Rajput; Hindu	11
12. Suket	420	Raja; Rajput; Hindu	11
13. Loharu	222	Nawab; Afghan; Muslim	9

States in relations with the Government of the Punjab

| 1. Bashahr | 3,820 | Raja; Rajput; Hindu | 9 personal |
| 20 non-salute states | | | |

States in relations with the Government of Bombay

1. Kolhapur	3,217	Maharaja; Maratha; Hindu	19
2. Idar	1,669	Maharaja; Rathor Rajput; Hindu	15
3. Khairpur	6,050	Mir; Talpur Baluch; Muslim	15
4. Rajpipla	1,518	Maharaja; Gohel Rajput; Hindu	13
5. Janjira	377	Nawab; Muslim	11
6. Cambay	350	Nawab; Mughal Persian; Shia Muslim	11
7. Baria	813	Raja; Chauhan Rajput; Hindu	9
8. Lunawada	388	Raja; Solanki Rajput; Hindu	9
9. Sachin	49	Nawab; African; Sunni Muslim	9
10. Sawantwadi	925	Sar Desai; Maratha; Hindu	9
11. Dharampur	704	Raja; Sisodia Rajput; Hindu	9
12. Bansda	215	Raja; Solanki Rajput; Hindu	9
13. Chhota Udepur	890	Raja; Chauhan Rajput; Hindu	9
14. Balasinor	189	Nawab; Pathan; Muslim	9
15. Sant	394	Raja; Parmar Rajput; Hindu	9
16. Mudhol	368	Raja; Maratha; Hindu	9
17. Sangli	1,136	Chief; Konkanasth Brahmin; Hindu	9
18. Jawhar	310	Raja; Koli; Hindu	9
19. Danta	347	Maharana; Parmar Rajput; Hindu	9
20. Bhor	925	Pant Sachiv; Brahmin; Hindu	9
132 non-salute states			

INDEX